International Kierkegaard
Commentary

International Kierkegaard Commentary

Philosophical Fragments
and
Johannes Climacus

edited by
Robert L. Perkins

MERCER

BL
51
.P54
1994

ISBN 0-86554-440-9   MUP/H351

International Kierkegaard Commentary
Philosophical Fragments
and
Johannes Climacus
Copyright ©1994
Mercer University Press, Macon, Georgia 31207 USA

Library of Congress Cataloging-in-Publication Data

Philosophical Fragments, and Johannes Climacus / edited by Robert L. Perkins
xii+291pp. 6x9" (15x22cm.)—(International Kierkegaard Commentary ; 7)
Includes bibliographical references and indexes.
ISBN 0-86554-440-9 (HC : alk. paper).
1. Kierkegaard, Søren, 1813–1855. Philosophiske smuler.
2. Kierkegaard, Søren, 1813–1855. Johannes Climacus.
3. Christianity—Philosophy—History—19th century.
4. Religion—Philosophy—History—19th century.
I. Perkins, Robert L., 1930– . II. Series.
B4376.I58   1994   Vol. 7
[BL51]
198'.9—dc20   93-48223

CIP

Contents

Acknowledgements

All the contributors to this volume would desire to make acknowledgments, but it is a privilege reserved for the editor. Those whom the contributors would have named will be satisfied to have served their friends and colleagues.

I have the privilege of thanking a number of persons at Stetson University who have supported my work in general and the *International Kierkegaard Commentary* in particular: H. Douglas Lee, president, Eugene S. Lubot, provost, Gary Maris, dean of the College of Arts and Sciences, and Christine A. Carlson, secretary of the Philosophy Department.

The advisory board and the volume consultant read all the contributions and offered valuable advice. Dr. Julia Watkin of Danish International Studies of the University of Copenhagen, was particularly helpful in suggesting possible authors and tracking down obscure matters in the text. The interest of Mercer University Press and especially the efforts of Mr. Edd Rowell are deeply appreciated. Princeton University Press gave permission to quote from *Philosophical Fragments* and the other translations to which they hold copyright.

The several contributors and I also thank our families for the lost evenings and other scattered hours while we pursued these tasks. Finally, I wish to thank my wife Sylvia Walsh, who has made our life together an unutterable joy.

Robert L. Perkins

Sigla

AN *Armed Neutrality* and *An Open Letter*. Trans. Howard V. Hong and Edna H. Hong. Bloomington and London: Indiana Univ. Press, 1968. (*Den bevæbnede Neutralitet*, written 1848–1849, publ. 1965; "Foranledigt ved en Yttring af Dr. Rudelbach mig betræffende," *Fædrelandet*, no. 26 [31 January 1851].)

C *The Crisis [and a Crisis] in the life of an Actress.* Trans. Stephen Crites. New York: Harper & Row, 1967. (*Krisen og en Krise i en Skuespillerindes Liv*, by Inter et Inter. *Fædrelandet* 188–191 [24–27 July 1848].)

CA *The Concept of Anxiety.* Kierkegaard's Writings 8. Trans. Reidar Thomte, in collaboration with Albert B. Anderson. Princeton: Princeton Univ. Press, 1980. (*Bergrebet Angest*, by Vigilius Haufniensis, ed. S. Kierkegaard, 1844.)

CD *Christian Discourses*, including *The Lilies of the Field and the Birds of the Air* and *Three Discourses at the Communion on Fridays.* Trans. Walter Lowrie. London and New York: Oxford Univ. Press, 1940. (*Christelige Taler*, by S. Kierkegaard, 1848; *Lilien paa Marken og Fuglen under Himlen*, by S. Kierkegaard, 1849; *Tre Taler ved Altergangen om Fredagen*, by S. Kierkegaard, 1849.)

CI *The Concept of Irony.* Kierkegaard's Writings 2. Trans. Howard V. Hong and Edna H. Hong. Princeton: Princeton Univ. Press, 1989. (*Om Begrebet Ironi*, by S. A. Kierkegaard, 1841.)

COR *The Corsair Affair.* Kierkegaard's Writings 13. Trans. Howard V. Hong and Edna H. Hong. Princeton: Princeton Univ. Press, 1982.

CUP *Concluding Unscientific Postscript.* Kierkegaard's Writings 12:1-2. Trans. Howard V. Hong and Edna H. Hong. Princeton: Princeton Univ. Press, 1992. (*Afsluttende uvidenskabelig Efterskrift*, by Johannes Climacus, ed. S. Kierkegaard, 1846.)

EO *Either/Or.* Kierkegaard's Writings 3 and 4. Trans. Howard V. Hong and Edna H. Hong. Princeton: Princeton Univ. Press, 1987. (*Enten/Eller* I-II, ed. Victor Eremita, 1843.)

EPW *Early Polemical Writings.* Kierkegaard's Writings 1. Trans. Julia Watkin.
Princeton: Princeton Univ. Press, 1990.

EUD *Eighteen Upbuilding Discourses.* Kierkegaard's Writings 5. Trans. Howard
V. Hong and Edna H. Hong. Princeton: Princeton Univ. Press, 1990.
(*Atten opbyggelige taler,* by S. Kierkegaard, 1843–1845.)

FPOSL *From the Papers of One Still Living.* See EPW.

FSE *For Self-Examination* and *Judge for Yourselves.* Kierkegaard's Writings 21.
JFY Trans. Howard V. Hong and Edna H. Hong. Princeton: Princeton Univ.
Press, 1990. (*Til Selvprøvelse,* by S. Kierkegaard, 1851, and *Dømmer Selv!*
by S. Kierkegaard, 1852.)

FT *Fear and Trembling* and *Repetition.* Kierkegaard's Writings 6. Trans.
R Howard V. Hong and Edna H. Hong. Princeton: Princeton Univ. Press,
1983. (*Frygt og Bæven,* by Johannes de Silentio, 1843, and *Gjentagelsen,*
by Constantin Constantius, 1843.)

GS *Edifying Discourses in Various Spirits* (*Opbyggelige Taler i forskjellig Aand,*
by S. Kierkegaard, 1847.). Part three, *The Gospel of Suffering,* and part
two, *The Lilies of the Field* (*Lidelsernes Evangelium* and *Lilien paa Marken
og Himlens Fugle*). Trans. David F. Swenson and Lillian Marvin Swenson. Minneapolis: Augsburg Publishing House, 1948.

JC See PF JC.

JFY See FSE.

JP *Søren Kierkegaard's Journals and Papers.* Ed. and trans. Howard V. Hong
and Edna H. Hong, assisted by Gregor Malantschuk. Bloomington and
London: Indiana Univ. Press, (1) 1967; (2) 1970; (3-4) 1975; (5-7) 1978.
(From *Søren Kierkegaards Papirer* I-XI³ and XII-XIII, 2nd ed., and *Breve
og Akstykker vedrørende Søren Kierkegaard,* ed. Niels Thulstrup, I-II,
1953–1954.)

JSK *The Journals of Søren Kierkegaard.* Trans. Alexander Dru. London and
New York: Oxford Univ. Press, 1938. (From *Søren Kierkegaards Papirer*
I-XI³ in 18 volumes, 1909–1936.)

KAUC *Kierkegaard's Attack upon "Christendom,"* 1854–1855. Trans. Walter Lowrie. Princeton: Princeton Univ. Press, 1944. (*Bladartikler* I-XXI, by S. Kierkegaard, *Fædrelandet,* 1854–1855; *Dette skal siges; saa være det da sagt,* by
S. Kierkegaard, 1855; *Øieblikket,* by S. Kierkegaard, 1-9, 1855; 10, 1881;
Hvad Christus dømmer om officiel Christendom, by S. Kierkegaard, 1855.)

LD *Letters and Documents.* Kierkegaard's Writings 25. Trans. Hendrik Rosenmeier. Princeton: Princeton Univ. Press, 1978.

LY *The Last Years.* Trans. Ronald C. Smith. New York: Harper & Row, 1965. (From *Søren Kierkegaards Papirer* XI^1-XI^2.)

OAR *On Authority and Revelation, The Book on Adler.* Trans. Walter Lowrie. Princeton: Princeton Univ. Press, 1955. (*Bogen om Adler*, written 1846–1847, unpublished, Søren Kierkegaards *Papirer* VII^2 235; VIII^2 B 1-27.)

PC *Practice in Christianity.* Kierkegaard's Writings 20. Trans. Howard V. Hong and Edna H. Hong. Princeton: Princeton Univ. Press, 1991. (*Indøvelse i Christendom*, by Anti-Climacus, ed. S. Kierkegaard, 1850.)

PF *Philosophical Fragments* and *Johannes Climacus.* Trans. Howard V. Hong
JC and Edna H. Hong. Princeton: Princeton Univ. Press, 1985. (Philosophiske Smuler, by Johannes Climacus, ed. S. Kierkegaard, 1844. "Johannes Climacus eller *de omnibus dubitandum est*," written 1842–1843, unpublished, *Søren Kierkegaards Papirer* IV C 1.)

PH *Edifying Discourses in Various Spirits.* (*Opbyggelige Taler i forskjellig Aand*, 1847.) Part one, *Purity of Heart* ["*En Leiligheds-Tale*"]. Trans. Douglas Steere. Second ed. New York: Harper & Row, 1948.

PV *The Point of View for My Work as an Author*, including the appendix "'The Single Individual' Two 'Notes' Concerning My Work as an Author" and *On My Work as an Author.* Trans. Walter Lowrie. London and New York: Oxford University Press, 1939. (*Synspunktet for min Forfatter-Virksomhed*, by S. Kierkegaard, posthumously publ. 1859; *Om min Forfatter-Virksomhed*, by S. Kierkegaard, 1851.)

R See FT, R.

SLW *Stages on Life's Way.* Kierkegaard's Writings 11. Trans. Howard V. Hong and Edna H. Hong. Princeton: Princeton Univ. Press, 1988. (*Stadier paa Livets Vej*, ed. Hilarius Bogbinder 1845.)

SUD *The Sickness unto Death.* Kierkegaard's Writings 19. Trans. Howard V. Hong and Edna H. Hong. Princeton: Princeton Univ. Press, 1980. (*Sygdommen til Døden*, by Anti-Climacus, ed. S. Kierkegaard, 1849.)

TA *Two Ages: The Present Age and the Age of Revolution. A Literary Review.* Kierkegaard's Writings 14. Trans. Howard V. and Edna H. Hong. Princeton: Princeton Univ. Press, 1978. (*En literair Anmeldelse. To Tidsaldre*, by S. Kierkegaard, 1846.)

TCS *Three Discourses on Imagined Occasions* [*Thoughts on Crucial Situations in Human Life*]. Trans. David F. Swenson, ed. Lillian Marvin Swenson. Minneapolis: Augsburg, 1941. (*Tre Taler ved tænkte Leiligheder*, by S. Kierkegaard, 1845.)

WL *Works of Love*. Trans. Howard V. and Edna H. Hong. New York: Harper & Row, 1962. (*Kjerlighedens Gjerninger*, by S. Kierkegaard, 1847.)

Introduction

Søren Kierkegaard's *Philosophical Fragments*, written under the pseudonym Johannes Climacus, confronts a fundamental issue of Western religious thought—fundamental, that is, since, at the latest, the conversion of Justinus Flavius ("Justin [the] Martyr," ca. 100–165). That issue is the encounter between the Christian religion and philosophic modes of thought. Climacus's examination of the relation of revelation (or faith) and reason (or philosophy) brilliantly combines an interest in the history of hierarchical thinking that characterizes long stretches of the history of philosophy since Plato with an interest in the relation of history and faith that is characteristic of modern times. In *Philosophical Fragments* these two themes are focused in the figure of Socrates whom Climacus uses as an ideal type or metaphor for the hybrid of modern thought that after Hegel must be called philosophical theology.

Climacus presents the contrasting position using another ideal type whom he calls "the Teacher," who turns out to be none other than Jesus of Nazareth though neither he nor the movement of which he is the reputed founder are ever named. The Teacher is the model for the mystery of the God-man that challenges the hierarchy of being and its doctrine of immanence by setting out the claim that the truth has been fully incarnate in history. The Christian mystery is presented as being utterly different from Platonic philosophy that claims that the ideal is outside history and that it suffers ontological and axiological diminution by immanent and graduated participation in history and matter. At issue in *Philosophical Fragments* is the cogency and appropriateness of the centuries-long effort by Christian thinkers to assimilate hierarchical thinking and the Christian revelation in spite of the deep differences between them. Of course, it was primarily the shared sense of the transcendent, the forms in Plato and God in Christian thought, that attracted the Christians to Plato. A second shared emphasis, the thought that the world made sense, was ordered and coherent, no doubt also deeply influenced those who tried to combine these two viewpoints into one coherent whole. How these two utterly different understandings of transcendence related to the world created many problems for all who participated in the discussion.

Dialectically intertwined in the discussion of the relation of Platonic metaphysics and Hebrew-Christian revelation is a second issue: the problem created by the claim of a historical revelation in Enlightenment and post-Enlightenment philosophy (PF, 1). By analyzing the import of the modal categories for historical knowledge in general and the Christian story in particular, Climacus forces his reader to rethink the relation of Christianity to the issues of historical knowledge. Climacus's synthesis of Platonic metaphysics and the Enlightenment forms of rationalism is unique in philosophical and theological thought, and the presentation is both terse and complex. These two clusters of concepts are set forth dialectically in Climacus's presentation of Socrates. The Socratic view of the world is taken as normative, and as a result the Christian categories are presented as paradox. This paradox is presented in such a way that the reasons for its inexplicability become clear. We come to understand why the paradox cannot be subsumed under the categories of philosophy, either Greek or modern. As a final irony, in a book filled with irony, Climacus forswears any intention of attempting to prove that either the Socratic or the Christian is the truer, only that they are different (PF, 111). Climacus offers us an either/or: either Socratic and Enlightenment rationalism or the Teacher.

By way of introduction I wish to review very briefly a few historic episodes of the relation of the Socratic, understood typologically as including both the hierarchical form of thought and the modern concept of history, to the Christian categories, and to indicate how the tension between them shapes some of the characteristic features of Western philosophy and its relation to religion and theology. I shall review a very small bit of the history of Neoplatonism and the rise of new modes of thinking in the late Middle Ages that led to modern philosophy. Recounting even this small part of the story will enable us to see more clearly how radical Climacus's either/or really is.[1]

Second, I shall examine some of the threads of the dispute between the Christian revelation and modern thought. I shall attempt to isolate the factor that enabled Climacus to unite the hierarchical forms of thought and modern historical thinking under the single ideal type, Socrates, and to show why and how, according to Climacus, modern religious thought must come to understand why the paradox is not philosophically understandable.

As mentioned previously, the conversion of Justin is decisive because he initiated the rapprochement between Neoplatonism and Christianity. Born in Palestine and educated in Ephesus, Justin sampled the prevailing schools of Stoicism, Aristotelianism, and Pythagoreanism before he became a Platonist. Soon thereafter he converted to Christianity, but when Justin became a Christian he did not stop thinking like a Platonist. Rather, his Platonism gained a new subject matter about which to think. A short time after his conversion he moved to Rome where he opened a school of "Christian philosophy"[2] which he supported with his own wealth. Justin urged that all that was true in pagan philosophy should be taken up into the larger and more inclusive truth of Christianity, only the errors being rejected. The moral idealism of Plato's Socrates was especially appealing to Justin. Socrates had been charged by the impious Athenians with impiety, the same charge brought against the Christians by the Roman government for attempting to proclaim, as Socrates had centuries earlier, the truth of the one God and the importance of the virtues in the achievement of human happiness. For Justin, the bond between the truth in pagan philosophy and the true religion was the Logos which

---

[1]Those who wish to follow this story in more detail should consult the near-classical works in the history of philosophy by Frederick Copleston and Etienne Gilson. For a more synoptic view, see James W. Jordan's *Western Philosophy from Antiquity through the Middle Ages* (New York: Macmillan, 1987). George Boas's introduction to his translation of Bonaventura's *The Mind's Road to God* (New York: Liberal Arts Press, 1953) is most insightful.

[2]Essays in this volume by Pattison, Dunning, Glenn, and Barrett contribute additional insights into the conceptual relations between Kierkegaard and the Platonic form of Christian philosophy.

enabled pagans to obtain the knowledge of the existence and nature of God but which had been fully present only in the incarnate Christ. Because of the universality of the Logos, some pagans were "Christians before Christ."

Justin's view of the Logos was, in all probability, more indebted to Philo than to the Fourth Gospel, for Philo's view and language were the common currency of Platonism at the time. Justin urges that the Logos is the intermediary between God and the world, and, at the same time, that there is no ontological distinction between the word and the unity of the forms the word expresses, a position that, if guarded, could and did contribute to the development of Logos Christology. However, when taken in a fashion that emphasizes the intermediary function of the word, as Philo and Plotinus did, the same set of analogies could and did lead directly to Arianism, the view that Christ was a creature and subordinate to God. Thus the most friendly encounter ever between Christianity and philosophy contributed to the development of both orthodoxy, through Justin, and heresy, through others who emphasized the more Plotinian understanding of the mediatory and subordinate function of the Logos even as they thought about the incarnate work of revelation.

Although many moderns have little or no sympathy for the theological and philosophical syncretism so apparent in Justin, it was common in that age and was a powerful force in the succeeding centuries in spite of the fierce opposition in the writings of Tertullian and a few others. Justin's martyrdom proves that the synthesis he worked out was not a speculative verbal game but rather an existential commitment.

Although Philo emphasized the notion of aspiration and ascent of the soul, Plotinus developed a more elaborate theory of emanation and descent which occurs prior to the return or ascent of the soul to the One. Both models were based on the analogy of Diotima's ladder (in Plato's *Symposium*). The theory of emanation, a metaphor invented by Plotinus, was more ontological and emphasized the diminution and corrupting of the purity of the one in a series of descending levels, each successive one of which departs further from the form, unity, and purity of the One than the previous level. The metaphor of ascent begins with the soul mired in matter and recounts its struggle and means of attaining again the vision of the unity of the One. Neither part of the metaphor of ascent or descent makes any sense apart from the other.

As his *Confessions* show, Augustine dramatizes both the analogy of descent (the fall into sin) and ascent (the soul's journey back to God). The story of salvation or psychological ascent appears to be close to Plato's intent, for "Diotima's ladder" in the *Symposium* is, after all, an analogy about the erotic ascent of the soul until it finally intuits the "single sea of beauty" (Plato) or "the great King Himself" (Philo). So indeed our hearts are restless until they repose in God, at least as Augustine understands metaphysics and the human passions as interpreted to him by the Neoplatonists and the Bible.

The syncretism of the Bible, the earlier theological tradition, Stoicism, Pythagoreanism, Roman skepticism, and neoplatonism that finds its classic expression in Augustine's *Confessions* is focused primarily on the struggle Augustine had with the intellectual conflicts in the late Roman Empire and the experience he had with his sexuality, which he interprets as a weakness if not bondage of the will. Throughout the *Confessions*, the unification of his personal powers proceed only as both intellectual and volitional issues are resolved, but the final climactic event is one that asserts the primacy of the will in the experience of personal repentance and the achievement of Socratic clarity about himself and/or forgiveness of his sins. The intimacy of the volitional and intellectual is one of the most remarkable achievements of his thought. The near seamless whole he creates between the Christian need for repentance for one's sins, the Socratic view of self-knowledge, and Plato's view of the ascent of the soul is evidence for most moderns of a deep tension between the religious and the philosophic sources of Augustine's thought. Nonetheless, throughout that period of philosophy's history we call "medieval," Augustine's synthesis sustained the understanding of the vital and viable unity of the religious, intellectual, and volitional aspects of the person.

Perhaps the clearest and most famous adaptation of Plato's complex model of ascent is in St. Bonaventura's *The Mind's Road to God*. In this work Bonaventura adopts what many may think of as a rather "churchy" Neoplatonism to present a theory of logical classes, a hierarchy of values (ethics), and a hierarchy of being (metaphysics). *The Mind's Road to God* is, no doubt, the ultimate and fullest development of the unity of the Neoplatonic vision of reality and the Christian view of the world. For this reason it is one of the most significant works in the history of philosophy and theology.

True to a fundamental root of the Franciscan order, Bonaventura bases his discussion on the analogy of seeing or vision that understands God as the light that makes all vision possible. Bonaventura's emphasis upon vision and sight suggests that all one must do to know something of God is to look at the world, for it contains traces of the divine. Such a view stands at the end of the long tradition that begins with Plato, who understood the intelligible ideas to be outside time and space but also manifest, in varying degrees, in the things of this world. Plotinus locates these forms within the One, whom he identifies with God. He understands the Craftsman (from Plato's *Timaeus*) as independent of and yet the instrument of the One in the fashioning of the world according to the intelligible forms. Bonaventura, extending the heritage of the Augustinian tradition, thought these forms to be contained in the word of God, expressed first in the creation but finally and ultimately in the flesh of Jesus. As a result, if one observes the world one can see traces of the divine, that become transparently clear in the divine Logos become incarnate.

Despite all the controversies between Bonaventura and Thomas Aquinas, the latter's thought also depended upon the vitality and continuity of the Platonic tradition. Thomas's fourth way, the proof for the existence of God based upon the notion of the gradation or the hierarchy of being, is indirectly related to the *Symposium* through Aristotle's *Metaphysics*. The proof also assumes the theory of the immanence of the eternal ideas in natural objects. This proof, so clearly indebted to the Neoplatonic tradition, is the foundation upon which all the other of Thomas's five ways are based. Thus the rivals of Paris, representing the traditions of Plato and Aristotle, share a dependence in vital areas of their thought, ultimately, on Diotima's ladder.

With the two major contenders for philosophic dominance in the leading university in Europe firmly supporting the Neoplatonic vision of the unity and order of being, it would seem that an established intellectual hegemony would continue to form the basis of philosophic and theological thought for ages to come. Such, however, was not to be the case, and in fact there was not even a hegemony evident at the time in Paris. I shall mention only three thinkers whose work challenged the basic Neoplatonic model of religious and philosophic reflection.

It was precisely this sense of the unity and gradation of being that is rejected in the work of Bacon, Scotus, Ockham, and others. Bacon, continuing the Franciscan interest in light, made numerous discoveries in optics and thought that good science would be a defense of religious faith. Speculatively he dreamed of automobiles and power-driven boats. He also urged the cultivation of several experimental sciences and thought that the results of related sciences (that is, medicine and nutrition) could be combined for purely practical and humane benefits. In defence of Bacon's acceptance of many alchemical views, we must remember that alchemy was accepted in the seventeenth century even by Boyle. What is important here, however, is that the hierarchical ascent of the soul and the ontological unity of the sciences simply disappear from view. Bacon's interests lie elsewhere.

Scotus begins a process of narrowing the power of reason in matters of faith. Scotus rejects the various views of the levels of being so dear to the Neoplatonists and the analogy of being as understood by Aquinas. Being or existence, Scotus argues, is a univocal concept, derived from sense experience and applicable to God in the same way it is to any empirical object. Although God's nature is still characterized by necessity and infinity, all differences between God and contingent things are a matter of essence, not existence. The will, moreover, has a more powerful liberty and authority over itself than even Augustine allowed. The will, contrary to Aquinas, can command the intellect to attend to this or that. This assertion of the primacy of the will rejects the view held since Plato and Aristotle that there is a natural and rational necessity that persons seek their happiness as it is, perhaps incorrectly, conceived. For Scotus, the will is "innately free," and seeks not only its own good (as Plato and Aristotle and their followers maintain) but is also just as capable of seeking the good of others simply because it is just and right.

Ockham continued the critique of scholastic metaphysics, asserting that universal terms do not name a common nature or

essence. Concepts are only names for particular subjects with indi-
vidualizing characteristics. Common or universal terms are the
result of our noticing resemblances among individuals. Metaphysics, knowledge, and action do not require the existence of the
intelligible ideas in any form discussed previously in the history
of philosophy. Moreover, the freedom of the will is a mere matter
of observation and requires no proof. The freedom of the will is a
condition of responsibility, and would be compromised if we had
a natural inclination or appetite that required us to act so as to
achieve our happiness. How we ought to live is determined by the
will of God, not by any concatenation of essences or natural laws.
These considerations leave philosophy with little to offer theology,
and little remains for theology except to explicate the logic of its
own categories and those of religious faith.

At the end of the labors of Bacon, Scotus, and Ockham the
whole great ladder of being, goodness, truth, and beauty lay in
ruins, a metaphor only the true believer will find overstated. Still,
it cannot be gainsaid that after their work, and that of many others
omitted here,[3] the nature of philosophy and its relation to religion
and theology changes dramatically, and one major reason is that
the Platonic model of thought had been marginalized by their
combined efforts. If anyone doubts this interpretation of the
matter, let that person explain, first, the subsequent emergence and
the near dominance of the utilitarian views of ethics and politics
in many regions after Hobbes; second, the ascendancy of science
as the primary model of thinking, as is apparent in the disputes
over the new astronomy and in Descartes, for whom God is little
more than a category that fills in the gaps in the system of science;
and, third, the transition of concern from the next world to this
world that accompanies the rise of the new economic and political
arrangements. All these changes are intellectually legitimated
without reference to the Neoplatonic tradition if not in outright
opposition to it.

---

[3]Another way of recounting the overcoming of the Neoplatonic model of
thinking would be to begin with the Latin Averroists and end with Nicholas of
Cusa.

The novelty of Kierkegaard's position is that he takes modern philosophy so seriously. His philosophic views do not attempt to resurrect any form of ancient or medieval thought. His efforts are not dedicated to any form of philosophy or theology that must be prefixed with the particle "neo." Kierkegaard is neither a Neoplatonist or Neothomist in philosophy nor a neoorthodox in theology. Kierkegaard's effort is new in its own terms and is not the revival of any other point of view. However, his thought is not dominated by the rise of modern science, although he is as cognizant of its achievements as any undergraduate and scholarly layman would have been at the time.

Johannes Climacus, Kierkegaard's pseudonym in *Philosophical Fragments,* points to one continuing, though quite well disguised, assumption from the hierarchical tradition in modern thinking about history. It is very important to note that the issue Climacus discusses was central to the debate about the use, uselessness, or harm of a new mode of hierarchical thinking for developing a Christian self-understanding. Instead of an ontological hierarchy based on Plato, the new form of hierarchy is based on the concept of time. There are three foci in this development. The first is the issue of the singularity of the historical event of the appearance of the God-man in history. The second issue relates to the cumulative achievements of history and culture that moderns call progress. The third has to do with the issues of historical knowledge. Just a brief word about each.

Kierkegaard accepted with little or no reservation the solutions to the great Christological controversies that led to the development of orthodoxy. At that time the difficulties had been caused by the absolute singularity of the event itself, or as expressed by Paul, the issue was that the Greeks seek wisdom and the Jews a sign. The last thing expected or acceptable religiously by the Greek and Jewish forms of thought was an individual human being who was thought to be the expression of God in the flesh. Both the Greek and the Jewish modes of thought found it irrational to claim that this supposed god-in-the-flesh died a felon's death. However, the solutions worked out during the era of the Christological controversies of the first five centuries of the common era had to be reaffirmed and redefined in the modern era in response to the terms of this age. Kierkegaard discovered deep within modern thought the difficulty of understanding the appearance of the God-man for reasons that bear some resemblance to the difficulties faced in the confrontation of the older hierarchical form of thought and the startling novelty of the Christian message.

The first issue, the historical appearance of the God-man, occasioned difficulty in the modern era because it is quite hard for modern thought to think the radically individual in a historical and/or sociological sense in spite of the "anthropocentric turn" supposedly injected in modern philosophy by Descartes. The habit of subsuming the individual into logical classes, as in hierarchical thought, gave way to subsuming the individual into sociological or historical groups among some thinkers of whom Kant is rather typical in his statistical analysis of the relation of free individual decision and sociological prediction. Thinkers like Condorcet, Herder, and Hegel thought of historical eras and peoples. Hegel did have a category of the "world historical individual," in which Jesus of Nazareth is not named. Thus it appears that the individual has no more status in modern thought than in the various forms of hierarchical thought it replaced. The figure of the God-man would be still more difficult to think than the ordinary individual, but in a certain sense the fate of both are related in modern thought; for the ordinary individual and the supposed God-man resist classification in unitive and numerical categories.

The second issue in modern historical thinking that makes it difficult to think the God-man is the modern concept of progress. The emergence of this concept is also a timely substitute for the hierarchical model of thinking. In hierarchical thought the "higher" has more ontological value than the "lower," a direct influence of the analogy of Diotima's ladder. In the concept of progress, the later is more developed, refined, rational, improved, and worthwhile. The "more" suggests a mere "quantitative" enhancement. It was an act of conceit and self-congratulation that the Enlightenment so designated itself and castigated the previous "dark ages." Such notions of historic improvement and self-complacency among the moderns are abundant, but the work of Lessing is most important here because it was so simply clear and had such an impact on the historical thought of Hegel. The latter had a concept of a telos, the fulfillment of personal freedom in societies, the reciprocity of the inner and the outer, that qualitatively differentiates him from most of the eighteenth-century philosophers of progress. However, such a telos places Hegel at an even greater disadvantage than that facing the eighteenth-century thinkers when it comes to being able to give centrality and ultimacy to the appearance of the God-man in history. If the higher values emerged in more recent times, or rather in the present, then the appearance of ultimate truth in the person of the God-man centuries ago is impossible. So for Hegel the reconciliation offered by the God-man was only a beginning, the ultimate completion of which occurs in the present—a word that for Hegel means a moving present and incomplete process.

The third issue, the question of historical knowledge, is a philosophic question and is not at all bibliographic or related to sources. Climacus asks, following Lessing, whether "a historical point of departure can be given for an eternal consciousness; how can such a point of departure be of more than historical interest; can an eternal happiness be built upon historical knowledge?" (PF, 1). Such questions lead directly to the consideration of the distinction between relations of ideas and statements about matters of fact and the modal considerations between possibility and necessity. In analyzing such questions Climacus analyzes the theory of the modal categories and the modern distinction between matters of fact and relations of ideas while at the same time he adapts these distinctions to elaborate the existential uniqueness and the philosophic ultimacy of the God-man. Climacus also recasts one of Lessing's assumptions about the reliability of direct eyewitnesses of an event by a far more subtle understanding of the problem of evidence than Lessing recognized. Because of his view that knowledge of matters of fact is at best only approximate, Climacus is much closer to Lessing, Kant, and other empirically minded thinkers of the eighteenth century than to Hegel, who felt that knowledge was present only when the necessity of the idea could be found.

Closely connected with but distinct from these considerations of historical knowledge is Climacus's concern for the logical coherence of the proofs for the existence of God. In this context, Climacus finds much he can appropriate from the Enlightenment, namely, its skeptical attitude toward these proofs. However, his critique of these proofs is closely connected to the critique of historical knowledge. In the ontological argument there is no appeal to factual being at all. The other proofs attempt to move from statements about contingent matters to justify statements about an eternal being, a clear jump from the finite to the infinite. Further, they beg the question, assuming the existence of the god whose existence they are intended to prove.

It is precisely his concern for the finite that causes Climacus to think that Socrates got most of the philosophic task correct. The Socratic emphasis upon existence is completely at odds with Plato's hierarchical metaphysics and modern speculation about the historical (CUP, 1:205). By making this distinction Climacus can retain the figure of Socrates while, at the same time, he jettisons the Platonic and Neoplatonic metaphysics along with the modern sense of the historical. Socrates then becomes the model of the subjective existing individual, the person who thinks the universal but who exists in time with tasks that require that he/she relate the universal to the particular conditions of one's personal inward development (CUP, 1:73). "The ethical is and remains the highest task assigned to every human being" (CUP, 1:151). This emphasis upon the ethical as a task that combines the universal and the individual connects, in Climacus's mind, the moral understanding of human existence that is continuous from Socrates through Kant and suggests the reasons why Climacus is perhaps the most controversial of Kierkegaard's pseudonyms.

The authors of the articles in this volume take up the issues discussed above along with many others. The cumulative effect of intellectually appropriating their efforts would be, first, an analysis of some of the crucial issues in logical theory, epistemology, personal identity theory, and religious language; and, second, a review of some further episodes in the history of philosophical theology offered here in a reversed chronological order. The contributors make no attempt to become edifying authors, but as one thinks philosophically one thinks about oneself, and that, Socratically, is to be edified.

Robert L. Perkins

1

Johannes and Johannes: Kierkegaard and Difference

Merold Westphal

Two of Kierkegaard's most widely read pseudonyms, Johannes de Silentio (as author of *Fear and Trembling*) and Johannes Climacus (as author of *Philosophical Fragments*) have more in common than their first names. Each presents two positions; following the pattern of *Either/Or*, let us call them A and B. This is not unusual. Philosophers often distinguish two positions in order to argue for either the truth of the one they hold or the falsity (perhaps inadequacy) of the one they do not. But the "arguments" of Johannes and Johannes are quite peculiar, for each seeks simply to show, without personally identifying with either position, that A is different from B and in showing wherein that difference lies.

This latter part of the project is, once again, not unusual. Philosophers often try to identify the precise point at which one position differs from another; but traditionally this is part of the process of trying to show that one is superior to the other. To locate the difference simply for the sake of showing that the two are different is indeed unusual. But this is precisely what Johannes and Johannes do. It is hard to think of philosophical arguments of this style with which to compare theirs. If contemporary philosophy revolves to a very considerable degree around the concept of difference, Johannes and Johannes, along with Kierkegaard, the producer/director of their performances, may be quite timely indeed.

In *Fear and Trembling*, Johannes de Silentio seeks to show the difference between the ethical and the religious. In *Philosophical*

Fragments, Johannes Climacus seeks to show the difference between recollection as the key to knowledge and revelation as the key to faith. We know that Kierkegaard is not neutral with respect to these differences. He thinks the religious is higher than the ethical and that, at least for authentic Christian faith, it is necessary to go beyond recollection to revelation.

But so far from allowing Johannes and Johannes to argue for these preferences, he does not even permit them to express their own preferences. This is not how he does it in *Either/Or*; there he does not resolve the tension between the two positions by telling us which to adopt, but he does allow A (the aesthete) and B (Judge William) to express their preferences with all the power at their disposal, and he allows Judge William to develop a rather sophisticated argument for the superiority of the ethical. But he keeps Johannes and Johannes on a tighter leash. The only "arguments" they are allowed to present remain entirely within the hypothetical.

In *Fear and Trembling*, Johannes de Silentio argues (in each of the three "problems") that the ethical is the universal, that if the universal is the highest human destiny, then Hegel is right, but Abraham is lost. If, on the contrary, Abraham is a hero and not a murderer, then the universal is not the highest and Hegel is lost. Either/Or. Either Hegel or Abraham, but not both. They are logical contraries. If H, then not-A; and if A, then not-H. The author might as well have been named Johannes de Hypothetico, for beyond these logical possibilities he posits no actuality. He takes no position.

In *Philosophical Fragments*, Johannes Climacus does the same. If knowledge is recollection, then the truth is within us, the teacher is only a midwife (the *maieutic* is the highest relation between humans), and the moment of learning, that is the historical setting of coming to the truth, is but an occasion and stands in no essential relation to the truth.

The thought experiment that lies at the heart of the *Fragments* is concerned with developing an alternative to this Socratic position. We deny one of the consequences (for otherwise we are back where we started with Socrates) and see that to be consistent we must deny all the others as well. If the truth is not in us the teacher must be more than a midwife and the moment of learning must be more than an occasion, accidentally related to the truth.

But while Johannes Climacus devotes considerable energy to working out this alternative in considerable detail, he neither affirms it nor argues for it. In his concluding "Moral" he writes, "This project indisputably goes beyond the Socratic, as is apparent at every point. Whether it is therefore more true than the Socratic is an altogether different question" (PF, 111). Either/Or. Either recollection or revelation. As candidates for the highest relation to the truth they are contraries. That's all.

These arguments are, to repeat, unusual. When, for example, Augustine draws essentially the same distinction in book 8 of the *Confessions*, it is in order to praise the faith grounded in revelation as "confession" and to condemn the knowledge grounded in recollection as "presumption" (at least as long as it takes itself, Platonically, to be the highest knowledge). There can be little doubt that Kierkegaard is, with a little help from Luther, an Augustinian. But he does not allow his pseudonym to take an Augustinian position. He only allows him to devote a lot of effort to a "thought experiment."

* * *

What is Kierkegaard up to? What is the strategy behind this staging? I want to suggest three answers to this question. I believe there is something right about each of them, but that only the third really answers the question.

According to the first answer Kierkegaard's strategy is dictated by his understanding of existential communication. He is as suspicious of the authority of the author as some of our contemporaries are, but for somewhat different reasons. Because he wants the reader to see for herself and to choose for herself, he resorts to pseudonyms so as not to place himself, his opinions, and his arguments between the reader and what Hegel would call *die Sache* (the matter at issue). Like the League of Women Voters, he wants his audience to be attentive to a debate that does not have the character of being set up by one of the parties to the debate. In the works in question, by contrast with *Either/Or*, he extends this tactic of authorial absence to the pseudonyms themselves, our friends Johannes and Johannes.

The second answer revolves around what we might call Kierkegaard's hermeneutical skepticism. In the *Philosophical Fragments* he allows Johannes Climacus to raise the topic of proving the existence of God (strictly speaking, "*the god*") in a context where the issue seems extraneous, or at least unnecessary (PF, 39). Can we prove the existence of God from his works? Only if we have "already in advance interpreted" them as his (PF, 40-41). To interpret the world or certain features of it as "works" and, moreover, as "works" whose only maker could be God is already to place an interpretation on them that is not necessary, to take them "as they do not appear directly and immediately" (PF, 42). If there is any sheer givenness, that is, if things ever do appear "directly and immediately," their nakedness renders impossible any inference from them to a divine maker.

This analysis is like the classical skeptical argument against the syllogism. Since I cannot know that all men are mortal unless I already know that Socrates, who is a man, is mortal, I must already know the conclusion of this famous syllogism to be true in order to know the truth of its universal premise. The argument is circular; it begs the question. But since, in the case Johannes presents, it is an act of interpretation that spoils the argument's innocence, it is the hermeneutical circle that we are dealing with and we can speak of a hermeneutical skepticism.

Now if Kierkegaard is impressed by the hermeneutical skepticism he permits Johannes to present, that would go a long way toward explaining the strategy we are considering. Johannes and Johannes are not allowed to present arguments against A and for B because such arguments will only convince the already converted, those already sharing the crucial but contestable interpretations that make them possible.

But, it may be answered, why then is Judge William allowed to argue for the ethical in *Either/Or*? One possible reply is that Kierkegaard adopted the hermeneutical skepticism presented by Johannes only after writing *Either/Or*. This would be a satisfactory answer if there were any reason to believe it true, but I am aware of no evidence in its favor.

A better answer begins by noticing that the hermeneutical skepticism of the *Philosophical Fragments* doesn't eliminate argument altogether; it just reminds us of the limits of argument. Hermeneutically speaking, all arguments are *ad hominem* arguments, and to have any force an argument must to some degree share an horizon of interpretation with those to whom it is addressed. By itself this wouldn't explain the difference between Judge William on the one hand and Johannes/Johannes on the other. But if we take into account an additional factor, it suggests an explanation.

For the aesthetic stage on life's way, the I is absolute; for the ethical the We is absolute, since Johannes defines the ethical not as the right simpliciter but as social morality, the right as defined by the beliefs, practices, and institutions of some actual society (Hegel's *Sittlichkeit*, Danish *det sædelige* or *Sædelighed*, FT, 55, including n. 7; usual translation: "ethical life"); and for the religious person God is absolute. It may well be that for the socialized human self the gulf between the I and the We is less than that which separates the self as both I and We from the God who transcends them both. In that case common hermeneutical ground might be found between Judge William and the aesthete more easily than between either of them and the knight of faith (and this in spite of the ease and volume of the Judge's God-talk). This would not eliminate all possibility of the latter presenting an argument for faith. In fact, I think Kierkegaard does just this in *The Sickness unto Death*. But it would provide reason to go slow in arguing for faith. It might be important, before attempting to do so, to call attention to the dramatic differences between social virtue and human understanding on the one hand, and faith and revelation on the other, which is precisely what Johannes and Johannes do. These differences define the hermeneutical situation within which argument and apologetics must operate.

This brings us to the third answer to the question, What is Kierkegaard up to? Like the previous answer, it replies that he is out to call attention to these dramatic differences, to dramatize them, we might say. But this is a different answer because it gives a different rationale for doing so. According to the second answer, the point of doing this is to render hermeneutical skepticism more concrete (and less negative) by applying it to the theory of the stages or spheres of existence. According to the third answer the point is to bring that skepticism still closer to everyday life by applying it to a contemporary, historical reality. As theory this reality goes under the name of Hegel; as practice under the name of Christendom.

Kierkegaard's strategy is to emphasize tension where the present age sees harmony, to juxtapose antitheses to its syntheses. The point of having Johannes and Johannes say that A and B are different, and leaving it at that, is to counteract the contemporary tendency, seen by Kierkegaard to be both strong and dangerous, to reduce those differences to identity. If, following a tradition often identified as postmodernism, we use the term "metaphysics" to designate the reduction of the other to the same, then Kierkegaard's strategy is to offer a critique of the metaphysics of modernity. This overcoming of metaphysics is motivated by the desire to confront modernity (and, very possibly postmodernity as well) with its other, to make philosophical reflection and social practice vulnerable to both God and neighbor in ways they have tended to foreclose.

* * *

We can say that the projects of the two Johanneses are similar in three respects: (1) they are content to argue that A and B are different, (2) these arguments can be viewed as a critique of metaphysics, and (3) they are immediately directed toward the modernity expressed by Hegel and by Christendom. But the two projects are more closely linked than that. I want to suggest that Johannes Climacus is trying to work out the epistemological ramifications of the critical social theory presented implicitly in the Abraham story as told by Johannes de Silentio.

To appreciate the nature of the latter it is important to remember that *Fear and Trembling* does not stage a confrontation between the right as such and the holy. Outside the text of *Fear and Trembling* I know of no evidence to suggest that Kierkegaard thought there was or might be a conflict between them; and inside the text of *Fear and Trembling*, no such confrontation takes place (though much of the literature renders itself irrelevant to the text by failing to notice this crucial fact).

When Kant talks about the moral law he has in mind a universal principle of reason that is dependent upon, embedded in, and relative to no particular social order or religious tradition. It is in itself so absolute that it can function as the criterion of what could count as divine. By contrast, when Hegel talks about ethical life (*Sittlichkeit*) as universal he has in mind the practices and institutions of some historically specific social order, along with its cultural traditions. Ethical life could be absolute, and thus the highest destiny for human persons, only if some specific social-cultural lifeworld had itself become absolute, had become, in biblical language, the Kingdom of God. It is to challenge just such a triumphalist assumption, present, he fears, both in Hegelian theory and in Christendom's self-consciousness, that Kierkegaard turns Johannes de Silentio loose on the story of Abraham.

Even before getting to *Fear and Trembling*, the attentive reader might have noticed that by the ethical Kierkegaard has Hegel and not Kant in mind. When, in *Either/Or*, he seeks to portray the ethical in contrast to the aesthetic, he creates Judge William, who presents no reflections on the moral law in its formal universality but two long and very Hegelian accounts of a particular social practice, monogamous marriage. But in *Fear and Trembling*, just to make sure we don't miss the point, he has Johannes (1) explicitly identify Hegel as the representative of the ethical three times (at the beginning of each "problem"), (2) regularly identify the ethical universal, not as abstract principle, but as the nation, the state, the church, and the sect (FT, 57-59, 62, 74, 79), and (3) explicitly identify the ethical with *Sittlichkeit* (FT, 55).

The question about the teleological suspension of the ethical, then, is not about a conflict between the right and the holy but about whether (a) the will of God might trump my society's best understanding and practice of the right or whether (b) my society might be so perfect an expression of the divine will that no tension between them is conceivable. In the first case my allegiance to my social order is only relative, while my allegiance to God is absolute; in the second case no such distinction is necessary or possible. The religious stage on life's way is defined by the former assumption, the ethical by the latter. (If this seems to imply that Kantian ethics belongs to the religious rather than to the ethical, so be it. It does fit much better within the framework of what Johannes Climacus will present as Religiousness A in *Concluding Unscientific Postscript* than it does within either Volume II of *Either/Or* or the portrayal of the ethical as the universal in *Fear and Trembling*.)[1]

---

[1]If there is a critique of Kantian ethics in *Fear and Trembling*, it is derivative from the critique of Hegel. Nothing in the text suggests a conflict between the will

On this account the ethical turns out to be ideological, the celebration and sanctification of some social status quo, while the religious turns out to be critical theory, a challenge to the pretense of finality in every established order. Critical theory becomes obsolete and ideology ceases to be a reproach just at that moment when some human society actually becomes legitimately final, the Kingdom of God. Another way to put this point is to say that we will all be Hegelians in heaven. But on earth. . . . That is the question Kierkegaard wants us to ponder, and he hopes that Johannes's reflection on the Abraham story will lead us to choose the religious as critique over the ethical as ideology.

The idea that Kierkegaard begins his career as critical social theorist in *Fear and Trembling* (if not in *The Concept of Irony*) is problematic to those for whom the concept of critical theory has been preempted by the Marxian and neo-Marxian traditions. How can this be a critical social theory if it does not thematize such issues as the relation between wage labor and capital, between civil society and the state, or between system and lifeworld?

Kierkegaard might well answer as follows.

> Read as I hope it will be read, *Fear and Trembling* is critical social theory in the same two ways that Marx's writings and those of his followers, including those of the Frankfurt School are: it points to a dimension of modernity that makes it hostile to truly human flourishing and it seeks to expose the ideological character of the theory that provides legitimation in spite of this defect. I invite Marxists (broadly speaking) to discuss with me whether the *most basic flaw* in modernity is some aspect of capitalism or its tendency to deify itself as history's *telos*, making itself immune to fundamental critique of any sort. But for Marxists (broadly speaking) to say that no theory is a critical theory that does not give a (broadly speaking) Marxist diagnosis of modernity is not

---

of God and what Kant purports to have found, the eternal and universally valid moral law. Kant would be in trouble (from the perspective of Abraham as hero) only if what he presents as Reason, pure and uncontaminated by time and history, is in fact some historically specific *Sittlichkeit* seeking to forget its human, all too human genealogy. It is precisely in the writings of Johannes Climacus that we find the suggestion that what presents itself as reason is only a particular human interpretation of the world. The real confrontation with Kant is in Climacus' reflections on reason (as recollection) and revelation, not in Silentio's telling of the Abraham story.

to win that debate but dogmatically to declare it already settled. It is to assume a priori (that is, uncritically) that problems in the spiritual realm cannot be as deep or deeper than problems in the material realm. But what if material injustice and oppression have their roots in spiritual pride?[2]

Those who are still skeptical might try the following experiment to test whether *Fear and Trembling* is critical theory. (1) First note the implication that from the perspective of the religious, your allegiance to your country can only be relative and never absolute (until that country actually is the Kingdom of God in its fullness). (2) Then make it a habit, whenever you say the pledge of allegiance to the flag, always to cross your fingers as a sign of your conditional commitment. (3) Do this especially on war related holidays and among God-and-country flag-waving patriots. (4) Make sure they notice what you are doing and explain to them that you are doing it because reading Kierkegaard has reminded you that your country is human, all too human, and that it is not worthy of unconditional allegiance.

* * *

We are now in a position to ask what might be meant by the claim that Johannes Climacus (in the *Fragments*) is trying to work out the epistemological ramifications of the critical social theory presented by Johannes de Silentio in *Fear and Trembling*. How does the dichotomy between recollection and revelation map onto that between the ethical and the religious?

Not directly. If *Fear and Trembling* points to the way in which revelation can be a challenge to the ultimacy of the ethical, the mention of Socrates, whom Climacus presents as the paradigm of the recollection thesis about knowledge, reminds us that social critique can come in this form too. The Socrates of the dialogues points to a knowledge which is both attainable through recollection and the basis for a powerful critique of Athenian *Sittlichkeit*. For

---

[2]For an example of the kind of (broadly speaking) Marxist response to Kierke-gaard I have in mind, see Steven Best and Douglas Kellner, "Modernity, Mass Society, and the Media: Reflections on the Corsair Affair," in *International Kierke-gaard Commentary: The Corsair Affair*, ed. Robert L. Perkins (Macon GA: Mercer University Press, 1990).

Socrates recollection gives us access to the eternal, under which everything temporal stands in judgment.

This means that there is a teleological suspension of the ethical in the dialogues. The lifeworld of the Athenian *polis* is not ultimate and absolute, but has as its destiny to transcend its natural historical accomplishments and atrocities in order to become the earthly embodiment of an eternal order to which it is responsible and over which it does not preside. In this way, but only in this way, can it find stability and its people happiness.

There is another version of knowledge as recollection present, though not named, in the *Fragments* (see PF, 182-83, 217). That would be Lessing. The questions on the title page about an historical point of departure for an eternal consciousness, how it could be of more than historical interest, and how historical knowledge relates to eternal happiness are motivated by his famous essay of 1777, *On the Proof of the Spirit and of Power* (PF, 1 and 273).

In discussing the attempt to argue for the truth of Christian faith on the basis of miracles and fulfilled prophecies, Lessing notes the problem of historical distance. "The problem is that reports of fulfilled prophecies are not fulfilled prophecies; that reports of miracles are not miracles."[3] For the sake of argument, however, he is willing to concede that such reports are "as reliable as historical truths ever can be." But they cannot be demonstrated and, consequently, nothing can be demonstrated by means of them: "*accidental truths of history can never become proof of necessary truths of reason*" (LTW, 53).

Lessing puts his point in the form of two rhetorical questions.

If on historical grounds I have no objection to the statement that Christ raised to life a dead man; must I therefore accept it as true that God has a Son who is of the same essence as himself? . . . If on historical grounds I have no objection to the statement that this Christ himself rose from the dead, must I therefore accept it as true that this risen Christ was the Son of God? (LTW, 54)

---

[3]*Lessing's Theological Writings*, ed. Henry Chadwick (Stanford CA: Stanford University Press, 1957) 52. Subsequent references in the text will be identified as LTW.

To intensify the issue, he notes that such claims are "inconceivable truths" and "something against which my reason rebels" (LTW, 53-54).

Not content to let us answer these questions for ourselves, Lessing gives us his own answer.

> But to jump with that historical truth to a quite different class of truths, and to demand of me that I should form all my metaphysical and moral ideas accordingly; to expect me to alter all my fundamental ideas of the nature of the Godhead because I cannot set any credible testimony against the resurrection of Christ: if that is not a μετάβασις εἰς ἄλλο γένος, then I do not know what Aristotle meant by this phrase. . . . That, then, is the ugly, broad ditch which I cannot get across, however often and however earnestly I have tried to make the leap. If anyone can help me over it, let him do it, I beg him, I adjure him. He will deserve a divine reward from me. (LTW, 54-55)

While Kierkegaard appreciates Lessing's acknowledgement of the ditch and the necessity of a leap, he would not be happy with this idea that human reason contains an a priori knowledge of God that is so ultimate and definitive that nothing that God could possibly do in history could affect it. To him this looks like a convenient device for locking God up, or better, locking God out of a world preinterpreted in our own image. So the *Fragments*, in presenting an alternative to Socrates, are simultaneously presenting an alternative to Lessing's (Leibnizian) account of our knowledge of God and to the whole Enlightenment project of which it is a classic expression.[4]

But here, as with Socrates, the point is not to preserve the teleological suspension of the ethical and its corollary that only God is absolute, while the universal (*Sittlichkeit*) is never more than relatively valid. For as with Socrates, there is a teleological suspension of the ethical in Lessing inasmuch as on his view reason puts us in touch with the eternal, to which every human community is answerable.

---

[4]As suggested in n. 1, this is the real confrontation with the moral and religious philosophy of Kant.

This is more than a logical possibility for Lessing, though the *Sittlichkeit* he has in mind is not that of the *polis* but that of the *ecclesia*. In *Nathan der Weise* he relativizes the particularity of the Jewish synagogue, the Christian church, and the Muslim mosque before the universality of the God available to all in the necessary and thus eternal truths of reason.

If we ask about the relation of *Philosophical Fragments* to *Fear and Trembling* with an eye to the former's concern for Socrates and Lessing, the answer would seem to be: very little. While the latter portrays Christian faith as an alternative to Hegelian civic virtue, the former portrays it as an alternative to pure reason as conceived by a precritical (pre-Kantian) and antihistorical (pre-Hegelian) Enlightenment.[5] Moreover, there is an irony in their juxtaposition. For while Johannes de Silentio portrays faith as essentially linked to a teleological suspension of the ethical, Johannes Climacus portrays it as the opponent of a Reason that makes such a suspension possible. For Socrates and Lessing it is precisely recollection that makes critical social theory possible. Is Kierkegaard a scattershot writer who shoots down his own trial balloons? a playful tease who ironically undermines all positions in order to become a lighter than air balloon himself?

This conclusion will recommend itself to those who find Kierkegaard irresistibly interesting (an aesthetic, or perhaps *the* aesthetic category) but who do not wish to take seriously his claim that

> I am and was a religious author, that the whole of my work as
> an author is related to Christianity, to the problem "of becoming
> a Christian," with a direct or indirect polemic against the
> monstrous illusion we call Christendom, or against the illusion
> that in such a land as ours all are Christians of a sort. (PV, 5-6)

Of course, Kierkegaard's reading of his authorship isn't absolute by virtue of his being its author. But a responsible reading will try to make sense of the author's self-interpretation rather than simply setting it aside on the basis of personal antipathy to his central concerns. Let us see whether such a charitable reading

---

[5]This account of pure reason as pre-Kantian and pre-Hegelian fits Kant's moral and religious philosophy as well as it fits Lessing's metaphysics. Both can be characterized as ontotheological. See n. 7.

of the *Fragments* can be found, one that will make it continuous with the "attack upon Christendom" unambiguously present in *Fear and Trembling*.

The first thing to note is that Socrates and Lessing do not represent Christendom. During what we might call the golden age of deism, there was an effort to develop a religion within the limits of pure reason that (1) was manifestly different from historic Christianity, yet (2) claimed to be, by virtue of its rationality, the highest form of Christian truth. But Kierkegaard did not write during the golden age of deism but toward the end of the golden age of Denmark. Neither in fact nor in Kierkegaard's interpretation is the Christendom that surrounded him the colonization of Christian faith by modernity in the form of precritical, antihistorical Enlightenment.

Moreover, Lessing was not part of that deism that claimed to be the highest form of Christianity. One of the things Kierkegaard most admired about him was his candor in noting the radical difference between the religion of pure reason and Christian faith. But after Lessing dug his ditch between them what would be the point of coming along and digging it again?

In other words, a *Philosophical Fragments* with Socrates and Lessing as its prime targets would seem to be both untimely (but not in the Nietzschean sense) and unnecessary. Perhaps Kierkegaard is just a literary gamester after all.

* * *

But the Preface makes it clear that Johannes thinks he is challenging the present age. What is more, he does so in language that is unmistakably Hegelian (PF, 6), and he presents himself as dancing with death, anticipating a theme he will make prominent in *Concluding Unscientific Postscript*, where the battle with Hegel and Christendom is at least as unmistakable as in *Fear and Trembling*. Is Hegel, even more than Socrates and Lessing, the target of the *Fragments*? The obvious advantage of such a reading is that it would restore continuity and (untimely) timeliness to the authorship. Since Hegel is, for Kierkegaard, the ideological culmination of Christendom, the confrontation with Christendom begun in *Fear and Trembling* would continue in the *Fragments* (as it clearly does in the *Postscript*).

Two important groups of evidence support this suggestion. First is the fact that Hegel's *Phenomenology of Spirit* concludes with a theory of absolute knowing spelled out in terms of recollection. While the concept of revelation appears in the penultimate chapter on religion, *Die offenbare Religion*, the transcendence of the limitations of the religious mode of knowing in absolute knowing is presented as recollection. Thus the concluding movement of the *Phenomenology* is from revelation to recollection. Not only does Climacus reverse the direction in the *Fragments*, but in place of the harmony posited by Hegel he presents a radical otherness that recalls the radical otherness of *Fear and Trembling*.

The Hegelian theory of absolute knowing as recollection is by no means a return to Socrates or Lessing. It occurs in the final paragraph of the *Phenomenology*, where in just over a page Hegel speaks no fewer than four times of recollection (*Erinnerung*).[6] Hegel spells out the distinctiveness of his concept by playing on etymologies. Recollection (*Erinnerung*) corresponds to the externalization or objectification (*Entäusserung*) of Spirit into time as history. So far from being a knowing that is independent of historical mediation and that elevates the knower into some eternal realm beyond history, for Hegel recollection is "comprehended History."

But while absolute knowing has an historical reference in some sense, Hegel insists that it also be characterized by universality and necessity, which Kant had clearly identified as the marks of the a priori. How this is possible Hegel seeks to show in Chapter Seven, where he describes the transformation of the religious form of knowing (*Vorstellung*) to the superior, philosophical form (*Begriff*).

The two central theses of this chapter on religion are: (1) Christianity is the revealed religion, and (2) the "incarnation of the divine Being . . . is the simple content of the absolute religion" (PS, 459). By the first of these Hegel does not mean anything like the traditional claim, presented in the *Fragments* as the alternative to Socrates, that knowledge of the Truth lies beyond the capacity of

---

[6]*Hegel's Phenomenology of Spirit*, trans. A. V. Miller (Oxford: Clarendon Press, 1977) 492-93. Miller translates the first three of these as "recollection," the fourth as "inwardizing." Subsequent references in the text will be identified as PS.

human reason, finite and fallen. He means rather that in Christianity, the divine Being becomes fully manifest and available to human knowledge.

But the religious form of this knowledge is "imperfect," "incomplete," "defective," "not spiritual," "not yet perfected" (PS, 462-63, 472, 477). For this reason everything depends on bringing our understanding of the second thesis, "the incarnation of the divine Being" to "a higher formative development of consciousness" above the "impoverishment of Spirit" represented by the religious understanding of God become human (PS, 463).

"The divine nature is the same as the human, and it is this unity that is beheld" (PS, 460). According to the religious understanding, this union of the divine and human takes place uniquely in Jesus of Nazareth. In other words, at this stage where it is "not spiritual," religious consciousness "knows the human form of the divine Being at first only as a particular, not yet as a universal, form" (PS, 472). For religion "Spirit as an individual Self is not yet equally the universal Self, the Self of everyone. In other words, the shape has not as yet the form of the Notion [*Begriff*], i.e., of the universal Self" (PS, 462).

This defect of religious thinking, its failure to see Jesus as Everyone, not human sinfulness, is what necessitates the death of Jesus. "In the vanishing of the immediate existence known to be absolute Being the immediacy receives its negative moment; Spirit remains the immediate Self of actuality, but as the *universal self-consciousness* of the [religious] community" (PS, 462). It is this relocation of the union of divine and human from the particularity of Jesus to the universality of the community that enables Hegel to make the following mind-boggling claim about the absolute essence, "This death is, therefore, its resurrection as Spirit" (PS, 471). The resurrection is not the return of Jesus but the permanence of his disappearance as an individual, leaving some human community as the locus of the unity of the divine and the human. This deifying of a human community is precisely the ethical of *Fear and Trembling*, to which the faith of Abraham is so starkly contrasted.

The other deficiency of religious representation is its lack of necessity. Because it

> interprets and expresses as a *happening* what has just been expressed [in Hegel's account of the community as divine] as the

> *necessity* of the Notion [*Begriff*], it is said that the eternal Being *be-*
> *gets* for itself an "other." . . . But the picture-thinking [*Vorstellung*]
> of the religious community is not this speculative thinking; it has
> the content but without its necessity, and instead of the form of
> the Notion it brings into the realm of pure consciousness the
> natural relationships of father and son. (PS, 465-66)

Hegel surely has a different theory of necessary truth from that
of Lessing and Leibniz, one that seeks to incorporate rather than
exclude the historical. But his theory, like theirs, entails that insofar
as the truth is necessary truth, it is within us and needs but to be
recollected. Even if such recollection is history comprehended
rather than abandoned, the point about recollection that is central
to Johannes Climacus in the *Fragments* remains the same.

Now it begins to look as if Hegel wrote the *Phenomenology* in
order to link Johannes to Johannes. In arguing that religious *Vor-*
stellungen must achieve the form of universality, he identifies what
he calls the higher truth of Christianity with what Johannes de
Silentio presents as the ethical in *Fear and Trembling*; and in seeking
to replace religious narrative with (his own very peculiar sort of)
conceptual necessity, he identifies his version of religious truth
with what Johannes Climacus presents as the Socratic recollection
motif in *Philosophical Fragments*. Since they are, in Hegel's text, two
sides of the same coin, that text invites us to read the works of
Johannes and Johannes as two sides of a single attempt to spell out
an alternative to an Hegelian understanding of Christianity.

As already noted, accepting such an invitation has two advantages. It binds the *Fragments* closely to its sequel from the pen of
Johannes Climacus, *Concluding Unscientific Postscript*, where Lessing
is something of a hero and the villains are Hegel and Christendom;
and, by linking the *Fragments* to *Fear and Trembling*, it supports
Kierkegaard's own claims about the unity and timeliness of his
authorship. In other words, it renders two authors more coherent,
Climacus and Kierkegaard.

Moreover, when *Philosophical Fragments* is read against the
background of the last chapters of the *Phenomenology*, its peculiar
style of philosophical argument becomes less perplexing. When
properly reinterpreted, according to Hegel's notion of the Notion,
the truth of religion is the following:

> Here, therefore, God is *revealed as He is*; He is immediately pres-
> ent as He is *in Himself*, i.e., He is immediately *present* as Spirit.
> God is attainable in pure speculative knowledge alone and *is*
> only in that knowledge, and is only that knowledge itself, for He
> is Spirit. (PS, 461)

In the pages that follow Hegel repeatedly notes that properly understood, religion is human self-consciousness rather than consciousness, that is, consciousness of itself rather than of an other (PS, 461-66, 471). If this were presented (a là Lessing) as an alternative to the Christian conception of the relation between God and humans, the task for a Christian thinker might be to try to show the superiority of the Christian conception.

But when this is presented as the Christian view of the matter, whose form has admittedly been altered but whose content has remained the same, the task of a Christian thinker is made much easier. It is only necessary to point out that and how A and B are different. As Johannes will put it in the *Postscript*, "Whether Christianity is in the right is another question. . . . But if Christianity is perhaps in the wrong, this much is certain: speculative thought is definitely in the wrong" (CUP, 1: 226). That is to say, while Climacus has no settled views on the truth value of either Christianity or Hegelianism as such, he holds that the latter is "definitely in the wrong" in presenting itself as identical with the former in content, if not in form. This is already his posture in the *Fragments*.

* * *

A second body of evidence in support of reading the *Fragments* as directed by Kierkegaard more at Hegel and Christendom than at Socrates and Lessing comes from the text of the *Fragments* itself. In addition to the already mentioned Hegelian allusions to the present age in the Preface, there are three themes that correspond (antithetically) to the three moments of the movement from religious *Vorstellung* to philosophical *Begriff* in the *Phenomenology*. That movement has just been described as one from particularity to universality, from contingency to necessity, and from consciousness to self-consciousness.

Over against the idea that the particularity of Jesus is replaced by the universality of the religious community as the locus of the unity of the divine and the human, Johannes emphasizes the historical particularity of the god in human form from start to finish. Chapters Four and Five of the *Fragments*, with their concern about the epistemic significance of historical closeness and distance would be meaningless if what were really at stake were the self-consciousness of the community. For even if the truth had come to be historically, it would now be present and available for recollective self-knowledge. But then the truth would be within us and we would be back with Socrates. The thought experiment would have failed to develop an alternative to his assumption.

Similarly, in the "Interlude," Johannes argues (with Lessing and against Hegel) that historical truths and necessary truths are mutually exclusive. In recollection we become "immediately contemporary" with the truth by virtue of its being directly present to us. For Socrates and Lessing this is by virtue of the way recollection lifts us out of history to participate in eternal truth. For Hegel this is by virtue of the fact that the truth has become our very being and is available to self-consciousness. But Johannes insists that the historical has "no immediate contemporary," whether it be ordinary historical facts or the extraordinary event of the Incarnation (PF, 87-88). Otherwise we would be back with Socrates.

Finally, against any hint that religious knowledge is self-consciousness, awareness or knowledge of self rather than of other, Johannes is equally clear that the thought experiment developed in search of a B different from the Socratic A posits the otherness of "the god" decisively and deliberately. Thus, for example, when "the god" who would be Teacher and Savior suffers death, Johannes distinguishes him from those for whom he dies as immortal and innocent over against their mortality and guilt (PF, 34). In a more sustained manner, in Chapter Three, he explores the idea of the unknown, the limit to what thought can think.

> What, then, is the unknown? It is the frontier that is continually arrived at, and therefore . . . it is the different, the absolutely different. . . . This human being is also the god. How do I know that? Well, I cannot know it, for in that case I would have to know the god and the difference, and I do not know the difference, inasmuch as the understanding has made it like unto that from which it differs. (PF, 44-46)

In a version of the Greek doctrine that like is known by like, Johannes here argues that the understanding can know God only to the degree that it finds or makes God to be like the human. Insofar as God is different, human understanding confronts the divine as beyond its powers.[7]

Johannes pushes this argument one crucial step farther by making sin the basis of the absolute difference between the divine and the human.

> But if the god is to be absolutely different from a human being [as the experiment seems at this point to require], this can have its basis not in that which man owes to the god (for to that extent they are akin) but in that which he owes to himself or in that which he himself has committed. What, then, is the difference? Indeed, what else but sin, since the difference, the absolute difference, must have been caused by the individual himself. . . . Thus the paradox becomes even more terrible . . . negatively, by bringing into prominence the absolute difference of sin and, positively, by wanting to annul this absolute difference in the absolute equality. (PF, 46-47)[8]

My suggestions in this essay for how best to read *Philosophical Fragments* can be summarized as follows.

(1) First note the peculiar form of argument adopted by Johannes Climacus, who, like Johannes de Silentio of *Fear and Trembling*, is content to call attention to the difference between positions A and B without arguing for either.

---

[7]In the attempt to keep the popular term "ontotheology" from being simply "a stick with which to thump upon my chosen opponents," Walter Lowe has offered a working definition of the term as follows: "any effort or tendency to think of God and the finite order in univocal terms." *The Wound of Reason: Theology and Difference* (Bloomington: Indiana University Press, 1993) 79. In this context we can say that the thought experiment of the *Fragments* explores a theological critique of ontotheology. The tendency to identify philosophical postmodernism with secular critiques of ontotheology fails to take sufficient account of the possibility introduced to us here by Kierkegaard, that there are religious motivations for challenging a theological metaphysics of presence.

[8]If the *Fragments* stress the paradox and the offense related to the negative moment, *The Sickness unto Death* develops the problematic, even offensive nature of the positive moment, the forgiveness of sins. For here reconciliation does not consist in the discovery that the difference was merely phenomenal; it is rather premised on the reality of sin as the "infinite qualitative difference" between God and the human self (SUD, 126; cf. 99, 121-22).

(2) Then note that *Fear and Trembling*, precisely by virtue of such an unusual argument, is a critical social theory directed against Hegel and an essentially Hegelian self-understanding of Christendom.

(3) Then note the evidence in support of the claim that *Philosophical Fragments* is more fruitfully read as directed against the same combination of Hegel and Christendom than as directed against Socrates and Lessing.

(4) Then draw the conclusion that *Philosophical Fragments* is a form of ideology critique, the attempt to work out the epistemological ramifications of the critical social theory presented in *Fear and Trembling*, by contrasting a theory of knowledge that tends to legitimize the deification of the Established Order, which Kierkegaard takes to be the blasphemy of Christendom, with a theory of knowledge that can support the teleological suspension of the ethical, the prophetic protest against the way Christendom takes God's name in vain.

2

Echoes of Absurdity:
The Offended Consciousness
and the Absolute Paradox
in Kierkegaard's Philosophical Fragments

Sylvia Walsh

Composed by a "loafer" who out of indolence produces "mere-ly a pamphlet" (nothing of "world-historical importance" mind you), *Philosophical Fragments* takes on the appearance of a jest (PF, 5). In reality it is deadly serious, as the "author," Johannes Climacus, stakes his life on it in a dance with the thought of death (PF, 8). Imaginatively constructing a "thought-project" concerning how truth is learned, Climacus admits that his proposal may make him look like "the most ludicrous of all project-cranks" (PF, 21). Yet he hopes to avoid outright derision from the reader with the further admission that the "fairy tale" narrated in the project is not his own but rather is plagiarized from the deity, who is the true author of the poem, or more accurately, "the wonder" that is poe-tized in it (PF, 26, 35). Climacus next indulges in a "metaphysical caprice" (*en metaphysisk Grille*) which, like the spiny hedgehog from which the word "caprice" is derived,[1] is designed to set our hair

---

[1]According to *Webster's New World Dictionary of the American Language* (Cleve-land and New York: World, 1964) "caprice" is derived from the Italian word *capriccio*, which is a combination of *capo*, from the Latin word *caput* or "the head," and *riccio*, meaning "curl," "frizzled," or literally "hedgehog." Hence "caprice" originally referred to "a head with bristling hair" and later became associated with the Italian word *capriola*, meaning "caper" or "leap," and in its verbal form *capriolare*, "to leap like a wild goat." In this way "caprice" came to mean a

bristling with its talk of an absolute paradox that is so curious, so ludicrous, and so unreasonable that the reader is required to lock everything out of his or her consciousness in order to get hold of it (PF, 37, 46). Then, in a short appendix to this caprice, we are entertained with a comic parroting or caricaturing of the absolute paradox in the form of an acoustical illusion, or, more accurately, two acoustical illusions. It is this parroting or echoing of the absolute paradox in the form of acoustical illusions that I want to investigate more closely in the present essay, arguing in the process that it is human understanding in the form of the offended consciousness, not the absolute paradox, that constitutes the absurd.

To support this contention and to show its congruency with other treatments of the absurd and the absolute paradox in Kierkegaard's thought, I shall draw upon the three additional writings in the Kierkegaardian corpus where these concepts are discussed: (1) *Concluding Unscientific Postscript*, which is also ascribed to Johannes Climacus; (2) Kierkegaard's unpublished response in his journals to the critique of *Fear and Trembling* by the pseudonymous writer Theophilus Nicolaus (theologian Magnus Eiríksson, 1806–1881); and (3) the discussion of offense under the pseudonym Anti-Climacus in *Practice in Christianity*.

"whim" or "idle, quaint, or curious notion" and refers to a sudden, apparently unmotivated turn of mind, emotion, or action caused by a whim or impulse. In preferring the word "caprice" as an English translation of the Danish word *Grille*, which appears parenthetically in the subtitle to the third chapter of the Danish editions of *Philosophical Fragments*, the new Princeton English edition by the Hongs thereby catches the ironically whimsical quality of the chapter that is missing in Howard Hong's previous revised translation of David Swenson's English version of the text (Princeton University Press, 1962) where the term "crotchet" is used instead. According to *Webster's*, this word "implies great eccentricity and connotes stubbornness in opposition to prevailing thought, usually on some insignificant point." "Crotchet," therefore, gives the impression of an oddball thinker who is somewhat set in his or her ways, whereas "caprice" suggests someone who is indulging in a playful philosophical game in the manner of the nineteenth-century German romantic ironists and the French postmodernists of the present age, only Johannes Climacus cloaks a true seriousness in his caprice, whereas the latter apparently do not except as their jesting is intended to have the negative effect of undermining the truth or validity of any project of thought or imagination.

I. The Absurdity of the Offended Consciousness
and the Absolute Paradox in Philosophical Fragments

The first acoustical illusion to which Climacus calls attention in the appendix to chapter 3 is prepared for and illuminated by way of an analogy of offense to unhappy love rooted in a misunderstood form of self-love. Like self-love, which deceptively appears to be active but is really a form of inner suffering, offense at its deepest level is a suffering, Climacus claims (PF, 49). Offense may take either an active or passive form, but since each form always involves an element of the other, even when offense is active it contains an element of weakness that makes it unable to free itself from suffering. Climacus wishes to establish the passivity or suffering character of offense in order to make the further claim that neither discovery of the absolute paradox nor taking offense at it originates in the understanding but rather comes into existence with the absolute paradox. Thus when Climacus speaks, as he does in the preceding chapter, of the understanding actively, passionately, paradoxically seeking to "discover something that thought itself cannot think," the unknown against which the understanding collides in this instance is not something it has discovered on its own even though it is in active pursuit of that which it does not know (PF, 37). When the understanding then exclaims that it has discovered a paradox which it cannot think or comprehend and becomes offended at it, this is, Climacus claims, an acoustical illusion resounding in the form of an echo of what the paradox announces to the understanding about itself, namely that it is a paradox.

Like any echo or acoustical illusion, however, the understanding distorts that which it imitates. Climacus thus likens offense to a caricaturing or parroting of the paradox, a copying of it "in the wrong way," so that offense is reckoned as an "erroneous accounting" and a "misunderstanding" of the moment or paradox (PF, 51, 52). But what does this mean? Does it mean that the paradox is not really a paradox? Does it mean that the understanding is wrong in thinking that it has discovered the paradox but right in declaring it to be a paradox? Does it mean that offense is simply the wrong response to the paradox?

Perhaps some light may be shed on these questions by considering another acoustical illusion that comes into play with reference to the paradox. Offense declares that the paradox is absurd, foolishness. But according to Climacus, this claim of the offended consciousness about the paradox is only an echo or counterclaim of what the paradox claims about the understanding. This time, however, the echo is not a copying of something the paradox announces about itself but rather of what the absolute paradox announces about the understanding. Instead of the paradox being the absurd, it is the understanding that is the absurd or has been made the absurd by the paradox. This would seem to be the conclusion to which we are drawn on the basis of the text thus far.

But the issue immediately becomes more complicated by the fact that Climacus goes on to say: "The understanding declares that the paradox is the absurd, but this is only a caricaturing, for the paradox is indeed the paradox, *quia absurdum*" (PF, 52). Now it sounds as if what offense says about the paradox is an echo or caricaturing of what the paradox is and proclaims about itself, not of the paradox's claim about the understanding as we were previously led to think. Climacus again reiterates that this is not something the understanding has discovered but rather is a discovery made by the paradox, which "now takes testimony from the offense" (PF, 52). But if offense constitutes an "erroneous accounting" of the paradox and copies it "in the wrong way," there must be some distortion in this testimony; otherwise offense is not wrong in its claim that the paradox is absurd, only wrong in thinking that it made the discovery on its own. Perhaps that is all the distortion amounts to, namely the illusion on the part of the understanding that it has discovered the paradox.

Climacus certainly leads us to think as much since he continues to emphasize that the discovery belongs to the paradox and that the understanding merely parrots it. How the paradox "discovers" (*opdaget*) itself or something about itself to the understanding is unclear to me, but perhaps Climacus means nothing more than that the understanding becomes cognizant of the paradox from the paradox, which announces itself as the absolute paradox to the understanding, rather than coming to this discovery by itself. That this is the case is suggested by subsequent passages in which the understanding is ushered to the "wonder stool" by the paradox and confirmed in everything it says about the paradox: "Now, what are you wondering about? It is just as you say, and the amazing thing is that you think that it is an objection, but the truth in the mouth of a hypocrite is dearer to me than to hear it from an angel and an apostle" (PF, 52). This passage suggests that what the understanding says about the paradox is true, even if it is parroted and intended as an objection. What then is the distortion that makes offense a wrong accounting of the paradox? Does it consist merely in the mistaken idea of the understanding that its charge of absurdity against the absolute paradox constitutes an objection to, rather than a confirmation of, its divine origin? Is it only a matter of who discovers the paradox? Surely there is more at stake than that.

Let me approach the problem, therefore, from another angle. Climacus states: "The offense remains outside the paradox, and the basis for that is: *quia absurdum*" (PF, 52). The first clause of this statement is reiterated twice in the course of the same paragraph, so it must be a claim Climacus wants to impress upon us. To illustrate what he means by this claim, Climacus introduces another term for the paradox, describing it this time as "the most improbable" in order to draw a contrast between the paradox and the understanding, which can deal only with that which is probable (PF, 52). The improbable is that which stands outside the realm of probability. Probability cannot deal with the improbable or rather can deal with it only by transforming it into something probable, ordinary, or trivial, hence abrogating it (PF, 52-53; cf. CUP, 1:211). As that which is the most improbable, therefore, the paradox stands outside the understanding as something it cannot understand. But notice that Climacus's claim is stated in reverse fashion: it is offense or the offended understanding that stands outside the paradox rather than vice versa. While the opposite is equally true, since it stands to reason that the paradox remains outside the understanding if the understanding remains outside the paradox, Climacus is primarily interested in determining how the understanding is related to the paradox rather than vice versa. If the understanding stands outside the paradox, the implication is that anything the understanding or offense has to say about it is suspect or a distortion in some fashion. Our problem is to determine the precise nature of this distortion.

II. The Absurd and the Absolute Paradox
in Concluding Unscientific Postscript,
the Response to Theophilus Nicolaus,
and Practice in Christianity

Since *Philosophical Fragments* is extremely sparse in what it has to say about the absolute paradox and the absurd, it may help to look briefly at Climacus's additional remarks about these categories in *Concluding Unscientific Postscript*. In this work Climacus suggests that the eternal essential truth becomes paradoxical either by being brought into relation to an existing individual, as in Socratic subjectivity, or by being placed in juxtaposition with existence by coming into existence itself, as encountered in Christian subjectivity (CUP, 1:205, 209). In the first instance, Climacus claims, the eternal essential truth is not in itself a paradox, but in the second it is. Furthermore, the second form of paradox is identified with the absurd, which is concretely defined here in terms of the historical fact "that the eternal truth has come into existence in time, that God has come into existence, has been born, has grown up, etc., has come into existence exactly as an individual human being, indistinguishable from any other human being" (CUP, 1:210). The eternal truth in this instance is absurd, Climacus claims, because "it contains the contradiction that something that can become historical only in direct opposition to all human understanding has become historical" (CUP, 1:211). Then he goes on clearly to equate this contradiction with the absurd: "this contradiction is the absurd, which can only be believed" (CUP, 1:211).

These later comments by Climacus indicate, first of all, that the absolute paradox is constituted by the juxtaposition of the eternal truth with existence or the historical, and this is consistent with the way he describes the paradox in *Philosophical Fragments*, where it is said that "the paradox specifically unites the contradictories, is the eternalizing of the historical and the historicizing of the eternal" (PF, 61). Second, they indicate that the absolute paradox itself is absurd because it involves the coming into existence of eternal truth or the god, whose being or essence is not subject to the contingencies of space and time. This would seem, then, to settle the issue about the absurdity of the absolute paradox. But if the absolute paradox is the absurd, why is the understanding declared absurd by the paradox when it claims the paradox is the absurd, foolishness? And why is this echo on the part of the understanding an "erroneous accounting" of the paradox, a misunderstanding of it?

Our original questions still stand and have not been clarified and answered by either *Philosophical Fragments* or *Concluding Unscientific Postscript*, at least not to my satisfaction. Let us turn, therefore, to another source of commentary on the paradox and the absurd, Kierkegaard's unpublished response to Magnus Eiríksson's pseudonym, Theophilus Nicolaus, preserved in the journals (*Papirer* X⁶ B 68-82; JP, 1:9-12 [78-81]; JP, 6:6598-6601 [68-69, 77, 82]). Although this response is directed to Nicolaus's review of Johannes de Silentio's *Fear and Trembling*, it ranges beyond the treatment of paradox and the absurd in that work to cover the use of these categories by other Kierkegaardian pseudonyms as well, including Johannes Climacus and Anti-Climacus. In fact, several of the journal entries constituting this response are attributed to Johannes Climacus.

In the first of these, Climacus points out that what he and Johannes de Silentio, neither of whom claims to have faith, call the absurd and the paradox, Theophilus Nicolaus regards not as absurd but as "the higher rationality" in a nonspeculative sense (JP, 6:6598). But Climacus claims that without the absurd serving as "the negative sign and predicate which dialectically makes sure that the scope of 'the purely human' is qualitatively terminated," there is no way of indicating that this higher reason lies on the other side of the human, "in the heavenly regions of the divine, of revelation," rather than on this side. The rationality of the content of faith might then be presumed to stand in continuity with human understanding and be subject to discovery through human reason rather than through revelation. In order to prevent this from happening, Climacus claims, the absurd is needed as a sign and category to exercise a "restraining influence" upon the believer. He then goes on to make the following crucial statement:

> When I believe, then assuredly neither faith nor the content of faith is absurd. O, no, no—but I understand very well that for the person who does not believe, faith and the content of faith are absurd, and I also understand that as soon as I myself am not in

> the faith, am weak, when doubt perhaps begins to stir, then faith
> and the content of faith gradually begin to become absurd for
> me. (JP, 6:6598)

This statement contains two important implications. First, it suggests that the absurd is a category of interpretation employed by human understanding, not a qualification of the absolute paradox itself as the content of faith. Second, the absurd more specifically is a category employed only by nonbelievers, not by believers. For believers, faith and the content of faith are not absurd even though the believer, like Abraham, appears to believe "by virtue of the absurd" to those who stand outside of faith. But Kierkegaard, speaking in another entry as Anti-Climacus in the response to Theophilus Nicolaus, goes on to point out that this is only how it looks *to a third person* who does not have the passion of faith (JP, 1:10). Neither Johannes de Silentio nor Johannes Climacus is a believer; thus they illumine faith only negatively, from the standpoint of an outsider, and should not be understood as describing the positive content of faith.

The absurd as a negative sign or determination of faith is nevertheless regarded by Anti-Climacus as an essential element in coming to faith, for several reasons. First, it assures that one has not overlooked any possibility of explaining the paradox or content of faith within the realm of what is possible from a merely human standpoint (JP, 1:9). Second, it assures that faith is not a (higher) form of knowledge, for only the passion of faith, not a better or higher understanding of the absolute paradox, is able to overcome the absurd (JP, 1:10; 6:6598). Third, and perhaps most importantly, it gives faith a double-sided or duplex character that is "more penetrating and dialectical and informed" than the view of faith as a higher form of rationality offered by Theophilus Nicolaus (JP, 1:10). In another journal entry of 1850 Kierkegaard laments the tendency of his time to present faith directly and in continuity with human understanding without the tension of the dialectical, suggesting that it results in an "unholy confusion" in speaking about faith (JP, 1:8). "The [immediate] believer is not dialectically consolidated as 'the single individual,' cannot endure this double vision—that the content of faith, seen from the other side, is the negative absurd," he complains (JP, 1:8).

In this duplex perspective, the absurd and faith are inseparable (JP, 1:10); one only comes to faith by way of the absurd and the possibility of offense, which always remains as a negative possibility in faith even though the believer no longer regards the content of faith as absurd. This is the same position we find Anti-Climacus taking in the opening summary of his exposition of the possibility of offense in relation to Christ in *Practice in Christianity*:

> Just as the concept "faith" is an altogether distinctively Christian term, so in turn is "offense" an altogether distinctively Christian term relating to faith. The possibility of offense is the crossroad, or it is like standing at the crossroad. From the possibility of offense, one turns either to offense or to faith, but one never comes to faith except from the possibility of offense. (PC, 81)

Anti-Climacus goes on to explore the possibility of offense in relation to Christ as a paradox or "sign of contradiction" in the form of a *qualitative* contradiction rather than as a logical or apparently logical contradiction concerning the speculative unity of God and human being:[2]

> In Scripture the God-man is called a sign of contradiction—but what contradiction, if any, could there be at all in the speculative unity of God and man? No, there is no contradiction in that, but the contradiction—and it is as great as possible, is the qualitative

---

[2]The nature of the contradiction that characterizes the absolute paradox in *Philosophical Fragments* and *Concluding Unscientific Postscript* and the God-man as a paradox in *Practice in Christianity* has been much debated in Kierkegaard studies. For a discussion of earlier scholarly treatments of this issue, see my dissertation under the name Sylvia Walsh Utterback, "Kierkegaard's Dialectic of Christian Existence" (Emory University, 1975) 190-92. For a more recent discussion of the contradictoriness of the absolute paradox in the Climacus writings, see C. Stephen Evans, *Kierkegaard's "Fragments" and "Postscript": The Religious Philosophy of Johannes Climacus* (Atlantic Highlands NJ: Humanities Press, 1983) 212-32. Evans takes the position that the absolute paradox is not a logical or formal contradiction but an apparent contradiction in the sense that "it necessarily *appears* to existing human beings as a contradiction" (222). While Evans also characterizes the paradox as a qualitative contradiction, he does so in a different sense than the one Anti-Climacus has in mind. Basing his view on the "infinite qualitative difference" between God and man because of sin, Evans states: "The contradiction in the paradox is a 'qualitative' contradiction wherein that which is absolutely unlike man (God) becomes man in order to abolish this unlikeness," as envisioned in the thought-project of *Philosophical Fragments* (229).

contradiction—is between being God and being an individual human being. (PC, 125; cf. 123 and 131)

As Anti-Climacus sees it, "Humanly speaking, there is no possibility of a crazier composite than this either in heaven or on earth or in the abyss or in the most fantastic aberrations of thought"—a viewpoint which echoes that of Johannes Climacus concerning the absolute paradox in his thought-project (PC, 82; PF, 37, 46). For Anti-Climacus, however, the possibility of offense is occasioned by the fact that an individual human being acts so as indirectly to suggest the quality of divinity in his being (in other words, one is offended by the "loftiness" of Christ) and by the fact that this man underwent humiliation and suffering, which are incongruent with the human conception of God (one is offended by his "lowliness") (PC, 82). In neither instance does the contradiction of the God-man have to do with the logic of the Incarnation, since Anti-Climacus is not concerned with a propositional truth claim but with the lofty actions and lowly condition of an individual human being that suggest the qualitatively contradictory makeup of his being. Furthermore, a logical contradiction is governed by the principle of contradiction, which excludes the possibility of the opposite of a proposition being true at the same time, whereas a paradox is distinguished precisely by the fact that both terms are regarded as being true at the same time. Like Virgilius Haufniensis, the pseudonymous author of *The Concept of Anxiety*, Anti-Climacus seems to assume a strict distinction between existence and thought or logic (CA, 9 and note 14). Logic pertains only to the realm of thought and cannot think the individual. Thus it can deal only with the concept of human being in general; that is, it universalizes human being whereas the union between God and human being Anti-Climacus is talking about is between God and an individual man. The qualitative contradiction this union posits is the greatest possible contradiction because qualitative opposites in existence cannot be mediated as they are in thought. As Johannes Climacus points out in *Philosophical Fragments*, thought cannot conceive an absolute difference between God and human being and tends, on the contrary, to assert a fundamental likeness rather than a contradiction between them (PF, 45).

III. Resolution of the Problem of the Absurdity of the Absolute Paradox

Factoring in these viewpoints, let us now return to the problem of the absurd in *Philosophical Fragments* with which we began. The problem, to restate it briefly, has to do with the charge and counter-charge of absurdity being voiced in a contest of echoing between the paradox and the understanding. The offended consciousness charges the absolute paradox is absurd, while the absolute paradox countercharges that it is the understanding which is absurd. But since the charge of the offended consciousness is only an echo of what the absolute paradox announces about itself, we are left wondering why the understanding is declared to be absurd in making this charge against the paradox, and further, why it is reckoned as an "erroneous accounting" of the paradox. *Concluding Unscientific Postscript* confirmed the absurdity of the absolute paradox but did not provide a satisfactory resolution of these questions. Kierkegaard's response to Theophilus Nicolaus carries us much further in this direction but further complicates the issue by requiring us to make a distinction between the believer and the nonbeliever when thinking about the absurd. Since Johannes Climacus is a nonbeliever, he speaks as one outside of faith who nevertheless succeeds in articulating the negative or obverse side of faith and the content of faith as it appears from the standpoint of human understanding. From this perspective, to declare the paradox to be absurd is undoubtedly a misunderstanding because human understanding stands outside the paradox and thinks the absurdity of the paradox constitutes an objection to it. Yet, according to Climacus, the absolute paradox proclaims itself to the understanding as the absurd and is a paradox precisely because it is absurd. Is this perhaps a further misunderstanding on his part, due to the fact that he is a nonbeliever? I think not, for Anti-Climacus is just as adamant as Johannes Climacus in proclaiming the contradictoriness and paradoxicality of Christianity. In fact, in the closing sentence of the response to Theophilus Nicolaus, Kierkegaard remarks:

> Incidentally, I would be glad to have another pseudonym, one who does not like Johannes de Silentio say he does not have faith, but plainly, positively says he has faith—Anti-Climacus—

repeat what, as a matter of fact, is stated in the pseudonymous writings. (JP, 6:6601)

In Kierkegaard's view, then, there is congruence and continuity between the pseudonyms on the absurdity of the paradox. Perhaps a clue as to how, in his mind at least, the apparent incongruities relating to the absurd in their accounts are resolved may be found in a journal entry of 1842–1843, predating the writing of *Philosophical Fragments* (JP, 3:3073). The content of this entry consists in Kierkegaard's reading notes on Leibniz's *Theodicy*, for example, the distinction Leibniz makes between what is above reason as opposed to what is against reason. For Leibniz, faith is above reason, which in Kierkegaard's judgment is equivalent to his own claim that Christianity consists of paradox. Since reason, as Leibniz understands it, involves "a linking together of truths (*enchainement*), a conclusion from causes," Kierkegaard concludes that faith "cannot be *proved, demonstrated, comprehended*" because there is a missing link. This means faith is a paradox and does not stand in continuity with reason, or at least not immediately so. Here we reach the point I want to emphasize in this entry. Kierkegaard goes on in these notes to state that Christianity *does* stand in continuity with reason, but it has "continuity only in reverse" (*bagvendt Continuitet*), that is, "at the beginning it does not manifest itself as continuity." The paradoxicality and unreasonableness or absurdity of Christianity thus constitute "the first form" of its appearance in world history and human consciousness (JP, 3:3073).

The notion of a "first form" of Christianity reappears in Kierkegaard's later religious writings and journals to indicate how Christianity combines both strictness and mildness, works and grace, law and gospel, and understands Jesus Christ as both the prototype and redeemer of humanity.[3] Ultimately, Kierkegaard contends, Christianity is all gentleness, love, grace, and consolation, but these factors are defined according to, or on the other side of, a dialectic in which "every qualification of the essentially Christian is first of all its opposite" (JY, 98). There are essentially four basic and decisive negative determinants of Christian existence which

---

[3]For a discussion of the way Kierkegaard sees Christianity combining these factors, see Utterback, *Kierkegaard's Dialectic of Christian Existence*, 335-52.

must be viewed and correlated in this dialectical manner: the consciousness of sin, the possibility of offense, dying away from the world or self-renunciation, and suffering. Through these factors the Christian stands indirectly related to or brings to expression in his or her existence the positive determinants of Christianity: forgiveness, faith, new life and hope, love, joy, consolation, and blessedness.[4]

Applying this dialectical framework to *Philosophical Fragments*, we may conclude, then, that Christianity appears in its first form as the absurd or a paradox to the understanding, but that is not its true or ultimate form, which is grasped only in faith. When the understanding declares the absolute paradox to be absurd, therefore, it is only an echo of what Christianity in its first form as absolute paradox proclaims about itself to the understanding. That echo is a caricature or distortion of the truth in being an acoustical illusion that originates from the paradox rather than from the understanding and in constituting an improper response to the paradox in the form of an offended consciousness rather than the happy passion of faith. But it is also a caricature because ultimately the absolute paradox, however improbable, absurd, contradictory, or paradoxical it appears to human consciousness, expresses only the *obverse* side of the truth, which is not only not improbable or impossible but is entirely possible because it is actual, having come into existence in the form of an individual human being in a decisive moment of time. From the standpoint of faith, all things are possible for God, even, we may presume, an entry into the forms and substance of the temporal order that are qualitatively different from the divine.

Our exploration of the perplexing little problem of the acoustical illusion in *Philosophical Fragments* has also shown, I think, that it is both appropriate and necessary to read this book in the context of Kierkegaard's other writings and not in isolation from them. Otherwise one may be tempted to take Climacus's views as fully representing the Christian position which he admittedly does not

---

[4]For a brief treatment of these dialectical factors in Kierkegaard's thought, see my article under the name Sylvia W. Utterback, "Kierkegaard's Inverse Dialectic," *Kierkegaardiana* 11 (1980): 34-54. For a more extensive treatment, see Utterback, *Kierkegaard's Dialectic of Christian Existence.*

subscribe to nor existentially reduplicate in his own life. Climacus gives us one side of the truth but not the whole truth as understood from a Christian perspective. It is perhaps with some justification, then, that his book should be taken lightly as the serious jest he claims it to be.

3

A Little Light Music:
The Subversion of Objectivity
in Kierkegaard's Philosophical Fragments

M. Piety

Kierkegaard referred to himself as "the Magister of Irony" (POV, 57),[1] not simply because, as Walter Lowrie points out, "the degree of Magister Artium had been granted him for his able dissertation on *the Concept of Irony*" (POV, 166n.15), but because many of his subsequent works were so thoroughly ironical.[2]

"The quality that permeates all irony," argues Kierkegaard, is that "the phenomenon is not the essence but the very opposite of the essence" (CI, 247). The irony of the *Fragments* must thus consist in an opposition between what is said directly in that work and what the reader is supposed to understand as the real meaning of the work. It may seem contentious to claim that the work has a "real meaning." As Sylvia Walsh has pointed out, however, Kierke-

---

[1]See also *Søren Kierkegaards Samlede Værker*, 1–14, ed. A. B. Drachman, J. L. Heiberg, and H. O. Lange, 1st ed. (Copenhagen: Gyldendal, 1901–1906) 13:552.

[2]The books and articles referring to irony in Kierkegaard's works are too numerous to be listed here, hence I will refer the reader to the following two bibliographies: Jens Himmelstrup, *Søren Kierkegaard International Bibliography* (Copenhagen: Nyt Nordisk Forlag Arnold Busk, 1962) and Aage Jørensen, *Søren Kierkegaard-literatur 1961–1970 . . . 1972–1980*.

One very helpful treatment of Kierkegaard's use of irony and, in particular, of the use he makes of irony through the agency of the pseudonym Johannes Climacus, does not, however, actually have "irony" in the title. This is C. Stephen Evans, *Kierkegaard's Fragments and Postscript: The Religious Philosophy of Johannes Climacus* (Atlantic Highlands, NJ: Humanities Press, 1983).

gaard does not embrace irony for itself, but only "as a strategy for dismounting untruth."[3] If she is correct, then the irony of the *Fragments* must represent Kierkegaard's attempt to dislodge some misconception relating to the issue with which it deals.

I

Climacus, the pseudonymous author of the *Fragments*, begins the work with an examination of the "Socratic question" (PF, 9) of whether or not the truth can be learned. On the Socratic account,[4] he explains, the learner is seen as *essentially* in possession of the truth, but *accidentally* in a state of forgetfulness. Hence, on this view, the learner does not actually need a teacher. "[T]he ignorant person," explains Climacus, "merely needs to be reminded in order, by himself, to call to mind what he knows" (PF, 9), and it would appear that anything from "a teacher" to the simple act of tripping over a stone could serve this purpose. Climacus's concern, however, is that such an interpretation of the relation of the individual to the truth appears to deprive the point in time at which the individual remembers the truth of any decisive significance. On this account, the moment (*Øieblikket*)[5] at which the truth is remembered becomes instantly hidden in the eternity of the truth which is remembered,

> assimilated into it in such a way that [the learner], so to speak,
> . . . cannot find it, even if [he] were to look for it, because [in
> eternity] there is no Here and no There, but only a *ubique et
> nusquam* [everywhere and nowhere]. (PF, 13)

---

[3]Sylvia Walsh, "Kierkegaard and Postmodernism," *International Journal for Philosophy and Religion* 29 (1991): 121.

[4]There is some question as to whether the position that Kierkegaard attributes to Socrates ought actually to be attributed to him. While this is not an insignificant issue, it has no bearing on the thesis being advanced in this essay, so I do not intend to address it here.

[5]This term should not be confused with "Moment." While both *Øieblik* and *Moment* are translated as "moment," the former refers to an instant or a point in time, while the latter is equivalent to Hegel's *Moment*, which is more properly translated as "stage" or "phase."

But if the individual has always known the truth, then it cannot be said that, at the moment he remembers this truth, he undergoes any substantive transformation like that traditionally associated with the transition from ignorance to knowledge.

Climacus speculates, however, that perhaps an alternative interpretation of the relation of the individual to the truth is possible, an alternative that would go "beyond" (PF, 11) the Socratic in that it would imbue the moment at which the truth was learned with decisive significance. If we are not to go back to the Socratic, argues Climacus, then the individual cannot be considered to be essentially in possession of the truth, but must rather be considered to be essentially *ignorant*. Hence, the only thing, on this view, that may serve to put the individual into the proper relation to the truth is a teacher. Here the teacher does not merely enlighten the learner, but rather effects a substantive transformation of him. That is, Climacus points out that if the learner is considered to be essentially ignorant of the truth, then it appears he cannot even be in possession of the condition for understanding it, "because [having] the condition for understanding the truth is like being able to ask about it—the condition and the question contain the conditioned and the answer" (PF, 14). Thus the learner needs to be given, not merely the truth, but also the condition for understanding it and to be made receptive to the truth in this way appears to involve a qualitative transformation of the individual.[6]

Climacus contends that if this alternative to the Socratic interpretation of the relation of the individual to the truth is correct, then he will have made an advance upon Socrates. That is, he will have gone beyond Socrates in that he will have imbued the point in time at which the truth is learned, insofar as it marks a qualitative transformation of the individual, with the essential or decisive significance that it lacked on the Socratic account.

It may occur to the reader, however, to question why the preservation of such significance for the moment at which the

---

[6]Compare this with the following remark written by Kierkegaard in his journal in 1848: "[T]he only fundamental basis for understanding is that one himself becomes what he understands and one understands only in proportion to becoming himself that which he understands" (JP 2:2299).

truth is learned would be considered to represent an *advance* over the Socratic account. A close examination of the alternative to the Socratic interpretation of the relation of the individual to the truth will reveal that significance is preserved for the moment only at great cost to the individual. That is, the individual, on this latter view, loses his autonomy with respect to his relation to the truth and becomes entirely dependent, in this relation, upon another who would be his teacher. Further, his existence, if and when he does come into possession of the truth, is punctuated by a radical discontinuity. He becomes, upon his reception of the truth, "a different person" (PF, 18). What, the reader may well ask, could possibly be the advantage in interpreting one's existence so that it is characterized by such dependency and discontinuity?

II

The *Fragments* is divided into several sections. The first part of the book describes the situation of the non-Socratic learner. Because this learner stands in need not merely of the truth but also of the condition for understanding the truth, and because the reception of this condition represents a *substantive transformation* of the learner and no mere human being would appear to be capable of effecting such a transformation, Climacus concludes that the teacher, on this view, must be "the god himself," and the learner "a follower" (PF, 18). The issue then concerns the nature of the relation of the follower to the god, that is, whether historical contemporaneity with the god can provide the individual with any advantage. In order to answer this question, Climacus undertakes, in chapter 4 of the *Fragments* (PF, 55-71), a close examination of the situation of "the contemporary follower" (PF, 55). But, of course, in order to answer the question satisfactorily, he must also examine the situation of the individual who is not a contemporary of the god, and this he does in the succeeding chapter (PF, 88-110).

Climacus decides, for reasons that cannot be obscure to any of his readers, that he will look, in particular, at the situation of the individual who lives exactly eighteen hundred and forty-three years after the death of the god.[7] He observes that in a play "there

---

[7]1843 is the publication date of the *Philosophical Fragments*.

may be an interval of several years between two acts" (PF, 72) and that "[t]o suggest this passage of time, the orchestra sometimes plays a symphony[8] or something similar in order to shorten the time by filling it up" (PF, 72). He thus decides to employ a similar tactic himself. That is, he decides to fill in the time which intervenes between the situation of the contemporary follower and the follower at second hand by briefly diverting the attention of the reader with a little light entertainment. This entertainment takes the form of an "Interlude" (PF, 72) inserted between the fourth and fifth chapters of the book and which examines the question of whether the past can be considered to be more necessary than the future, or whether the possible, by becoming actual, becomes more necessary than it was.

I contend that the question with which the "Interlude" is concerned is by no means unrelated to the problem of the *Fragments*, that is, I believe that what is said in the "Interlude" represents a deliberate attempt, on Climacus's part, to subvert the pretended objectivity of the work as a whole. Climacus contends that he is not biased in the direction of either of the interpretations of the relation of the individual to the truth that he presents in the *Fragments*. He is simply, he contends, engaged in a "Thought Project" (PF, 9) in which outcome he has no essential interest. I shall argue, however, that to accept what is said in the "Interlude" is to express an implicit preference for the alternative to the Socratic interpretation of the relation of the individual to the truth.

The significance of the "Interlude" is that it involves the implicit assumption that time is real. But this is precisely what the Socratic interpretation of the relation of the individual to the truth rejects. Climacus contends, at the beginning of the *Fragments*, that he is going to set out to determine whether there is a way to interpret the relation of the individual to the truth that will imbue "the moment" with essential or decisive significance. He does not argue, however, that such an alternative to the Socratic interpretation, is necessarily more true. This is an issue that, it appears, is

---

[8]The Danish term here is *"en Symphoni"* which, in nineteenth-century Danish, could mean anything from a large orchestral piece to the more modest compositions. It appears that the latter usage was more common than the former. I am indebted to Bruce Kirmmse for this information.

left unresolved even at the end of the *Fragments*. But the thesis of the "Interlude"—that is, that the actual is no more necessary than the possible, or that nothing comes to be through necessity—depends, for its validity, upon the implicit assumption that the "the moment," that is, the temporal aspect of existence, has essential significance.

III

I mentioned above that it might well occur to the reader to question why Climacus would consider that an interpretation of human existence that would preserve essential significance for the temporal aspect of that existence, would represent an advance over one that did not. Temporality, or change in which temporality is quite often considered to consist, involves some rather problematic concepts, that, in turn, appear to present an intractable set of problems for philosophers. As a result, there is strong tradition among philosophers to discredit this aspect of human existence, a tradition that reaches back through the history of philosophy as far as Parmenides.[9]

Parmenides contends that either a thing *is*, and then "it is impossible for [it] *not to be* (ἡ μὲν ὅπως ἔστιν τε καὶ ὡς οὐκ ἔστι μὴ εἶναι), or it *is not* (ἡ δ' ὡς οὐκ ἔστιν)."[10] Thus, for Parmenides, nothing can be understood to *come to be*. What is true, or what is real, he argues, is what is "uncreated and imperishable" (ἀγένητον and ἀνώλεθρόν).[11] Reality is timeless and unchanging. Consider the following fragment.

> It never *was*[12] nor *will* be, since it *is* now, all together, one, continuous. For what birth will you seek for it? How and whence did it grow? . . . [W]hat need would have driven it [to be] later rather than earlier, beginning from nothing to grow? Thus it

---

[9]The rejection of the reality of time is characteristic of all of what is referred to as Eleatic philosophy as well as most of analytic philosophy of time.

[10]G. S. Kirk, J. E. Raven, M. Schofield, *Presocratic Philosophers* (Cambridge: Cambridge University Press, 1983) 245; italics added.

[11]Ibid., 248.

[12]I have italicized this word, and all the other words in this passage that appear in italics, in the hope that this will make what is a very difficult passage a little easier to understand.

must either *be* completely or not at all . . . [f]or if it *comes into*
being, it *is not*: nor *is* it if it is ever *going to* be in the future. Thus
coming to be is extinguished and *perishing* is unheard of.[13]

The difficulty is that the claim that something can *come to be*
appears to commit one to the counterintuitive view that one can
get something from nothing. Climacus acknowledges this difficulty, but he attempts to escape the problem by contending that there
is a difference between *absolute* non-being and the non-being that
represents *potential* being. Climacus argues in the "Interlude" that

> this non-being [*Ikke-Væren*] that is abandoned by that which
> comes to be [*det Tilblivende*] must also be. . . . But such a being
> [*Væren*] that nevertheless is a non-being is possibility [*Muligheden*]
> and a being that is being is indeed actual being [*virkelige Væren*]
> or actuality [*Virkeligheden*] and the change of coming to be is the
> transition from possibility to actuality. (PF, 73-74)[14]

Thus Climacus escapes the charge that in maintaining the reality
of time he is trying to get something from nothing by contending
that possibility is a kind of non-being that differs from the non-
being that is purely nothing. But it would not appear that he has
actually advanced beyond Socrates, in that it might still be argued
that what appears to *come to be* in fact *is* already in the form of
possibility, and that the change is thus merely in the *appearance* of
the thing and not in its essential being or *reality*.

It would seem that there is no way, objectively, to resolve the
above dispute. That is, the difficulty reduces to the issue of how
one interprets the expression "possible." According to Aristotle,
there are at least two senses of the term, and in one sense it is
appropriate to speak of the necessary as being, or as having been
possible—that is, it would appear self-contradictory to speak of the

---

[13]Ibid., 249-50.

[14]I have altered the translation slightly. The Hong translation has "all coming
into existence" where I have "all coming to be." The Danish is actually *Alt*
Tilblivelse. *Tilblivelse* may be translated into English as "birth," "origin," "genesis,"
or "creation." Thus the above quotation may be translated literally as "all birth,
generation or creation is a *suffering*." The Hong translation is not incorrect. I have
altered it because "existence" (that is, *existents*) is a technical term for Kierkegaard,
which does not actually appear in the passage in question, and because the altera-
tion makes the similarity with the above fragment of Parmenides more apparent.

necessary as being, or as having been, *impossible*. Hence, on this view, one could speak of a particular historical event as having been "possible" at the point before it became actual, and yet still understand this process of actualization as one of necessity. But this is precisely the sort of talk that Climacus wants to avoid because it reduces the phenomenon of the *coming to be* of an event to something of merely *accidental* significance. That is, on this view, insofar as an event would be understood to be necessary, it would not need to become actual in order to negate the possibility of any other event or course of events. It is thus a matter of indifference, on this view, whether a particular event is possible, or has already been actualized. In either case there would be only one possibility that could be actualized.

But, again, it is precisely this sort of indifference that Climacus desires to overcome. Hence he concludes that Aristotle is mistaken in his view that there is a sense in which possibility may be predicated of the necessary.[15] The necessary cannot come to be, or cannot be understood as ever having been possible, argues Climacus, because

> [c]oming to be is a change, but since the necessary is always related to itself and is related to itself in the same way, it cannot be changed at all. All coming to be is a *suffering* [*Liden*], and the necessary cannot suffer, cannot suffer the suffering of actuality—namely, that the possible . . . turns out to be nothing the moment it becomes actual. . . . [Hence, he concludes that] [p]recisely by coming to be, everything that comes to be demonstrates that it is not necessary, for the only thing that cannot come to be is the necessary because the necessary *is*. (PF, 74)[16]

But if nothing can come to be through necessity, then everything which comes to be must do so through freedom. Thus Climacus concludes that the change (κίνησις)[17] of "coming to be" must be grounded in freedom and not in necessity.

Everything that comes to be, argues Climacus, is "*eo ipso* historical" (PF, 75). Mere phenomenal change is not equivalent, on

---

[15]PF, 75.

[16]See n. 13 above.

[17]See J. Heywood Thomas, "Logic and Existence in Kierkegaard," *Journal of the British Society for Phenomenology* 2 (1971): 3-11, for Kierkegaard's views on κίνησις.

Climacus's view, to κίνησις. The changes that characterize nature, like, for example, those associated with the changing seasons, do not, on Climacus's view, come about through freedom but are determined by the essence of nature itself.[18] What can be said to "come to be" is thus not an event in the sense of natural events like storms or earthquakes, but rather acts, or events that involve human agency.[19] But if such acts, or *historical* events, come about through freedom, it would not be appropriate to say, prior to their appearance, that they existed in the form of possibility; one would say rather that *possibility* existed.

It will perhaps help make this point clearer if we consider a particular historical example. Take, for instance, the abolition of slavery in the United States. One could not consider, prior to this event, that the event existed already, in the form of possibility; one would consider rather that such an event was possible, or that the possibility that such a thing might happen existed. But to say that *possibility* exists, rather than that an *event* exists in the form of possibility, is to say that at that particular point in time, any number of different events could be actualized. But if this is truly what it means for something to be "possible," then the process of coming into existence—that is, the transition from possibility to actuality—is not something of merely *accidental* significance, as is maintained on the Socratic view, but concerns rather the very *essence* of human existence.

IV

The question now becomes: What significance does what is said in the "Interlude" have in relation to the *Fragments* as a whole? It is clear that the question with which the "Interlude" is concerned is *not* unrelated to the problem of the *Fragments*, as Climacus maintains. If the reader accepts what is said in the "Interlude," then it would appear that he is precluded from accepting the Socratic account of the relation of the individual to the truth. But *must* the reader accept what is said in the "Interlude"?

---

[18]See PF, 75-76 for Climacus's views on nature.

[19]Climacus's use of κίνησις here is thus related to Aristotle's use of the expression κίνησις πολιτείας to refer to political change or revolution.

Climacus offers an argument for the views he expresses in the "Interlude," but this argument is far from conclusive. The reader is still free to reject the view that the transition from possibility to actuality constitutes a *substantial* or *real* change. Climacus argues that the necessary cannot come to be because coming to be is a change and the necessary cannot change. But if one subscribes to the aforementioned sense of "possible," then one may simply argue that coming to be does not actually constitute a change in any substantial sense.

Climacus's rejection of this sense of "possible" appears to stem from an intuition that this is not what we normally mean when we use the expression. But even if his intuition is correct, we should not automatically assume that our language always provides us with an accurate representation of reality. It is not legitimate to conclude from the fact that we understand or use the term "possible" in a particular way, that this tells us something about the true character of existence. It may be that, in fact, nothing is possible in the sense in which we most often use the term.

If one accepts what is said in the "Interlude," then the effect that this has upon the *Fragments* as a whole is clear. Climacus claims that what he presents in the *Fragments* is a disinterested or objective account of what he considers is an exhaustive treatment of the ways in which an individual may be related to the truth. A close examination of the "Interlude" reveals, however, that what is offered in the *Fragments* is by no means as disinterested or objective an account as Climacus claims. If one accepts what is said in the "Interlude" concerning the nature of the transition from possibility to actuality, then one is committed to the position that the temporal aspect of human existence is of essential or decisive significance. We have seen, however, that the Socratic interpretation of the relation of the individual to the truth deprives temporality of such significance. Thus, if one accepts what is said in the "Interlude," then it would appear that one is precluded from accepting the Socratic interpretation of the relation of the individual to the truth. But why would Climacus deliberately subvert the objectivity of the *Fragments* in this way?

V

Climacus does not actually identify the alternative to the Socratic account of the relation of the individual to the truth as the specifically Christian account until the end of the *Fragments*.[20] That it is the Christian account is, according to Climacus, not a fact that can have been obscure to any of his readers. It may occur to the reader, however, to question why Climacus would be concerned to contrast the two accounts in this way. The answer is that the "Socratic" account has a much broader significance than is immediately apparent. This account represents for Climacus the traditional *philosophical* interpretation of the relation of the individual to the truth, an interpretation that, as we have seen, may be traced back through the history of philosophy to Parmenides. It is not simply Parmenidean, however. The traditional philosophical position is that all that is required in order for one to come to know the truth is the possession of the faculty of reason. Insofar as one possesses this faculty, one may be said to be in possession of the truth. That is, reason, on the traditional philosophical view, represents the condition for understanding the truth and, again, according to Climacus, "the condition for understanding the truth is like being able to ask about it—the condition and the question contain the conditioned and the answer" (PF, 14). Thus, insofar as *every* human being is considered to be rational, if a particular individual fails to come to understand the truth, this failure must be viewed as a phenomenon of merely *accidental* significance; for, on this view, he must be understood to have been *essentially* capable of coming to understand the truth, even if he *accidentally* failed to realize this potential.

What Climacus has done in the *Fragments* is to contrast what he considers to be the philosophical interpretation of existence with the Christian interpretation. Readers familiar with the references to "stages" of existence in many of Kierkegaard's pseudonymous works[21] may wonder at Climacus's contention that the above

---

[20]PF, 109.

[21]References to these "stages" are too numerous to mention. The reader may refer, however, to *Either/Or*, 2 vols., trans. Howard V. Hong and Edna H. Hong

interpretations actually exhaust the possibilities for the manner of one's relation to the truth. One would think, for example, that the relation of the aesthete to the truth would be different from that of the ethicist, or, more particularly, that the relation of either of these two to the truth would be different from that of the "religious" individual—meaning here the individual who exemplifies what Climacus characterizes in the *Postscript* as "religiousness A" (CUP, 1:555-61, 572).[22] It is important to remember, however, that, for Kierkegaard, there are ultimately only two stages of existence, non-Christian and Christian, and it is not really important which "stage" of existence one exemplifies if that stage is not the Christian one.[23] All non-Christian "stages" of existence are the same in that they consider that the relation of the individual to the truth is one of immanence. Hence they all fundamentally reduce to the Socratic.

The irony of the *Fragments* is that the work purports to be an objective juxtaposition of the interpretations of existence examined therein when, in fact, it is not. The reader may wonder *why* Climacus would so carefully, and indeed artfully, create in the *Fragments* such a discrepancy between the works *appearance*—that is, its pretended objectivity—and its *real* bias. I believe the answer lies in Kierkegaard's views regarding indirect communication.

There are a number of reasons why the reader might prefer the Socratic account of the relation of the individual to the truth to the Christian account. Apart from the conceptual or theoretical difficulties associated with the idea of change (which difficulties we looked at above in connection with Parmenides), the Christian interpretation of existence, insofar as it considers the individual to be essentially ignorant of the truth, places him in a position

---

(Princeton: Princeton University Press, 1987); and to the *Stages on Life's Way,* trans. Howard V. Hong and Edna H. Hong (Princeton: Princeton University Press, 1988).

[22]See also SV VII, 488-90; 498.

[23]Consider, for example, the following quotation: "in the solemn silence before God, the can be no doubt about it. There is an either/or: either God/or . . . the rest is indifferent" (CD, 333).

It is also important, in this context, to be aware that Kierkegaard divided his authorship into two groups: "aesthetic" and "religious" (PV, 13; JP 6:6347) and not three or four as the theory of the stages of existence might suggest.

"outside the truth" (*uden for Sandheden*) (PF, 13), which is to say, in a state of error or "untruth" (*Usandheden*). But to be in a state of error, in this way, implies that there is something fundamentally *wrong* with one's subjective existence, and this is not a thesis that anyone is going to be particularly anxious to accept. What is *wrong*, of course, is, for Kierkegaard, that one is sinful and it is precisely this sinfulness that keeps one from being willing to accept the truth about one's subjective situation when it is presented in a straightforward manner. "[D]irect communication," argues Kierkegaard, "presupposes the receiver's ability to receive is undisturbed. But here such is not the case" (POV, 40).[24] Indeed, there is a sense in which it would not even appear possible for the reader to accept the Christian interpretation of existence, unless he had *already* received the condition for understanding it. That is, even our understanding of ourselves as sinful is, for Kierkegaard, something we are unable to come to on our own but which must be supplied to us by God.[25]

VI

It is my contention that Climacus believes that it is not possible to resolve the debate between the Socratic, or the traditional philosophical interpretation of existence and the Christian interpretation through a purely objective consideration of the two positions. A purely objective consideration of these two positions would not even appear to be possible insofar as the truth in question concerns the nature of one's subjective existence—that is, whether it is one of truth or error—and hence the character of one's subjective experience must enter in as a criterion for choosing between the positions.

---

[24]SV XIII, 541.

[25]We can understand ourselves as outside the truth without previously having received the condition for understanding this truth. We cannot, however, understand ourselves as in such a position through our own fault, and this is precisely what Kierkegaard maintains that sin is: to be in error through one's own fault. It is the consciousness that one is in error through one's own fault, that marks the substantive transformation of the individual identified above, for it is "with this consciousness that he takes leave of his former state" (PF, 19).

I believe Climacus uses the "Interlude" to make an implicit appeal to the subjective experience of his reader in order to find out whether that experience is one of freedom or of necessity. That is, it appears he inserts the "Interlude" into the *Fragments* in order to see how the reader will react to it. Will he accept it as making sense of his experience, which is to say, does he have the impression that his existence is characterized by a multiplicity of possible courses of action, only one of which can be actualized by any particular choice, or does he have the impression that in any particular instance there is, in fact, only one thing that he can actually choose to do?[26]

Both the Socratic/philosophical and the Christian accounts of the relation of the individual to the truth view the truth as eternal, but only the Christian interpretation, on Climacus's view, preserves any reality for *time*. It is the Christian interpretation of existence, however, that considers the individual to be in a position of untruth or error. Hence it would seem, paradoxically, that time can only be real for an individual who is in a state of untruth. So if the reader of the *Fragments* chooses the Christian interpretation of existence in order to preserve the reality of time, he does so at the cost of understanding himself as fundamentally outside the truth or in error. But this is, of course, according to Kierkegaard, exactly how he *should* understand himself. That is, it is Kierkegaard's belief that we are all subjectively in a state of sin and that hence we must pay close attention to the character of our subjective experience—in this case, to its temporality—in order for the truth of our existence to become manifest to us. And this truth is precisely that we are in a state of untruth. Hence, if we approached the question of the nature of our relation to the truth purely *objectively*, that is, if our pursuit of the truth of our existence were carried out in abstraction from our *subjective* experience, then this truth would be something that we could never come to know. So in desiring to make an

---

[26]My temptation is to consider that such a perception of freedom as was described above is a universal characteristic of human experience. One of my colleagues has informed me, however, that his experience is precisely the opposite. He claims that his impression is that his choices are, in fact, *determined* by the "kind of person" he is and that thus the future is, for him, already determinate.

advance upon Socrates, Kierkegaard does not merely, like Climacus, hope to learn something about the nature of human existence, he hopes to help the individual come to a more adequate understanding of his subjective situation—that is, that he is in a state of untruth.

Conclusion

The debate between the Socratic or philosophical interpretation of the relation of the individual to the truth and the Christian interpretation cannot be resolved objectively because this debate ultimately concerns the individual's subjective situation. Indeed, if it were not for the desire to imbue the moment with essential or decisive significance, which is to say, if it were not for the desire to preserve the reality of time—which desire stems from the character of our subjective experience—there would be no debate, no sense in which another interpretation of existence could be said to go beyond the Socratic.

It would certainly have been possible for Kierkegaard to have stated the above thesis in a straightforward manner, but, again, Kierkegaard's views on the nature of communication commit him to the view that this would be less effective than presenting the thesis in a manner that appeared antithetical to its actual content. A direct presentation would by no means compel the reader to accept the thesis and it might possibly even provide him with an opportunity to defend himself against such acceptance. Thus it would seem that Kierkegaard practically orders his reader to try to resolve this debate in an objective fashion, precisely in order to help him to understand that such a resolution is impossible.

The "Interlude" has long been appreciated by Kierkegaard scholars as an extremely important section of *Fragments* and the *Fragments* has, in turn, long been appreciated as one of Kierkegaard's most important works. If the interpretation offered above is correct, then it is clear that the irony in the *Fragments* consists in this discrepancy between the work's *form*—that is, its claim to objectivity—and its *content*—that is, its implicit bias. It is, however, "the most common form of irony," according to Kierkegaard, "to say something earnestly that is not meant in earnest. The second form of irony, to say in a jest, jestingly, something that is meant in earnest is more rare" (CI, 248). It is clearly the latter form of irony that permeates the *Fragments*. That is, the irony here is not employed simply for its own sake, but is used by Kierkegaard rather as a heuristic device, a device that would help him to reveal indirectly to his reader, a truth about his existence of which he was previously unaware.

4

Apologetic Arguments
in Philosophical Fragments

C. Stephen Evans

It is not hard to show that Kierkegaard was no friend of apologetic arguments for the truth of the Christian faith.[1] Statements of hostility to apologetic arguments are numerous in many of Kierkegaard's works. In *Practice in Christianity,* the Christian pseudonym Anti-Climacus says that the attempt to prove that Christ is God is blasphemy from the viewpoint of faith (PC, 29). Those who argue for the truth of Christianity from its long endurance in the world are "betraying, denying, abolishing Christianity" (PC, 144). In *Concluding Unscientific Postscript* Johannes Climacus treats attempts to prove the truth of the Scriptures as a symptom of the loss of faith (CUP, 1:30). In *Works of Love* Kierkegaard pronounces "woe to the person who could make the miracles reasonable" (WL, 193).

Nor is this antiapologetic attitude absent from *Philosophical Fragments.* *Fragments* contains a well-known critique of theistic arguments in chapter 3 (PF, 39-44). Later, the pseudonymous author Johannes Climacus discusses the question of whether the god who has become a human being in order to bring humans the

---

[1]By an "apologetic argument" I mean any argument intended to show the truth or reasonableness of Christian faith. This includes arguments designed to remove objections by clarifying Christianity so as to resolve apparent inconsistencies and eliminate misunderstandings. I regard arguments of this type as not merely directed to unbelievers, but as having value to believers as well. As will become apparent, Kierkegaard seems to have a narrower concept of apologetic argument, but my broader use will turn out to be essential to remove an apparent tension in his writings.

truth would offer some kind of "accommodation" for the sake of enabling people to recognize him as the god. He concludes that any such accommodation will be of no value to anyone who lacks the condition of faith and in fact is "elicited from him [the god] only under constraint and against his will, and it may just as well alienate the learner as draw him closer" (PF, 56). So much for historical apologetics.

If we make the reasonable assumption, confirmed by Climacus himself, that the thought-project of the book is intended to illustrate the relation between Christianity and human reason, then it seems safe to conclude that *Fragments* is hostile to arguments designed to show that Christianity is objectively true. Rather than arguing for the truth of Christian faith, *Philosophical Fragments* seems far more concerned to highlight the offensive character of Christianity. It is natural for philosophers to try to give explanations of difficult doctrines and arguments for their truth, Climacus says, "for is that not what philosophers are for—to make supernatural things ordinary and trivial?" (PF, 53). Climacus, however, insists that the thought-project he spins out as an analogue to Christianity necessarily contains the possibility of offense, a claim echoed by Anti-Climacus for Christianity itself in *Practice in Christianity* (PC, 81).

The "Moral" of *Philosophical Fragments*, though it does not attack apologetics, would seem at least to disavow any apologetic aims in the book. Here Climacus says that his thought-project "indisputably goes beyond the Socratic." However, this "going beyond" has nothing to do with arguing that the invented thought-project is truer than the Socratic perspective: "Whether it [Climacus's project] is therefore more true than the Socratic is an altogether different question, one that cannot be decided in the same breath" (PF, 111).

Given the antiapologetic claims that are pervasive in Kierkegaard's authorship and prominent in *Philosophical Fragments*, it is very surprising to discover that the book contains a number of arguments that look very much like apologetic efforts. I shall briefly look at some apparent apologetic arguments in *Philosophical Fragments*, arguments that on the surface seem aimed at showing that something like Christianity is true.[2] I shall then try to draw some conclusions about the nature of apologetic arguments in relation to the possibility of offense. Do the arguments given by Climacus undermine his rejection of apologetics? Or do they show that his rejection of apologetics is not a blanket condemnation, but a rejection of a specific kind of apologetics? I shall argue that the latter is the case, and that Climacus allows "room" for a kind of apologetic argument that still holds open the possibility of offense.

Four Apologetic Arguments in Philosophical Fragments

I shall consider four arguments. Three are locatable at specific texts; the fourth is an "argument" that is implicit in the structure of the book as a whole. Each of the first three arguments occurs in a kind of dialogue with the "interlocutor" who appears to challenge Johannes Climacus from time to time in the book.

The "No Human Author" Argument. At the close of the first chapter, "Thought-Project," the interlocutor breaks in and accuses Climacus of setting forth as his own invention what is common knowledge, when Climacus presents his account of the god as the indispensable teacher of humans sunk in error. According to the objector, Climacus is like "a vagabond who charges a fee for showing an area that everyone can see" (PF, 21). Climacus responds with ironical penitence: "Maybe so. I hide my face in shame." (PF, 21). The penitence hides a point; having admitted that he is not the real author of the project, Climacus goes on to extend to the interlocutor the honor of the authorship. On the assumption that the interlocutor will decline the courtesy, Climacus broadens his offer: "Will you then also deny that someone has invented it, that is, some human being?" (PF, 21). Astonishingly, Climacus assumes that the interlocutor will not accept any human author, and uses the admission to mitigate the plagiarism charge: "In that

---

[2]Throughout this essay I assume that the "thought-project" Climacus spins out in *Philosophical Fragments* is intended as an analogue to Christianity, and that comments on such matters as the relation between the thought-project and reason are intended to illuminate the situation of Christianity.

case, I am just as close to having invented it as any other person" (PF, 21).

Climacus obviously thinks that his thought-project is the work of the god. Furthermore, he claims that the content of the hypothesis somehow enables people to know this: "Everyone who knows it [the thought-project] also knows that he has not invented it" (PF, 22). This "oddity" that everyone who knows about the project also knows that it is not of human authorship "enthralls" Climacus so much that he concludes that it constitutes a kind of proof of the hypothesis: "It tests the correctness of the hypothesis and demonstrates it" (PF, 22).

There are a number of ways of articulating the argument sketched here by Climacus, but on one reading it corresponds pretty closely with one traditional type of apologetic argument for Christianity. Theologians have sometimes argued that the Christian faith is simply not the sort of thing that unaided human reason could ever have invented. The supernatural origin of Christian faith is attested by its content. Thomas Aquinas, for example, in the *Summa Contra Gentiles*, cites the fact that the Christian revelation includes "truths . . . that surpass every human intellect" as evidence that one can reasonably accept the Christian revelation as coming from God.[3] Put baldly, the form of the argument would be something like this:

1. A religious claim of type X could not have been invented by any human being, but only by God.
2. Christianity makes a claim of type X.
3. This religious claim of Christianity could only have been invented by God.

What is "X" in this argument? It's not altogether clear, but a plausible answer would be the claim made by the thought-project that humans are caught in an error that they cannot overcome themselves, but can only overcome through the teaching of the god.[4] The argument occurs immediately after a passage in which

---

[3]Thomas Aquinas, *Summa Contra Gentiles*, bk. 1, chap. 6, trans. Anton C. Pegis (New York: Doubleday, 1955) 72.

[4]An alternative, perhaps equally plausible interpretation, is to view the "X" as simply the difference between the Socratic and Christian views that the chapter

Climacus discusses birth and rebirth. A person who has been born can know that he or she was born; an unborn person can have no such consciousness. Similarly, a person who has been reborn can be conscious of the rebirth, and that the previous state that made the rebirth necessary was a state of "not-being" of a sort (PF, 20-21). So perhaps Climacus is suggesting that the Christian claim that humans are caught in "original sin," so that they are spiritually dead and completely incapable of overcoming their problem, is not one that could "naturally" occur to any human being, but can only be known after God has revealed it.

I shall not comment on the strength of this argument or any of the others Climacus recounts, nor shall I discuss the objections to which it may be vulnerable. My purpose in this paper is neither to do apologetics nor to do it in, but to think about the legitimacy of apologetics as a general enterprise within the general framework of Kierkegaardian views of faith and reason.

The Argument from the Uniqueness of the Incarnation. Climacus gives a very similar argument at the close of the second chapter, "The God as Teacher and Savior." The interlocutor once more accuses Climacus of plagiarism. Climacus once more confesses that he is not the author of the poem, but forces the question as to who the author is, since it would be curious indeed to have a poem without a poet (PF, 35). This time Climacus specifically attributes to the interlocutor the accusation that Climacus has stolen his poem from the god, rather than any human being or the human race in general (PF, 35-36). In reflecting on this point Climacus is once more transported: "But then my soul is also gripped with new amazement—indeed, it is filled with adoration, for it certainly would have been odd if it had been a human poem" (PF, 36).

The amazement reflects the theme of chapter 2, which contains an imaginative sketch which fleshes out the bare-bones logical structure of chapter 1. Here the god decides to become the teacher out of self-giving love, and wills to express that love through a decision to take on the lowly station of the learner who is in error.

---

as a whole tries to make clear. I prefer the narrower interpretation since it makes the argument more precise and easier to evaluate.

So we have here an argument structurally similar to the previous argument; the content of the Christian revelation is itself evidence for its supernatural origin, only here the content which serves as the locus of the argument is the story of the incarnation. No human being, says Climacus, could have hit upon such an idea. "Presumably it could occur to a human being to poetize himself in the likeness of the god or the god in the likeness of himself, but not to poetize that the god poetized himself in the likeness of a human being" (PF, 36).

I shall again resist the temptation to discuss the plausibility of this claim about the uniqueness and unimaginability of the incarnation. Climacus has no qualms about accepting the claim and drawing some rather extravagant conclusions, however. The person who has had this story confided to him by the god is pictured by him as adoringly echoing 1 Corinthians 2:9 by confessing that "this thought did not arise in my heart." Rather, this thought is "the wonder" or "the miracle" [Vidunderet] (PF, 36).

The Argument from Offense. The third apologetic argument in *Fragments* that I wish to discuss is contained in the section entitled "Offense at the Paradox (An Acoustic Illusion)," which is the appendix to chapter 3. Climacus has argued that when the learner encounters the incarnation of the god, two passionate responses are possible. The happy encounter between the disciple and the god occurs in the passion of faith; the unhappy relation characterized by misunderstanding is termed offense. The thrust of this section is that the objections to the incarnation made by the offended consciousness are not what they appear to be. Offense literally does not understand itself (PF, 50).

Offense rejects the incarnation, described as the "paradox" of the god as a human being, because it sees such a paradox as absurd. Offense thus thinks it has "got the goods" on the paradox, has subjected it to critical scrutiny and found it wanting. The response of the paradox is that offense is merely echoing, in a distorted and therefore confusing form, what the paradox says about itself. The "objection" that offense raises is simply the correct self-understanding of the paradox, echoing back in a misleading form. When offense claims that the paradox is absurd, the paradox makes a vigorous response:

> The understanding has not discovered this; on the contrary, it was the paradox that ushered the understanding to the wonder stool and replies: Now, what are you wondering about? It is just as you say, and the amazing thing is that you think it is an objection, but the truth in the mouth of a hypocrite is dearer to me than to hear it from an angel or an apostle. (PF, 52)

It is for this reason that Climacus claims that "offense can be regarded as an indirect testing of the correctness of the paradox" (PF, 51).[5]

Where is the apologetics here? The argument seems to be something like this. The kind of objections raised against belief in the incarnation are an indirect confirmation of its truth. A genuine revelation from God, a supernatural revelation that is truly "the wonder" (*Vidunderet*) would be something that human reason could not be expected to comprehend. Thus, when human reason pronounces that it cannot make sense of the incarnation, this is precisely what one would expect if the incarnation were a divine revelation. The descriptions of the paradox given by the offended person are then helpful in two ways. First, they echo and thus confirm the assertion of the incarnation to be a divine revelation and not a human invention. Secondly, they represent the kind of response one would expect from an encounter with a genuine revelation, and thus they provide at least weak confirmation that this revelation is genuine.

In effect Climacus argues that the very improbability of the incarnation to human understanding is a mark of its truth. A person who wanted to make up a story would make up something much more plausible. The paradox, however, says that "comedies and novels and lies must be probable, but how could I be probable" (PF, 52). An argument that is roughly similar to this one is again present in Aquinas, who argues that the content of the Christian revelation is so contrary to a human being's natural disposition to believe that the fact that people can be brought to

---

[5]We must be careful here not to misunderstand the reply of the paradox. The paradox is agreeing, not that it is in fact absurd, but that it necessarily appears absurd to the reason or understanding. We must leave open the possibility that to the person of faith, the person who is not offended, the paradox is not absurd.

assent to it is itself the "greatest of miracles." Aquinas here contrasts Christianity with Islam, which he argues contains the kinds
of claims likely to be accepted by "carnal men" and is supported
by the kind of proofs "as could be grasped by the natural ability
of anyone with a very modest wisdom."[6]

The Argument of the Book as a Whole. This last argument from
the appendix to chapter 3 casts an illuminating ray on the structure
of *Philosophical Fragments* as a whole. Although the book seems to
eschew any apologetic argument in the "Moral," more than one
reader has seen the book as a whole as a sustained argument for
the plausibility of an orthodox Christian view of the incarnation,[7]
and this despite the claim of the author that the attempt to make
the "paradox" probable is wrongheaded (PF, 94-95)! The fact that
this kind of reading is even possible suggests that the pose of neutrality with respect to Christianity on the part of Climacus may be
ironically deceptive.

A review of the book as a whole might be helpful in
suggesting how it may appear to have an apologetic thrust.
Chapter 1 describes the "thought-project" that is clearly supposed
to be an analogue to Christianity as a logically consistent, coherent
alternative to the Socratic perspective on "the Truth" and how the
Truth is to be gained. Not only is this Christian analogue internally
consistent; some of what may appear to be its most objectionable
features, such as its postulation of a condition of error that humans
cannot overcome themselves, are presented as logically essential if

---

[6]Aquinas, *Summa Contra Gentiles,* bk. 1, chap. 6 (Pegis trans., 72-73).

[7]Of course there is some debate as to the range of an "orthodox Christian view
of the incarnation." Climacus certainly makes no attempt to clarify the incarnation
precisely, so it is not possible to say, e.g., that only fully Chalcedonian formulations of the doctrine qualify as orthodox. However, he says enough to make it
clear that some formulations would not count as orthodox. In particular, interpretations of the incarnation that understand Christ's divinity as a special, intensified
case of a general divine-human unity (e.g., "Christ had a specially high sense of
the consciousness of God that is potentially present in all humans") will not qualify as orthodox precisely because they are clearly Socratic. For Climacus the incarnation must be understood in a way that implies that Christ was uniquely divine,
and not as simply as Christ possessing, in an exceptionally high or even unparal-
leled manner, some divine quality that generally belongs to the human race.

Christianity (to avoid the clumsy locution "Christian analogue") is to be something genuinely different from pagan, Greek thought. Certainly the claim that Christianity is not the same thing as Greek thought is not implausible, so the argument of chapter 1 can be read as deducing from this plausible claim some of the main features of Christian faith.

Chapter 2 goes even further and actually attempts in some sense to make the incarnation plausible. Chapter 1 argues that any genuine alternative to Socrates will have God as our teacher. Chapter 2 argues, at least poetically and persuasively, that we can only make sense of this supposition by postulating an incarnation of God in human form. Only self-giving love could motivate the god to become our teacher, and self-giving love would desire a union with the beloved that could only be achieved by the lover taking on the condition of the beloved.

Chapter 3 rejects natural theology, as we noted at the beginning of the paper, but it does much more than this. It confirms the inability of reason to come up with any true knowledge of God on its own, and thus once more points to the reasonableness of looking to revelation as the only path to knowing God. Though chapter 3 insists that the incarnation is a paradox, and that reason may well be offended by it, it insists just as strongly that offense is not the only possible reaction. Reason and the paradox may also be on good terms, a condition that is made possible when reason "wills its own downfall" (PF, 47). Climacus also tells us that reason and the paradox can be happily joined when the understanding "surrenders itself" (PF 54), or steps aside (PF 59). It seems significant that it is reason itself that does the surrendering and stepping aside. The implication of this is that though the paradox cannot be understood by reason, reason can understand this fact. Climacus seems to be arguing that it can be reasonable for reason to recognize the limits of reason.

The appendix to chapter 3, as we have seen, defuses the objections made by the offended consciousness by arguing that these claims are unoriginal echoes of what God's revelation itself contains. Moreover, the objections represent precisely the kind of reaction one would expect from humans who are naturally prone to believing they are self-sufficient, humans who are insulted by a revelation that implies the opposite.

Chapters 4 and 5, as we have seen, imply that historical apologetics is pointless. Faith in the God is produced by a firsthand encounter with the incarnate God, and historical evidence is neither necessary for such faith nor sufficient for it. However, even here, the thrust is not solely antiapologetic. Many critics of Christian faith would argue that its historical claims cannot be reasonably believed because the historical evidence is insufficient. The point of Climacus's argument is that such an objection to Christian faith is misguided, because the ground of faith is not evidence of this type at all. The lack of such evidence is not the basis of offense, and the lack should not be seen as a problem for Christianity. Hence the overall message of the last two chapters seems designed to undermine one common objection to Christianity. They at least seem to contain a negative apologetic argument, an attempt to undermine an objection to faith.

Thus, *Philosophical Fragments* as a whole, read from beginning to end, seems as if it could be designed to make Christian faith more plausible, despite the repeated claims to the contrary. The ease with which the book can be read as an apologetic argument suggests that this reading may not simply be an example of "deconstructing the text" by making its author say the opposite of what is intended. It suggests that apologetics of a sort may be what the author intended.

Apologetics in a Nonfoundationalist Key

Even if I am wrong in suggesting the plausibility of such a reading of the book as a whole, there still remain the specific apologetic arguments we discovered sprinkled throughout the book. How can the polemic against apologetics in *Philosophical Fragments* be reconciled with the apologetics the book itself contains?

Of course one could just say that the two cannot be reconciled. Johannes Climacus is a self-described humorist and perhaps would not be troubled by the constraints of logical consistency. He condemns apologetics but engages in it himself. I cannot speak for others, but I myself would not find this kind of inconsistency to be particularly humorous. Humor as incongruity should no more be confused with logical inconsistency than profundity should be confused with obscurity.

I find much more interesting the suggestion that there may be different kinds of apologetics. Perhaps the kind of apologetics that Climacus and Kierkegaard would censure is significantly different from the kind they engage in, so different that it did not occur to either that the kind of apologetic argument they presented *was* a form of apologetics.

To flesh this suggestion out, we need an illuminating characterization of what the two kinds of apologetic argument are like. I think there are two reliable clues we need to keep clearly in mind to do this. One is the ineliminability of faith. Climacus wants to say that the possession of faith is an essential prerequisite for grasping the truth of Christianity. Hence we can safely conclude that any form of apologetic argument that appears to make faith unnecessary or even to lessen the need for faith would be the kind of apologetics that Climacus wishes to reject.

The second clue is closely tied to the first, and concerns the possibility of offense. Climacus holds that the possibility of offense is inherent in authentic Christianity. In fact, he even holds, as we have seen, that the reactions of the offended consciousness to the claims of Christianity are a kind of confirmation of its truth. So it is safe to say that Climacus will condemn any apologetic argument that seems designed to eliminate or even to lessen the possibility of offense.

So now our questions are as follows: "Can we imagine a type of apologetic argument that seems designed to make faith unnecessary and offense impossible? Also, can we imagine another type of apologetic argument, one that *requires* faith and does *not* diminish the possibility of offense?" I think we can understand what arguments of both of these types would look like.

Roughly, I think that arguments that are designed to eliminate the necessity for faith and lessen the possibility of offense are arguments that are presented within the framework of the epistemology of classical foundationalism. To give content to this suggestion, and ultimately to characterize in a concrete way the type of apologetic argument I have in mind, I must say in a brief manner what I mean by "classical foundationalism."

First, classical foundationalism, in the sense I have in mind, is of course a form of foundationalism. That is, the classical foundationalist pictures knowledge as something like a building, and affirms that a building needs foundations. Translating the metaphor, the foundationalist recognizes that although we hold some beliefs on the basis of others, the process of justifying our beliefs by giving reasons for them cannot go on forever. Somewhere the chain of justification must end, and it ends in those beliefs (or items of knowledge) that are foundational to all of the rest.

How does the *classical* foundationalist differ from others? Alvin Plantinga has characterized classical foundationalism as a doctrine that puts restrictions on what may properly be foundational to what may be termed a person's noetic structure. Specifically, the classical foundationalist says that the foundations of knowledge must be highly secure; good buildings require good foundations. Hence, Plantinga describes two forms of classical foundationalism, each based on a conception of what beliefs are properly basic: ancient and medieval classical foundationalists accept as properly basic only propositions that are "either self-evident or evident to the senses," while modern foundationalists accept as properly basic only propositions that are "either self-evident or incorrigible."[8]

If one asks what motivates foundationalism in both of these forms, I think that the most plausible answer is a desire to avoid error. The classical foundationalist wants certainty in some sense of that word. If I base my beliefs on what is less than certain, then there is a real chance I may be mistaken. To avoid this, I must root my beliefs in certainties, the kind of thing any sane rational person who is in the appropriate position can understand and recognize as true.

Foundationalist Apologetic Arguments. If we translate classical foundationalist epistemology into apologetic arguments, then it is easy to see that these arguments appear to violate the two constraints on permissible apologetics that we drew from Climacus.

---

[8]Alvin Plantinga, "Reason and Belief in God," in *Faith and Rationality*, ed. Alvin Plantinga and Nicholas Wolterstorff (Notre Dame IN: University of Notre Dame Press, 1983) 58-59.

Such arguments appear to lessen the need for faith and they appear to make offense less possible. Aquinas, for example, seems to say that faith and knowledge are mutually exclusive in the sense that what we know by "vision" or "sight," or what we know by philosophical demonstration we can no longer be said to believe on the basis of authority.[9]

Two kinds of arguments will serve as illustrations of the kind of apologetics that I believe Climacus would find repugnant. One would be attempts to prove the existence of God, where this project is construed as an attempt to show that the existence of God can be logically deduced from premises that can be known with certainty by any sane rational person. The "Five Ways" of Thomas Aquinas can be construed in this way. (I shall not attempt to say whether this is how Aquinas himself construed them.) The first of the arguments Aquinas presents begins with a premise that is alleged to be "certain and evident to our senses," and each of the others begins with a claim that is thought to have a similar degree of certainty.[10] The soundness of the arguments seems to imply that although it is possible and even permissible for a person to believe in God by faith, faith with respect to belief that God exists is not necessary for the person who has grasped the soundness of the proofs. So the arguments can be construed as making faith unnecessary, at least for some people. Furthermore, the arguments would also seem to eliminate the possibility of offense. It is hard to see how any reasonable individual could find rationally offensive what is rationally demonstrable and certain.

It seems pretty clear from chapter 3 of *Philosophical Fragments* that Climacus does find attempts to prove God's existence in this manner wanting (PF, 39-44). However, despite the historical importance of these arguments in philosophy, I believe they are not the best illustration of the kind of apologetics that Climacus finds objectionable, because they do not involve in an essential way the concept of offense. For Climacus, and for Kierkegaard generally,

---

[9]See Thomas Aquinas, *Summa Theologica*, 1.q.2, art. 2; 1.q.12, art. 13. (Found, e.g., in *Basic Writings of Saint Thomas Aquinas*, ed. Anton C. Pegis [New York: Random House, 1945] 21, 111.)

[10]Aquinas, *Summa Theologica*, 1.q.2, art. 3. (Found, e.g., in Pegis, *Basic Writings of Saint Thomas Aquinas*, 22-23.)

offense is not an attitude inspired merely by belief in God, but one that has as its focus the specific belief that God has become a human being, which Climacus generally calls the "paradox."

There is a long tradition of historical apologetics within Christian thought, attempts to defend the historicity of the incarnation of God as Jesus. Someone who held a classical foundationalist epistemology and who held that historical knowledge was objective in character would very likely hold that these apologetic arguments shared that objective character. Someone who held a positivist or quasi-positivist view of historical knowledge, for example, might even construe such arguments as "scientific" in character.[11] If one simply looks at the historical evidence for the miracles performed by Jesus, the claims about himself that those miracles attest, and especially the evidence for the resurrection of Jesus, then the divinity of Jesus can be seen as the most reasonable conclusion one could draw from the facts, even if it is conceded that in historical matters strict proof is impossible.

There seems little question that Climacus finds such arguments mistaken and wrongheaded. He says unequivocally in chapters 4 and 5 of *Fragments* that without the condition of faith any historical evidence of this type is of no value (PF, 62, 64, 69). To buttress his case he gives thought-experiments. For example, a contemporary of the god's appearance who hired a hundred secret agents to observe the god's every movement accurately could wash his hands of the charge of historical ignorance, but would by no means necessarily be a disciple of the god (PF, 59-60). A tyrant from the next generation who seizes and interrogates all the surviving witnesses is similarly protected against historical inaccuracy but is by no means closer to faith (PF, 92). Climacus finds historical arguments from the consequences of Christian faith, such as its long endurance in the world and supposed beneficent transforming power, to be even more dubious and less convincing (PF, 94-98).[12]

---

[11]For an example of a Christian apologist who seems to hold to such a view of history as scientific in character, see John Warwick Montgomery, *The Shape of the Past: An Introduction to Philosophical Historiography*, vol. 1 of *His History in Christian Perspective* (Ann Arbor: Edwards Brothers, 1962).

[12]See also the quick dismissal of this kind of argument in *Concluding Unscientific Postscript* (CUP, 1:46-49).

Insofar as such historical arguments purport to establish their conclusions on the basis of objective evidence, they certainly appear to make faith unnecessary. They make it appear that a person's ability to believe that Jesus Christ is divine depends solely on that person's intellectual acuity; moral and spiritual qualities seem to drop out of the picture as irrelevant, except to the degree that a lack of such qualities might interfere with a person's intellectual equipment operating in a proper manner. Furthermore, it is hard to see how they preserve the essential character of the possibility of offense, since they seem designed to show that a belief in the divinity of Jesus is the most logical conclusion a rational person who is aware of the evidence could draw. It seems safe to conclude, therefore, that it is this type of argument that Climacus has in mind when he condemns apologetics.

Apologetics in a New Key: Nonfoundationalist Arguments. If one grants that an accurate characterization has been given of the type of apologetic argument Climacus wishes to reject, then the question remains as to what kind there might be that he could accept. I think that Johannes Climacus gives us a helpful clue here in his discussion of the physicoteleological argument, or argument from design, for God's existence. While Climacus is very critical of those who put forward this argument as deciding the question of God's existence, he makes an apparently favorable comment about Socrates, who is credited with having invented the argument. Socrates did not assume that the question of God's existence is one that must be left undecided prior to the argument, but "constantly presupposes that the god exists, and on this presupposition he seeks to infuse nature with the idea of fitness and purposiveness" (PF, 44).

One might well wonder about the value of an "argument" that appears to rest on the assumption that its conclusion is true, but let us put aside that worry to deal with later. The immediate point I wish to make is that Climacus does not seem to object to an argument that in some sense rests on faith rather than being a replacement for faith. The argument that Socrates is credited with advancing is clearly not one that would convince any sane, rational person of its conclusion, nor does it appear intended to accomplish this. Rather the argument itself seems to rest on a risky assumption, a presupposition of Socrates that is not self-evident, evident to the senses, or incorrigible.

Now if we construe Socrates' argument as blatantly circular, it seems a pointless enterprise. On the assumption that God exists, it is possible to infer that God exists. But I think such a construal would miss the point of what Socrates is credited with in this case. Climacus says that Socrates begins with the presupposition that God exists, and that nature is God's handiwork. On this assumption, he "reads" or interprets the natural world as showing signs of fitness and purposiveness. Perhaps the suggestion here is that these signs might not have been noticed if Socrates had not come to the natural world with this prior assumption. Clearly, the "data" or "evidence" Socrates discovers would not look very impressive to a classical foundationalist, since it is not the product of a purely objective, presuppositionless observer.

Before agreeing that Socrates' argument is therefore worthless, it would be well to remind ourselves that classical foundationalism has taken some hard knocks in recent philosophy. It might in fact be difficult to find someone today who would accept the possibility of a purely objective, presuppositionless observer. It is a commonplace of contemporary theories of perception that what a person is able to perceive does depend partly on the expectations, basic beliefs, and conceptual apparatus of the observer. Socrates certainly is not "neutral" in viewing the world as he does, but that does not imply that the picture of the world he develops is one he has simply invented or projected on to his experience. The "subjective" states of Socrates do not have to be seen as a "distorting veil," as is assumed so often by classical foundationalism. Rather, the "subjectivity" that Socrates brings to his experience of the world might be an enabling factor, providing Socrates with the skills and abilities needed to recognize features of the world that would otherwise be unnoticed.

This argument of Socrates is a nonfoundationalist one in at least two respects. First, the truth of at least one of the premises, in this case that nature is purposive, can be recognized only by certain people, people who approach their experience with the right sort of subjectivity. Secondly, even for those people, this premise is not self-evident, evident to the senses or incorrigible, nor does it appear to be deducible from premises that meet this standard. Not everything about our experience of nature supports this perspective, and it is possible for one to understand how others might reject the claim, and even to imagine oneself coming to reject the claim.

Nevertheless, I would claim that the argument is not necessarily pointless or viciously circular. One might wonder about this, given the way Climacus construes the argument. As he describes Socrates' procedure, Socrates begins with the assumption that God exists, and with this assumption experiences the natural order as showing evidence of divine handiwork. Is this not circular reasoning?

It is easy to state the argument in such a way that it is not formally circular. For example, one could reason that (1) nature shows purposive design; (2) purposive design is the work of a creative intelligence; hence (3) nature is the work of a creative intelligence. The argument is clearly not formally circular. However, Climacus seems to suggest that the acceptance of the first premise is tantamount to accepting the conclusion. This might suggest that the argument is pointless if not circular, because it will only be accepted as sound by someone who already accepts the conclusion.

It does not follow that the argument is pointless even if it is true that the first premise will only be accepted by a person who already accepts the conclusion. The argument might still have value in helping such a person better understand his or her belief; the value of the argument might lie in articulating what was only implicit in the conviction, and in helping the individual to see the links between belief in God and certain experiences of the natural order. Nor is it true that the argument will have no evidential force in this case. The links between experience and the belief that the argument helps make clear may support the belief. Even if it is true that those links will only be noticed by someone who already holds the belief, that does not mean the links are not real. Nor does it mean that they have no value in strengthening the belief, helping the believer "see" the ways in which nature points to the truth of the belief. The fact that those links may not be noticed by others in no way shows that they have no epistemic force.

Furthermore, it is not clear that such experiential links will necessarily only be noticed by someone who already holds the belief. Even if a belief in the purposiveness of nature is tantamount to seeing nature as the handiwork of God, and hence implicitly contains belief in God as an element, it is possible that someone may have failed to notice the connection. Belief in God may be *implicit* in belief in the purposiveness of nature, but what is implicit in a belief may not always be obvious, and the value of the argument might lie precisely in making what is implicit explicit. Someone may still object that the argument will not be convincing to everyone, but only to those with the right "faith." However, in this context that is not a demerit, since we set out precisely to see if an apologetic argument that is nonfoundationalist could be envisaged, and therefore the argument should not be evaluated by the criteria employed by classical foundationalism.

So I would claim that the physicoteleological argument that Climacus attributes to Socrates provides a model of an apologetic argument that has genuine epistemic worth and yet would be acceptable to Climacus. The argument is acceptable because it does not attempt to eliminate or replace faith, but explicitly posits faith as a necessary condition for the acceptance of the argument. But what of the possibility of offense?

To deal with offense, we must shift our attention from discussion of natural theology, where offense really has no place,[13] to discussion of the incarnation. I believe that the Socratic theistic argument we have examined does provide a model for understanding the apologetic arguments offered by Climacus himself. The central argument we saw at the conclusion of the first two chapters of *Fragments* revolved around the claim that the content of the "thought-project" Climacus ironically claims to have invented is such that no human being could have invented it. I think it is safe to say that this claim is not one that is self-evident, evident to the senses, or incorrigible. Nor do I think it is likely that anyone will produce an argument for this claim from premises that are acceptable to classical foundationalists. Hence I think that it is very likely that this argument is, like Socrates' reputed bit of natural theology,

---

[13]Of course some contemporary thinkers, such as feminist theologians and process theologians, may be "offended" in some senses by classical theism and by classical natural theology, but they are not offended in the technical sense of Climacus.

one that will only be acceptable to someone who already has a certain degree of faith that the story is indeed one revealed by God.

Just as was the case for the Socratic argument, this does not imply that the argument is circular or pointless. Certainly, it is not difficult to formulate the argument in a way that is not formally circular. And even if it is true that only the person who already has faith that God has become a human being will be able to recognize the remarkable features of the story that point to a non-human author, it does not follow that the argument is pointless. The features of the story that the argument (or a suitably developed version) might highlight and enable the person of faith to recognize may be genuine features of the story, and they may indeed truly point to a divine author. What is implicit in accepting the story may not always be explicit to the individual who accepts the story, and thus the argument may have genuine value in strengthening and confirming an acceptance of the story.

But what of offense? Is such an argument an attempt to do away with the possibility of offense? Of course the person who believes the story is one that God has authored is not offended, but that is not surprising. Climacus does not say that the person of faith is offended. What is necessary is not offense but the possibility of offense. It seems to me that an argument of this sort, which is only likely to be acceptable to a person of faith, in no way diminishes the possibility of offense. In fact, such a possibility may be strengthened by the argument, insofar as the argument highlights a feature of the Christian story that is more than a little difficult to swallow. Someone who finds it preposterous that a human being could be divine is not necessarily going to find it less preposterous to be told that this is a truth which God has revealed to us humans, and that it is a story that no human being could have invented.

The argument of Climacus that offense itself provides a confirmation of the truth of the incarnation demands a similar analysis. I cannot conceive of any reading of this argument that would sound convincing in a classical foundationalist context. On the other hand, for a person of faith, it may indeed be revealing and significant to notice that the objections of the offended consciousness are precisely what one would expect if a divine revelation were genuine, and that these objections are a kind of confused echoing of part of the content of that divine revelation.

Do such apologetic arguments commit the sin of the other kind of apologetic argument? Specifically, do they make the grasping of religious truth a purely cognitive matter that seems divorced from the possession of moral and spiritual qualities on the part of the believer? I think it is easy to construe the arguments in such a way that they do not do this. All one must do is further specify the nature of the faith that is regarded as a condition for accepting the arguments. If faith is a complex condition that includes basic moral and spiritual dispositions, then of course it follows that one cannot grasp the force of the arguments apart from the possession of those qualities.[14] Describing faith in such a way is of course independently motivated and not an ad hoc move; the theologian has plenty of reasons to regard faith as more than simply accepting certain propositions without conclusive evidence. Rather, faith must be seen as consisting partly in such things as a receptive openness to the mysterious aspects of human experience, an unselfish willingness to consider whether one's own attempts to dominate the world are an expression of sinful pride, and an attitude of hope towards the possibility of a life of eternal love for oneself and for other human beings. It may well be that people with such qualities are the kinds of people who get transformed by God in the course of their experiences and form the kinds of beliefs about themselves and the universe that are tantamount to belief in God.

I conclude that Climacus is not inconsistent in putting forward apologetic arguments while condemning classical foundationalist apologetics, so long as the apologetic arguments put forward are nonfoundationalist in character. Once this is recognized, the possibility opens of recasting other traditional apologetic arguments in a nonfoundationalist mode, such as historical arguments that appeal to miracles or which suggest that the transformed lives of the apostles can be seen as evidence for the resurrection of Jesus.

---

[14]For an excellent account of Kierkegaard's view of faith that shows how subtle it is by highlighting the role of faith as a transformation of the imagination rather than simply an act of will, see M. Jamie Ferreira, *Transforming Vision: Imagination and Will in Kierkegaardian Faith* (Oxford: Oxford University Press, 1991).

I do not think, however, that this is a possibility that Climacus or Kierkegaard foresaw, and perhaps it is not one they would have welcomed. However, I do not see that they have any real grounds for rejecting such a recasting of traditional apologetics, provided the arguments are carefully construed in such a way that they can be seen to presuppose and not replace faith. Given the fact that many people today find it difficult to accept miracles, so that the presence of miracles in a narrative is itself grounds for questioning the veracity of the narrative, it is not hard to see how this requirement could be fulfilled. I would insist once more that even if such arguments only have value to people of faith, and this assumption could certainly be challenged, it still may be true that their value to people of faith is great.[15] Evidence that is only recognizable to people of faith may still be evidence. I conclude that someone who accepts the basic complaint of Climacus and Kierkegaard against apologetic arguments need not reject all apologetics. Rather, apologetic arguments of a nonfoundationalist type are perfectly consistent with a Kierkegaardian perspective on faith and reason.

---

[15]For a detailed discussion of the possible value of historical apologetic arguments within the framework of Johannes Climacus's basic views on how faith in an incarnate God is formed, see my *Passionate Reason* (Bloomington: Indiana University Press, 1992).

5

A Paradox of Personal Identity in Kierkegaard's Philosophical Fragments

George Connell and Heather Servaty

In the first two chapters of *Philosophical Fragments*, Kierke-gaard's pseudonym Johannes Climacus purportedly draws out the central Christian tenets from the mere hypothesis that the moment in time may have decisive significance. Beginning with Meno's question as to whether the truth may be learned, Climacus traces a dialectical pathway that leads him, by the end of chapter 2, to the god becoming the lowest of the low and the servant of all so as to teach the truth. Absolutely crucial to this line of reasoning is Climacus's identification of untruth as sin. Only thus does the initially epistemological question of learning the truth become, fundamentally, a question of soteriology. But in identifying untruth as sin, does Climacus blame the victim? On what basis does he point an accusing finger at the learner-to-be? Climacus's answer comes in a single dense, problematic but crucially important paragraph.

Now, inasmuch as the learner exists [*er til*], he is indeed created, and, accordingly, God must have given him the condition for understanding the truth (for otherwise he previously would have been merely animal, and that teacher who gave him the condition along with the truth would make him a human being for the first time). But insofar as the moment is to have decisive significance (and if this is not assumed, then we do in fact remain with the Socratic), he must lack the condition, consequently be deprived of it. This cannot have been due to an act of the god (for this is a contradiction) or to an accident (for it is a contradiction that something inferior would be able to vanquish something superi-or); it must therefore have been due to himself. If he could have lost the condition in such a way that it was not due to himself, then he would have possessed the condition only accidentally, which is a contradiction, since the condition for the truth is an essential condition. The untruth, then, is not merely outside the truth but is polemical against the truth, which is expressed by saying that he himself has forfeited and is forfeiting the condition. (PF, 15)

The argument here for the self's responsibility for its existence in a state of untruth parallels closely an argument Augustine develops in his dialog *On Free Choice of the Will*.

> Augustine. For the present, we can be certain that whatever be that nature which, by right, is superior to the mind strong in virtue, it cannot be unjust. Therefore, even though it may have the power to do so, it will not force the mind to serve lust.
> Evodius. No one will hesitate to admit this.
> Augustine. Since, because of justice, whatever is equal or superior to the mind that possesses virtue and is in control does not make the mind a slave to lust; and since, because of its weakness, whatever is inferior to the mind cannot do this . . . therefore it follows that nothing can make the mind a companion of desire except its own will and free choice [*voluntas et liberum arbitrium*].[1]

Despite this argument's august lineage, it appears to leave Climacus impaled on the horns of a dilemma. On the one hand, he has to argue that having the truth is *essential* to human existence. Only thereby is he able to pin the blame for its loss squarely on the self. On the other hand, if the truth is an essential attribute of humanity, then it would seem that the self that surrendered it couldn't persist to reacquire it through the benevolent intervention of the teacher. Climacus's argument seems here to rest on the incoherent notion of a particular individual maintaining her identity through a process of initially having, then surrendering, and then reacquiring one of her essential properties. In the paragraph quoted, Climacus infers the self's prior possession of the truth from the fact that possession of the truth is essential to that self. The assumption behind this inference seems to be that an entity must have possessed all of its essential properties at some time in

---

[1]Augustine, *On Free Choice of the Will*, trans. Anna S. Benjamin and L. H. Hackstaff (Indianapolis: Bobbs-Merrill, 1964) 21-22.

the past even if it no longer possesses all of them in the present. Climacus does well to keep this assumption implicit!

Focusing on this apparent incoherence will show how dis-analogous two of Climacus's examples are to the process in question. To illustrate how a self could voluntarily surrender something and yet not have the ability voluntarily to reacquire that thing, Johannes Climacus speaks of a child who chooses to spend a gift of money on a toy but then decides he prefers a book. The importuned book dealer responds:

> My dear child, your toy is worthless; it is certainly true that when you still had the money you could have bought the book just as well as the toy, but the awkward thing about a toy is that once it is purchased it has lost all value. (PF, 16n)

Similarly, a knight offered favorable terms by one army on the day of a battle tries in vain to accept the offer once the battle is over and he, having joined the opposing side, lies manacled in the victorious king's dungeon.

As useful as these examples are in showing that what is freely done can't always be freely undone, they are fundamentally dis-analogous to the condition of the learner on Climacus's hypothesis. Neither ownership of a toy or a book nor joining a particular army is an essential human attribute, so there is no problem involved in the self same boy and the self same knight persisting through their respective unfortunate decisions. And should the book dealer grant the wish of the boy or the victorious king free the knight, there is no difficulty involved in the persistence of either self through the respective events. But the learner supposedly loses and then regains the truth, a condition that Climacus asserts is constitutive of the learner's very humanity. And for a human to lose that which makes her human is surely to cease to be herself.

Or are we too hasty in this judgment? Have we failed to distinguish between a property's being essential to an object's continued membership in a sortal class (here, that of human beings) and a property's being essential to the self-identity of an object? It is easy to overlook this distinction since there is such substantial overlap between the two types of essential properties. Most often, when a thing ceases to belong to the natural kind to which it has thither to belonged, it simply ceases to be. (And, of course, vice versa.) But this overlap isn't complete. Depending on which criterion of personal identity one accepts, one can construct a scenario in which the humanity of an individual is retained through some change but in which there is a loss of personal identity. For example, if someone were to undergo a total loss of memory and a radical change of character, it can plausibly be argued that we should view the pre- and post-change phases of that single human life as two distinct persons. Similarly, depending on one's criterion of personal identity, one may be able to construct a scenario in which an individual ceases to be human but continues to exist as the same person he was while still a human. For example, a prince turned into a frog by a wicked witch is no longer human but is still himself. When reading fairy tales, we accept without hesitation the idea that one and the same individual originally was a human prince, then was tragically transformed into a frog, but finally is restored to both his princeliness and humanity by the kiss of a maiden.[2]

Perhaps we have here the relevant analogy to the self's loss and recovery of the truth. (After all, Climacus, like his creator, Kierkegaard, loves fairy tales, especially ones involving royalty, mistaken identity, and love.) Is Climacus supposing that the self, in misusing its freedom and surrendering the truth, ceases to be human but continues to be the self that it is until and through its transformative encounter with the teacher? If so, then perhaps he can escape the dilemma on whose horns he seems so dreadfully impaled. In order to establish the self's responsibility for its condition of untruth, he points out the essential link between the self's original humanity and the condition for understanding the truth. Recall that he says that not to have been given the condition for understanding the truth would have left the self an animal. If the condition is essential to the self's humanity, not to its personal identity, then the self could survive both its self-induced alienation

---

[2]Our reference to fairy tales in assessing criteria of personal identity is in keeping with the widespread use of quite fantastic thought-experiments in the philosophical literature on this subject. For a telling critique of this heavy reliance on fantastic thought-experiments, see Kathleen Wilkes, *Real People: Personal Identity without Thought-Experiments* (Oxford: Oxford University Press, 1988).

from the truth (=dehumanization) and its unmerited restoration by the teacher.

Unfortunately, this suggestion is no sooner raised than dismissed. Let us look again at the first sentence of the paragraph we are scrutinizing.

> Now, inasmuch as the learner exists [*er til*], he is indeed created, and, accordingly, God must have given him the condition for understanding the truth (for otherwise he previously would have been merely animal, and that teacher who gave him the condition along with the truth would make him a human being for the first time). (PF, 15)

The parenthetical phrase is clearly counterfactual, indicating that the self, even in the depths of its untruth, isn't merely animal. Climacus appears genuinely committed to the following inconsistent claims: (1) the possession of the truth is that which distinguishes humans from animals, (2) the teacher brings the truth to the learner who has forfeited the truth, and (3) the learner is human and not animal in the period between her forfeiting of the truth and her restoration by the teacher.

Rather than entering a plea of paradox here so as to excuse ourselves from the task of making sense of Climacus's argument, we should invoke the principle of hermeneutic charity and do what we can to resolve the apparent incoherence. Since the issue is fundamentally one of personal identity, we need to determine Climacus's views on the subject and, specifically, to ascertain what criterion of identity he employs. A natural way to undertake this task is to ask whether Climacus would or could have accepted one of the familiar theories of personality identity articulated in Western philosophy since Locke raised the question.

At first glance, the criterion of bodily continuity appears compatible with the Kierkegaardian anthropology shared by most of the pseudonyms and certainly by Johannes Climacus. The conception of human beings as psychophysical syntheses that is most fully worked out in Anti-Climacus's *Sickness unto Death* is already sketched out in the unpublished *Johannes Climacus*.[3] Further, the

---

[3]See below in this essay for a discussion of the substantial agreement between the anthropology of *Johannes Climacus* and that of *The Sickness unto Death*.

existentialist themes that resonate through Climacus's discussions in the *Concluding Unscientific Postscript* are, implicitly and explicitly, polemics against Cartesian dualism and Idealistic conceptions of the transcendental ego. Since our embodiment is, on Climacus's view, an essential dimension of our selfhood, it would seem that bodily continuity is a plausible candidate for his criterion of personal identity.

But recall the questions Climacus places on the title page of *Fragments*: "Can a historical point of departure be given for an eternal consciousness; how can such a point of departure be of more than historical interest; can an eternal happiness be built on historical knowledge?" Despite the intentional vagueness of "eternal consciousness" and "eternal happiness," the intelligibility of these questions certainly seems to depend upon the intelligibility of the self surviving its biological death. Since Climacus argues in *Postscript* that an objective, conceptual analysis of the notion of personal survival of death cannot settle the issue conclusively, either positively or negatively, it is clear that he does not accept bodily continuity as his criterion of personal identity.[4] To assert consistently the objective uncertainty of personal survival of death, he must adopt a criterion of personal identity that leaves such survival an open question. But even if one associates eternal happiness with the idea of a resurrected body, there seems no plausible way to state this view in terms of bodily continuity. First, continuity appears to be broken during the interval between death and resurrection. Second, the material body of this life and the spiritual body of the life to come seem too radically dissimilar to be identical in any meaningful sense.

While the bodily continuity criterion nicely reflects Climacus's belief that humans are psycho*physical* syntheses, it fails to allow for the transfer of the self from one body to another involved in the resurrection of the dead. What Climacus needs is a criterion of personal identity that requires the self to be embodied but which does not tie the self to a particular body. Functionalism seems tailor-made to play this role.

---

[4]See CUP, 1:171-77.

In the first instance, functionalism is a theory of mind rather than of personal identity. Sydney Shoemaker, one of its prominent advocates, writes:

> What various versions of [functionalism] hold in common is that every mental state is a 'functional state,' i.e., a state which is definable in terms of its relations (primarily its causal relations) to sensory inputs, behavioral outputs, and (especially) other functional states. A mental state is individuated, and constituted as being the particular mental state that it is, by its place in a complex causal nexus of states.[5]

This theory of mind rather directly suggests a theory of personal identity. Two mental states are co-personal (=are states of an identical person) if and only if they are functionally related to each other, that is, if they are so connected as jointly to cause successor mental states and behaviors.

Note that this criterion of identity exhibits both of the qualities Climacus needs. First, its focus on behavioral outputs requires the self's embodiment. Second, its total neutrality as to the specific character of the states that produce the successor mental states and behavioral outputs leaves it great flexibility to accommodate the "body transfers" involved in resurrection. Shoemaker describes the following scenario to help us imagine such a transfer.

> Imagine a society living in an environment in which an increase in some sort of radiation has made it impossible for a human body to remain healthy for more than a few years. Being highly advanced technologically, the society has developed the following procedure for dealing with this. For each person there is a stock of duplicate bodies, cloned from cells taken from that person and grown by an accelerated process in a radiation proof vault, where they are then stored. Periodically a person goes into the hospital for a 'body change.' This consists in his total brain-state being transferred to the brain of one of his duplicate bodies. At the end of the procedure, the original body is incinerated.[6]

Now, if the resulting self forms beliefs and performs actions as a result of relating functional states produced by both pre- and post-

---

[5]Sydney Shoemaker and Richard Swinburne, *Personal Identity* (Oxford: Basil Blackwell, 1984) 92.
[6]Ibid., 108-109.

transfer experiences, then those states are co-personal and the person-stages in which the experiences occurred are stages of a single, subsisting self. To use an example of Shoemaker's, if prior to such a body transfer a person agreed to meet a friend for lunch at a specific time and place and after the transfer acted to be at the rendezvous at the appropriate time, then the functional state recalling the agreement and the functional state of knowing the current time and location are functionally related and co-personal. Thus, the self that agreed to the meeting and the self that showed up for lunch are the same self despite the total absence of bodily continuity.

While Shoemaker accepts a materialist theory of mental states that would leave little room for belief in resurrection, the preceding scenario shows that functionalism is consistent with such resurrection. It seems perfectly plausible that God could transfer a self's functional states (whatever their character) to a new spiritual body, thereby securing the continued existence of the person.

Despite its attractive flexibility, functionalism is ill-suited to be Climacus's criterion of identity. What is functionalism if not a contemporary version of the Hegelian maxim that the inner is the outer and the outer the inner? ("The inner" would designate functional states and "the outer" the causal inputs and behavioral outputs in terms of which functionalists define and identify functional states.) One can plausibly read Kierkegaard's entire pseudonymous literature as a sustained polemic against Hegel's maxim. Note that both Johannes the Seducer in *Either/Or* and the knight of faith described in *Fear and Trembling* present similar conventional exteriors but conceal utterly discrepant subjectivities behind their innocuous appearances. In "A Glance at a Contemporary Effort in Danish Literature" in the *Postscript*, Climacus explicitly associates himself with the other pseudonyms' attacks on the maxim.[7] Furthermore, in the *Postscript* as a whole, he develops a theoretical grounding for the radical incommensurability of subjectivity and objectivity, of personal identity and public behavior. He writes:

> The less externality, the more inwardness. That the most passionate decision occurs in a person in such a way that it is not detected at all is something profound and wonderful. (CUP, 1:382)

---

[7]See, e.g., CUP, 1:259-61.

We cannot plausibly attribute a neobehaviorist criterion of personal identity to the great theoretician of interiority and the incognito of faith.[8]

Given Climacus's emphasis on subjectivity, we would do well to consider the primary subjectively oriented criterion of personal identity: memory. Locke, the original formulator of this criterion, writes:

> For, since consciousness always accompanies thinking, and it is that which makes every one to be what he calls self, and thereby distinguishes himself from all other thinking things: in this alone consists personal identity, i.e. the sameness of a rational being; and *as far as this consciousness can be extended backwards to any past action or thought, so far reaches the identity of that person; it is the same self now it was then; and it is by the same self with this present one that now reflects on it, that that action was done.*[9]

That is, person A is identical with person B if and only if A recalls an experience of B's or vice versa.[10]

As stated, the memory criterion is impossibly stringent. Even advocates of the memory criterion have long accepted the need to weaken Locke's strong version of the criterion to handle such difficulties as Reid's gallant colonel objection and the obvious fact that none of us remembers all our past experiences all the time. Surely the *possibility* of remembering prior states is enough to establish the relevant continuity of consciousness. That is, person

---

[8]Merold Westphal has plausibly argued that Kierkegaard later found it necessary to back away from the radical disassociation of subjectivity and action: in the last years of his life, Kierkegaard espoused a radical Christianity in which believers would necessarily find themselves in open conflict with the established order and especially its ecclesial buttresses. See Merold Westphal, "Kierkegaard's Teleological Suspension of Religiousness B," in *Foundations of Kierkegaard's Vision of Community: Religion, Ethics and Politics in Kierkegaard,* ed. by George B. Connell and C. Stephen Evans (Atlantic Highlands NJ: Humanities Press, 1992).

[9]John Locke, *Essay Concerning Human Understanding,* bk. 2, chap. 27, §9 (many editions); our italics.

[10]Henceforth, we will omit the "or vice versa" to reduce the unwieldiness of our statements of the memory criterion.

A is identical with person B if and only if A either actually recalls or has the potential to recall an experience of B's.[11]

Such a modified version of the memory criterion lends itself quite well to at least some aspects of *Fragments*. Specifically, Climacus discusses as a coherent option the Socratic model of learning in which the recollecting self is identical to itself in its preamnesic phases even before it recollects what it knew in those states. Clearly, no bodily criterion of identity will do here since the recollecting self supposedly recalls what it knew in its disincarnate, prenatal phases. And, by hypothesis, there is not yet any actual recollection of those phases. Neither will it do to reformulate the memory criterion in terms of a chain of conscious states each linked by an actual memory to predecessor states: if the trauma of incarnation/birth is sufficiently great, it might break all actual memory links. It is the self's capacity, given proper prodding and prompting, to recollect what it learned during its preincarnate phases that plausibly establishes identity, even if the self never actually carries out such a recollection.

Careful attention to the phrasing of the prior paragraph reveals the need for a slight but significant emendation in our statement of the memory criterion. In discussing the identity of the Socratic learner with its preincarnate phases, we emphasized the self's recollection of knowledge acquired during those phases, not recollection of those phases themselves. That is, even if the self doesn't remember viewing the forms, its present recollection of *what* it then learned is sufficient to establish identity. This fits with our intuitions concerning cases of amnesia. For example, in Alfred Hitchcock's film *Spellbound*, the character played by Gregory Peck suffers severe amnesia. Ingrid Bergman, playing a psychiatrist, asks Peck how he would diagnose a pain in the upper right quadrant. When Peck immediately answers that he would suspect either pneumonia or gall bladder trouble, the two know that Peck

---

[11]In this and in subsequent statements of the memory criterion, our references to experience and to memories of experiences should be understood as assuming the first person character of those experiences and memories of experiences. Thus, it is not necessary to stipulate as do some writers that A remembers an experience of B *as B*.

is a doctor.[12] This example vividly illustrates the fact that "total" amnesia is seldom really total. While the amnesiac may be unable to recall any *episodes* from his past, he retains much of the knowledge learned in that past. He still knows his language, his trade, the customs of his country. It is plausible to assert that recalling such content suffices to establish identity with the past phases in which the content was learned even if the episodes and experiences of that past are beyond recall. Thus we restate the memory criterion: person A is identical with person B if and only if A actually or potentially remembers either an experience of B's or the content of an experience of B's.

But does the memory criterion as now stated work as well on the alternative hypothesis that the self doesn't recollect the truth but genuinely learns it? It would appear not since Climacus differentiates the Socratic and Christian hypotheses precisely by reference to the possibility of recollecting the truth. For him to establish the identity of the Christian self in its three phases (truth-untruth-regained truth) by reference even to potential memory certainly seems to abrogate the Christian hypothesis that the truth can be learned, to reduce untruth from total alienation from the truth to temporary amnesia, and to return to the Socratic.

Perhaps, however, he could adopt the memory criterion as modified above and still avoid collapsing the Socratic and Christian hypotheses by insisting that each conceives of potential memory in a fundamentally different way. On the Socratic hypothesis, the self is capable of recollecting the truth on its own. Though a maieutic teacher may prompt the recollection, that prompting is a mere occasion, of disappearing significance, since the recollecting self always and ineluctably possesses the truth. But on the Christian hypothesis, the self has radically alienated itself from the truth so that it doesn't even know its untruth and is oriented polemically against the truth. On its own, the learner is utterly incapable of recollecting the truth it previously surrendered. It can't even remember surrendering it, since to remember that forfeiture would involve remembering what was forfeited. But

---

[12]We owe this example to Walker Percy who discusses this and other instances of amnesia in his *Lost in the Cosmos* (New York: Farrar, Straus & Giroux, 1983).

when the teacher, the god-man, transforms and recreates the self in the moment, the self regains the condition for understanding the truth. That is, with divine assistance, it is restored to its prelapsarian condition and knows once again what it once knew. That is, with God's help, the learner remembers the truth. Since Climacus asserts that God is strictly egalitarian and doesn't play favorites on the basis of contingent differences between persons,[13] consistency demands that he hold that all people have the potential to enter a saving relation to the god-man, the teacher. This, however, raises the question of the status of persons who are born prior to the advent of the teacher or who are so geographically removed from the scene of that arrival that they never have an opportunity to respond to news of the teacher with either faith or offense. It is a measure of Climacus's commitment to an egalitarian conception of God that he postulates a postmortem opportunity for decision for all those denied such an opportunity in this life.[14] In thus positing that all people have the potential to enter a saving relation to the god-man, Climacus also posits the possibility of recovered memory of either the prelapsarian phases of each person's life or, more plausibly, the content of those phases, the truth. And this, on a suitably modified version of the memory criterion, suffices to establish identity.

Questions remain, however, as to the suitability of even this version of the memory criterion to Climacus's Christian thought-experiment. First, for those selves that refuse or squander their opportunity for restoration, for those selves who are offended by the teacher or for those lukewarm, spiritless selves who acknowledge the teacher "to a certain degree," the possibility of recovered memory of the truth is irretrievably lost at death.[15] Such

---

[13]"Let the learner be X, and this X must also include the lowliest, for if even Socrates did not keep company solely with brilliant minds, how then could the god make distinctions?" (PF, 31)

[14]"If [the teacher and the learner] were to meet in another life, that teacher would again be able to give the condition to the person who had not received it. . . . " (PF, 17)

[15]This is the point of Climacus's repeated contrasting of religiousness A and religiousness B on the basis of their respective stances toward time: one's years between cradle and grave are revoked as jest in religiousness A since nothing one can do will change one's essential relation to the eternal; in contrast, religiousness

a self must still be identical with the self that sacrificed the truth or else its eternal alienation from the truth is unjust. Second, Kierkegaard holds out the prospect that God, in forgiving sin, blots it out of his mind completely, forgets it entirely.

> Up to now I have armed myself against my depression with intellectual activity which keeps it away—now, in faith that God has forgotten in forgiveness whatever guilt I have, I must try to forget it myself, but not in any diversion, not in any distance from it, but in God, so that *when I think of God I may dare think he has forgotten it and in that way myself learn to dare to forget it in forgiveness.* (JP, 5:6043; our italics)

Despite the fact that the guilt is forgotten by both God and the redeemed self, that self must be identical with the self that committed the sins from which it is redeemed, else redemption is impossible because unneeded. Thus, if one postulates that Climacus would accept his creator's view of forgiveness, there seem to be unrecalled and unrecallable stages of the lives of both the blessed and the damned. Even if one refuses to admit the Kierkegaardian view of divine forgiveness as relevant to an investigation of Climacus's views, the parallel case of those who are eternally alienated from the truth suffices to call the memory criterion into question.

Perhaps some version of the criterion employing counterfactual clauses could be formulated to handle such objections: person A is identical with person B if either (1) A remembers an experience or content of an experience of B's or (2) A could remember an experience or content of an experience of B's on her own or with suitable prompting by another or (3) A could remember an experience or content of an experience of B's if A were transformed suitably by God or (4) A could have remembered an experience or content of an experience of B's if A had accepted God's initiative to transform A or (5) A could have remembered an experience or content of an experience of B's if A had rejected God's initiative to transform A.

Aside from the intuitive implausibility of such a tortuous criterion, there is further reason for thinking any version of the memory

---

B places infinite significance on one's temporal existence since one's eternal blessedness is at stake.

criterion unsuitable: its one-dimensional focus on the self's relation
to its past. John Perry writes:

> [T]here is nothing in Locke's account of personal identity to ex-
> plain *why* I care what happens to me tomorrow. That I will be
> run over by a truck means, says Locke, that the person who is
> run over by a truck will remember thinking and doing what I am
> thinking and doing now. But why would I care especially about
> that? Why should a person who is having such memories be of
> any more concern to me than anyone else?[16]

Perry is charitable to Locke here in not asking whether that future
run-over self will be doing any remembering at all! But the real
point of Perry's criticism is that it is implausible and arbitrary to
explain the self's concern for its future states wholly in terms of its
relation to past states. What is it that uniquely privileges the reten-
sive temporal ekstasis over the protensive?

In asking this question, we come face to face with the total un-
suitability of the memory criterion to Climacus's thought. Throughout *Fragments* and *Postscript*, Climacus continuously sets future-ori-
ented Christian existence over against various past-oriented forms
of selfhood, the Socratic, the humoristic, the immanent religious,
and (if one is charitable enough to call forgetfulness a form of selfhood) the Hegelian. In lampooning the Hegelians, Climacus specifically attacks the "anticipatory recollection" that the defender of
the memory criterion must invoke to account for our concern for
our futures:

> The speculative absentmindedness may be psychologically ex-
> plained only by the constant association with world history, with
> the past. Instead of really being aware of himself as one who is
> living in the present and has the future before him, in order thus
> to come to the point of being psychologically able to reproduce
> the individual element, which is only one factor among others in
> world history, the speculative thinker mingles everything and
> wants to anticipate his own pastness—in order then to act,
> although it seems fairly easy to understand if a person has first
> become something past, then he has acted. (CUP, 1:146)

---

[16]John Perry, "The Importance of Being Identical" in *The Identities of Persons*,
ed. Amelie Oksenberg Rorty (Berkley: University of California Press, 1976) 68.

If the memory criterion has the wrong orientation, it nonetheless has the right focus: continuity of consciousness. Climacus's concern is for his own happiness, his own eternal consciousness. Recall the questions on the title page of *Fragments*. There Climacus asks about the possibility of a *future* blessedness. He asks the same question in *Postscript*, albeit in a more personal manner:

> I, Johannes Climacus, born and bred in this city and now thirty years old, an ordinary human being like most folk, assume that a highest good, called an eternal happiness, awaits me just as it awaits a housemaid and a professor. I have heard that Christianity is one's prerequisite for this good. I now ask how I may enter into relation to this doctrine. (CUP, 1:15-16)

For such a future blessedness to be his, there must be some sort of continuity between the consciousness that enjoys that felicity and the self that anxiously questions the possibility of and conditions for that felicity.

But how to explain the present self's identity with its future (as well as past) phases so as to make sense of this concern? We want to suggest that Climacus (and Kierkegaard with him) answers this question by inverting it. Rather than explaining concern in terms of identity, Climacus explains identity in terms of concern. It is the self's concernful relation to its past, present and especially future that establishes the self's identity, not vice versa. To explain and document this radical solution to the issue of personal identity, we turn first to the final dense pages of the unpublished manuscript *Johannes Climacus or De omnibus dubitandum est*.

In *Pars Secunda* of the manuscript, Climacus gives up his efforts to make sense of the statements about doubt made by presumed philosophical authorities, especially Hegelians, and strikes out on his own. Since he views doubt as a subjective determination, he rejects any and all empirical approaches to the question and resolves instead to "search out *doubt's ideal possibility in consciousness*" (JC, 166). He writes, "The possibility of doubt . . . lies in consciousness, whose nature is a contradiction that is produced by a duplexity [*Dupplicitet*] and that itself produces a duplexity" (JC, 168). Climacus identifies the two relata of this duplexity as reality (or immediacy) and ideality (or language). While he is cryptically laconic here, it is clear that realty/immediacy typically denotes the brute here-now givenness of the self's present, its facticity, while ideality/language denotes the self's openness to the nonactual, the possible. While both aspects of experience are essential conditions of consciousness, they are not mutually sufficient. When considered strictly alone, when abstracted from the fuller reality that is consciousness, the reality/ideality pairing is reflection, which Climacus describes as the mere possibility of consciousness (JC, 169).

Despite its inability to exist on its own, reflection may describe the full extent to which consciousness is employed at a particular moment, as when the self is engaged in objective knowing. When the two opposed terms, reality and ideality, are to be compared, one of the two must be selected as the standard against which the other is judged. When ideality is measured against reality, the result is the project of objective knowledge, the disinterested attempt to construct a system of knowledge (the ideal) that accurately reproduces its object (the real).[17] In objective knowledge, the knower drops out of the picture as insignificant and so we remain within the dichotomous structure of reflection.

When reality is measured against ideality the picture is different. Climacus asserts in the *Postscript* that the only reality the self can reflectively engage without thereby converting it to ideality is its own existence. Thus, only when the self sets about conforming its personal existence to its ideals, its own imagined futures, does it genuinely measure the real by the ideal. This activity, however, is ethical and presupposes *interest*, a third element altogether alien to the simple juxtaposition of ideality and reality that is reflection. It is this tripartite schema, ideality, reality, interest, that Climacus designates as consciousness. He writes:

> Reflection is the possibility of the relation. This can also be stated as follows: Reflection is *disinterested*. Consciousness, however, is the relation and thereby is interest, a duality that is perfectly and with pregnant double meaning expressed in the word "interest" [*interesse*, being between]. Therefore, all disinterested knowledge (mathematics, esthetics, metaphysics) is only the presupposition of doubt. As soon as the interest is canceled, doubt

---

[17]In this instance, "the real" is used more broadly to designate all that is actual, not simply the self's facticity.

is not conquered but is neutralized, and all such knowledge is simply a retrogression. Thus it would be a misunderstanding for someone to think that doubt can be overcome by so-called objective thinking. Doubt is a higher form than any objective thinking, for it presupposes the latter but has something more, a third, which is interest or consciousness. (JC, 170)

Climacus here sketches in broad strokes a theory of consciousness that is very suggestive for our inquiry into personal identity. Consciousness is not a passive, disinterested knowing but the interested projection of futures and enactment of projects. The self, reflecting on itself as it is and as it has been, imaginatively projects ideals of itself as it can and should be. To our question, "Why should I care about a particular future self in a way I care about no others?," Climacus could answer that the present self is the self it is in major part because of its imaginative projection of and interested relation to that future self. Thus the present self's concernful relation to its future phases explains rather than is explained by the identity of the self at those two times.

Those familiar with *The Sickness unto Death* will recognize the above theory of self as substantially identical with Anti-Climacus's anthropology. Granted, the terminology is very different, but in almost every instance one can readily pair terms and phrases from *Johannes Climacus* with their synonyms in *The Sickness unto Death.* Where Climacus speaks of consciousness, Anti-Climacus speaks of the self. Where Climacus speaks of an interested relating of reality and ideality, Anti-Climacus speaks of a relation that relates itself to itself. This latter formulation reflects Anti-Climacus's view that the self both as it is and as it will be is a synthesis of the finite and infinite, the temporal and the eternal. Where Climacus speaks of reflection as the dichotomous possibility of consciousness, Anti-Climacus speaks of negative thirdness as an unposited synthesis of the elements of selfhood. And Climacus's ultimate description of consciousness as the interested relating of reality and ideality corresponds perfectly to Anti-Climacus's positive thirdness.

Two aspects of this shared theory of selfhood are especially worthy of note. First, it betokens a profoundly relational metaphysics. Granted, all plausible metaphysics recognize the existence of relation. But most metaphysics make substance primary and then account for relation in terms of juxtapositions of substances. Here, however, the "relata" aren't substances; rather they are inseparable aspects of a relation that is irreducibly basic. That is, the self exists only as the interested relation of the self as it is to the self as it may or will be. To separate either aspect from the relation is impossible since neither could be what it is apart from the relation. The present self wouldn't be the self that it is if its horizon of futurity were to vanish, and it is hard to say what a possible self is if it is not the anticipated future of some actual self. Poul Lübcke's comments on Anti-Climacus's relational theory of the self are to the point here:

> Strictly speaking, talk of a synthesis or a relation is misleading since it implies that there are two distinct relata which enter into some relation or other in which they "synthesize" with each other. In this sense, chlorine and sulfur stand in relation to each other and synthesize as sulfuric acid. But it is clear that this is not the sort of relation to which Anti-Climacus refers. Rather, . . . one ought to say that the *pair* finitude/infinitude *taken as a whole* represents one aspect under which a human's life can be characterized in as much as the life is located on a scale with pure finitude and pure infinitude as extremes.[18]

Lübcke's focus here is a bit different from ours since he is discussing the relation of finitude and infinitude in the present self whereas we are discussing the relation of the present self to the future self. Nonetheless, his point is relevant since he is arguing, as are we, that the relations constitutive of the self do not involve separable, substantial relata but are irreducibly basic.

The second striking feature of Climacus's and Anti-Climacus's shared view of the self is its emphasis on event. The self is not a passively persisting substance or a static relation between substances but the ongoing event of self-relation. Thus, in asking about Climacus's understanding of self-identity, we should inquire into the identity-conditions of the ongoing event of self-relation that is the self.

These points call into question the framework in which our paradox of personal identity has been stated. Our aporia arose when we noted that Climacus seems bound to describe "the truth"

---

[18]Poul Lübcke, "Selvets Ontologi hos Kierkegaard," *Kierkegaardiana* 13 (1984): 53; our translation.

as both an essential and an accidental property of the self. But what happens to this apparent paradox if we challenge the underlying notion of the self as a substance and "the truth" as a property? Further, until we have a better idea of what it means to characterize an event of self-relation as true or untrue, we can't be at all sure whether Climacus's account is paradoxical or perfectly coherent. How exactly is Climacus using "the truth" and how does it fit into his distinctive theory of the self as the event of self-relation?

The most (in)famous of Climacus's statements on this topic is surely his claim in *Postscript* that "truth is subjectivity." While many have read this as an endorsement of radical relativism, more attentive interpreters have shown it instead to betoken an overriding emphasis on existential appropriation: it is not enough to know the truth, one must live it.[19] This conception of truth as appropriation fits perfectly with the relational theory of self we have attributed to Climacus: appropriation is the reduplication of the ideal in the real, the possible in the actual; it is the interested self's continuous struggle to realize its imagined futures.

Does this construal of "the truth" help us to untangle the knots we have found in the opening chapters of *Fragments*? In large measure, it does. The problem on which we have focused is Climacus's insistence *both* that truth is an essential attribute of the self *and* that it may be lost and reacquired. As long as we interpret his claims in terms of a substantial self and its essential or accidental properties, Climacus's statements remain stubbornly nonsensical. But when we think of truth as the event of interested self-relation, Climacus makes much more sense. Truth is an essential attribute of human selves in that the self *is* the event of interested self-relation. But since the self is free, the exact quality of its self-relation is in its own hands. The self can responsibly undertake its task of self-relation or it can evade, ignore or rebel against it. In the former case, the self exists in the truth, in the latter, in untruth. That is, Climacus equivocates on "the truth." On the one hand, it designates the irreducibly basic event of self-relation that is the

---

[19]For a balanced discussion of the meaning of the claim that truth is subjectivity, see C. Stephen Evans, *Kierkegaard's Fragments and Postscript: The Religious Philosophy of Johannes Climacus* (Atlantic Highlands NJ: Humanities Press, 1983).

self. In this sense, the truth is an essential attribute of human selves. On the other hand, truth designates the normative modality of that relation of the self to itself and untruth all of the host of distorted and disturbed modalities of self-relation.

But we no sooner resolve one problem than we raise a new one. The construal of "the truth" we have put forward threatens to abrogate Climacus's carefully tended separation of the Christian and the Socratic hypotheses. For if "the truth" designates only appropriate self-relation, what reason do we have to believe that the learner needs the teacher to regain the truth? As Climacus shows in *Postscript*, the case for responsible self-relation, the case for being a subjective thinker, can be made in purely immanent terms without reference to a divine teacher. Further, Climacus articulates a theory of indirect communication whereby one person can Socratically occasion another's self-concern. What becomes of Climacus's hypothesis in *Fragments* that the learner lacks the truth and only the divine teacher, the god-man, can restore it? Clearly, some additional connotation attaches to "the truth" as used in *Fragments*. What this additional connotation is becomes clear when we recall the parallelism of Climacus's and Anti-Climacus's anthropologies. In the famous opening of *The Sickness unto Death*, Anti-Climacus asserts that the self's relation to itself is simultaneously a relation to God:

> A human being is spirit. But what is spirit? Spirit is the self. But what is the self? The self is a relation that relates itself to itself.
> . . .
> Such a relation that relates itself to itself, a self, must either have established itself or have been established by another.
> If the relation that relates itself to itself has been established by another, then the relation is indeed the third, but this relation, the third, is yet again a relation and relates itself to that which established the entire relation.
> The human self is such a derived, established relation, a relation that relates itself to itself and in relating itself to itself relates itself to another. . . . (SUD, 13-14)

In *Fragments*, Climacus identifies the truth as proper god-relation by (purportedly) drawing out the implications of the idea that the truth may be learned. If the truth is truly to be learned, then the teacher does not simply bring the truth but is the truth for the learner. For the learner to reacquire the truth she has forfeited, she must enter and remain in the appropriate relation to the teacher. Since this restoration involves the recreation of the learner, only the god can be the teacher. Since the god's only possible motivation is love, and love seeks love, Climacus concludes that the teacher's goal in the transformative encounter is winning the love of the learner. Accordingly, this love is what Climacus cryptically designates as "the truth." As clever as his chain of reasoning is here, we find it far more plausible to regard this as the exposition of a presupposition rather than a genuine derivation.

Just as Climacus equivocates in using "the truth" to designate both self-relation generally and the normative mode of self-relation, he similarly equivocates in using "the truth" to designate the god-relationship. Noting this equivocation helps resolve his apparent inconsistency as to whether "the truth" is an accidental or essential property of the self. First, "the truth" is essential to the self in that the self stands related to God as inevitably and unavoidably as it stands related to itself. Second, "truth" and "untruth" equivocally designate proper and improper modalities of the underlying, inevitable relation to God just as they designate proper and improper modalities of relation to self.

These two levels of equivocation on "the truth" are not evidence of terminological sloppiness on Climacus's part. Rather, they capture an ambiguity Climacus believes to inhere in the situation of conversion. In one sense, the learner exists prior to receiving the truth from the teacher. Else we would have to speak of creation rather than conversion. But so profound is the transition from untruth to truth that Climacus compares it to birth, to the transition from nonbeing to being.

> Inasmuch as he was in untruth and now along with the condition receives the truth, a change takes place in him like the change from "not to be" to "to be." But this transition from "not to be" to "to be" is indeed the transition of birth. But the person who already *is* cannot be born, and yet he is born. Let us call this transition *rebirth*. (PF, 19)

To demonstrate further the correctness of our interpretation of "the truth" as used in *Fragments*, we will clarify three otherwise problematic passages in the paragraph under scrutiny. The first sentence of that paragraph runs:

> Now, inasmuch as the learner exists [*er til*], he is indeed created, and, accordingly, God must have given him the condition for understanding the truth (for otherwise he previously would have been merely animal, and that teacher who gave him the condition along with the truth would make him a human being for the first time). (PF, 15)

Climacus goes out of his way here to introduce the idea of God as creator and humans as created so as to set, at least implicitly, the context within which to understand "the truth." No previous passages prepare for this allusion to the Judeo-Christian doctrine of creation; if we took Climacus's conceit of conducting a thought-experiment seriously, we should heartily protest such an unmotivated introduction of theistic presuppositions. But, of course, he pleads guilty to just such charges of illicit introduction of borrowed ideas at the end of almost every chapter of *Fragments*.

A second problematic passage our interpretation clarifies runs thus:

> If he could have lost the condition in such a way that it was not due to himself, then he would have possessed the condition only accidentally, which is a contradiction, since the condition for the truth is an essential condition. (PF, 15)

What is especially curious here is Climacus's suggestion that the truth is an essential condition, not an essential condition of some type of thing. Typically, properties can be both accidental and essential depending on the kind of thing of which it is a property. Thus, three-sidedness is an essential attribute of triangles but an accidental property of signs. But Climacus asserts that the truth is an essentially essential attribute: to have it is to have it essentially. And this makes perfect sense if "the truth" designates relation to self and to God. Since these sorts of relations are constitutive of the selves that have them, they couldn't possibly cease to stand in these relations and still exist.

The last sentence of the paragraph similarly represents an interpretive problem until it is viewed in light of the view of the self we have sketched above. The sentence runs:

> The untruth, then, is not merely outside the truth but is polemical against the truth, which is expressed by saying that he himself has forfeited and is forfeiting the condition. (PF, 15)

How is it that a self can continue forfeiting that which it has for-feited? This apparent paradox makes sense when we recall that untruth is not the simple absence of truth. Rather, untruth is a dis-tortion in the self's relation to itself and to God. Since the self is the ongoing event of relation to itself and to God, this distortion is itself ongoing. Untruth is not a passively suffered legacy of some past mistake, it is a present and active misrelating of the self to itself and to the power that created it.

Our apparent paradox of self-identity was insoluble so long as we thought of truth as an ordinary property that one gains and loses. But once we think of the matter in terms of Kierkegaard's relational metaphysics, as soon as we think of truth and untruth as modalities of an unbreakable relation of the self and God, we find that what appeared incomprehensible was actually an admir-ably concise if cryptic encapsulation of Kierkegaard's understand-ing of the human condition.

In resolving this apparent difficulty, we have accomplished three things: (1) we have rendered more intelligible a crucial para-graph in Climacus's "deduction," showing it to assume a theory of the self shared by a number of pseudonyms and Kierkegaard him-self, (2) we have shown that this Kierkegaardian theory of the self suggests an approach to the issue of personal identity that is radi-cally distinct from of those most frequently proposed in Anglo-American discussions of that issue, and (3) we have illustrated that the principle of hermeneutic charity, the assumption that Kierke-gaard and his pseudonyms express coherent ideas even when they seem to be stating bald paradoxes, is far more heuristically pro-ductive than its alternative.

6

Forstand *in the Swenson-Lowrie Correspondence and in the "Metaphysical Caprice"*

Andrew J. Burgess

Good translations are like window glass: look into them and only the meaning of the original text shines through. The translator's labor is transparent. When the manuscript is delivered to the publisher the reasons for interpretive decisions are omitted, except perhaps, in problematic cases, as translator's footnotes.

The case of the translation of *Forstand* in the third chapter of *Philosophical Fragments* is an exception to the usual rule. From 1933 to 1939 the two main translators of Kierkegaard into English, David Swenson of the University of Minnesota and Walter Lowrie of Princeton University, set out to coordinate their translation principles and terminology. During a period of seven years the two men wrote more than a hundred letters, many of them several pages long and all of them written with the kind of care one expects from a public scholarly exchange. As Howard Hong once remarked, with a correspondence like this underway it is a wonder the two ever had time to translate!

On most points Swenson and Lowrie reached agreement, but regarding the Danish term *Forstand* they could not. Swenson argued for translating the word as "reason," Lowrie as "understanding." At issue was a question at the heart of *Fragments*. Is the paradox of the incarnation beyond the limits of the *Forstand*? Yes, said Swenson; that is what *Fragments* is all about. No, said Lowrie, for in that case Christian faith would be nonsensical, like a belief in square circles.

Fortunately in this instance the reasoning behind the translation was preserved. After Swenson translated *Fragments* he also published his side of the argument from his letters with Lowrie, and although Lowrie did not publish his letters others such as Howard Hong have taken up the discussion. The Hong *Fragments* translation sides with Lowrie in translating *Forstand* as "understanding" rather than "reason," mainly because of Swenson's apparent later change of view on the issue (JP, 3:906-907nn.). The new translation is thus a suitable occasion for taking up the question again and, by asking about the remaining issues of the controversy, to contribute to an ongoing discussion of the book, particularly the key third chapter, the "Metaphysical Caprice."

Understanding and Reason

The real issue between Swenson and Lowrie never was just the translation of a word, on which both were prepared to compromise, but the question of how to present the book's attack on intellectualism without using terminology that would lead the English reader to think it irrationalist. The challenge they faced was one that translators and interpreters of *Fragments* have struggled with ever since.

The distinction between understanding and reason has a complex history. Reason is autonomous, declared the Enlightenment, and the principles of reason are the final court of appeal. In the *Critique of Pure Reason* Kant develops this Enlightenment conviction with a distinction between two "faculties," understanding (*Verstand*) and reason (*Vernunft*). While the understanding is limited to employing concepts to constitute our experience, there is also a higher faculty, reason, that operates on concepts to organize them systematically. In the hands of the nineteenth-century Idealist philosophers, the faculty of reason assumes an ever more glorious role. With Hegel, for example, understanding and reason are stages in the development of mind. The understanding is the stage that regards opposites as mutually exclusive, whereas the reason is the more advanced stage that rises to the identity of opposites, where the law of contradiction no longer holds.[1]

The currents from Germany washed also upon the shores of mid-nineteenth-century Denmark. Through the 1833–1834 lectures of his teacher H. N. Clausen, Kierkegaard encountered Kant, but he seems to have been unimpressed by Clausen's presentation of Kant (JP, 2:1305 [1834]; cf. JP, 3:2713 [1839]). For Kierkegaard during this period, the Hegelianism of his tutor H. L. Martensen was a much more live option than Kant or Clausen. By 1837, indeed, Martensen was the talk of the theological students in Copenhagen with his proposal to "go beyond" Hegel. In place of the "autonomous" reason of Hegel, he argued for a "theonomous" reason that "mediates" the differences between Hegelian speculation and biblical revelation, so that each may serve as ground for the other.[2] Under the influence of Bishop J. P. Mynster, Martensen began in 1842 to mute his Hegelianism and to point out the advantages of the method of "mediation" for peaceful resolution of ecclesiastical disputes—a politic tack, surely, for someone who himself probably aspired to become bishop.[3] During this period Kierkegaard came to reject with increasing vehemence Martensen's deliberate blurring of the distinctions between reason (in Hegel's sense) and Christianity. As *Philosophical Fragments* put it in 1843, there can be no mediation between Socrates and Christ. Autonomy and theonomy are incompatible. Either/or!

The Swenson-Lowrie Correspondence

How could this strident cry by *Philosophical Fragments* be put into terms understandable in a new language? That was the challenge faced by Swenson and Lowrie in the early 1930s, as they proposed to translate the whole Kierkegaardian corpus.

---

[1]A brief account of the Kantian and Hegelian background of this distinction, and Kierkegaard's relation to it, is found in Robert Widenmann's "Kierkegaard's Terminology—and English," *Kierkegaardiana* 7 (1968): 118-24.

[2]Handwritten copy of Martensen's 1837 lectures on dogmatics, Det Kgl. Bibl., Add. 134; cited in J. H. Schjørring, "Martensen," *Kierkegaard's Teachers, Biblioteca Kierkegaardiana* (Copenhagen: C. A. Reitzels, 1982) 10:187.

[3]Schjørring, ibid., 194-95.

The question of the translation of the word *Forstand* entered the correspondence in the summer of 1935, as Swenson laid the groundwork for translating *Philosophical Fragments* and *Concluding Unscientific Postscript*.[4] Lowrie's reply on 7 September urges Swenson to reconsider the terminology for several reasons:

> If Kierkegaard had used Fornuft instead of Forstand, I might have felt compelled to translate the word by "reason," although I should have felt it a hard compulsion, seeing that for several generations past the best English writers have so carefully established and maintained (in opposition to the vulgar usage) a distinction between the reason and the understanding which relieves the believer in the paradox from the grim necessity of asserting that he believes contrary to Reason, and consistently opposes to faith, not the Reason (which in view of this distinction is conceived of as unimpeachable authority), but the Understanding.[5]

Forstand and *Fornuft* are the key terms here. *Forstand* is the Danish cognate of the German word *Verstand*, and *Fornuft* the cognate for the German word *Vernunft*. By distinguishing the two terms Lowrie believes he has protected the third chapter of *Fragments* from the charge of irrationality and, although the letter goes on to acknowledge that his proposed usage may have problems in some parts of the chapter (such as with regard to the question of "understanding the Paradox"), he continues to insist on the word "understanding" as the proper translation of *Forstand*.

The five points of Swenson's long reply on September 14 are well known to Kierkegaard scholars from their inclusion in his classic work *Something About Kierkegaard*.[6] The fourth point, which Swenson finds to be the most compelling reason to reject translating *Forstand* with "understanding," is precisely the argument Lowrie has put forward in its favor:

---

[4]This correspondence is kept both at the University of Minnesota Library and at the Princeton University Library, but the numbering of the letters differs. Permission for the use of this material has been given by the University of Minnesota Archives, used for this study, and by the literary executor of Walter Lowrie.

[5]Walter Lowrie, correspondence, Univ. of Minn. #33, Princeton #30.

[6]David Swenson, *Something about Kierkegaard* (Macon GA: Mercer University Press, 1983; ROSE ed. [with additions] of 1945 rev. and enlarged ed. from Augsburg Publishing House, Minneapolis) 218-22.

If I use the word *Understanding* in Chapter III, I am aware that I will evoke the suggestion that human nature contains a higher principle, the Reason, which does not need to be set aside, and for which the Absolute Paradox is not paradoxical. I am convinced that such a thought is flatly contradictory of the entire spirit, purpose, and letter of Kierkegaard's work. If there is such a principle in me, then there is no Absolute Paradox, then the Teacher is not God, then the entire virile Christian terminology of the new birth, of the believer being a new creature, etc., falls down like a house of cards, and becomes mere rhetorical exaggeration, an immature and irrelevant adornment of what is essentially the Socratic position.[7]

The two men are here in direct disagreement: Lowrie prefers the term "understanding," because that usage leaves room for someone to think that there is another higher principle, the reason; while Swenson insists on the term "reason," precisely in order to prevent anyone from thinking in this way.

In support of his view Swenson questions whether *Fragments* allows for any distinction between reason and understanding, and he concludes by elaborating the concept of *Forstand* in response to the objections raised. The supposed distinction between reason and understanding is not supported by the text, he says. The Kantian distinction between reason and understanding is irrelevant here, the Hegelian distinction is explicitly repudiated by Kierkegaard, "the Scandinavian languages, like the English, do not in daily use make any distinction in principle between *Fornuft* and *Forstand*," and the common verbal distinction in English between what is privately understandable and what is universally rational does not apply to what Kierkegaard calls the "Absolute Paradox."[8] However one translates *Forstand*, whether as "reason" or "understanding," the term "does not stand for an abstract human faculty, like the function of thinking in categories (Kant), or the power of general ideas (the soul, in Plato), and so forth."[9] Swenson thus feels he is in agreement with the main body of English usage when he says that the word "stands for the essential and reflective common

---

[7]Ibid., 219-20.
[8]Ibid., 218-19.
[9]Ibid., 220.

sense of mankind, in which each individual participates, though of course, with respect to his actual as opposed to his ideally potential grasp, at any one time, only imperfectly."[10]

Lowrie replies to Swenson in a letter on September 22:

> You give so many reasons for preferring "reason" that I despair of persuading you against it. But though the reasons you advance are all of them good reasons, they do not avail to persuade me to change my purpose to use "understanding." For my heart has reasons that reason knows not of. To state my case very briefly: "to believe against *reason*," is popularly understood to include the agility the White Queen boasted of, "to be able to believe fifty impossible things in a minute," or, as S.K. frequently puts it, "to make two and two make five." That is what he *doesn't* mean by the Paradox.[11]

Lowrie's point is apt: a translator who made *Fragments* advocate logical contradictions would betray the book's intent. "The danger of misinterpretation seems to me to lie on that side. Whichever word we use, the danger of reducing everything to the Socratic is sufficiently guarded against by the vigor of S.K.'s expressions."[12]

Later Lowrie brings forward another argument, in a letter dated September 30: "If, as you are inclined to think, the Scandinavia [sic] languages make no distinction between Fornuft and Forstand, why is it that S.K. does not use these words interchangeably, but (in the contexts we are interested in) uses exclusively Forstand?"[13] There must, Lowrie believes, be some kind of distinction between reason and understanding implicit in Kierkegaard's usage here, or *Fragments* would not be so careful to use one word and not the other.

On October 3 Swenson replies to both of these questions. With regard to the question about contradiction, he agrees with Lowrie that there can be no contradiction or opposition between revelation and mathematical or logical truth. What *Fragments* describes as *For-*

---

[10]Ibid.

[11]Walter Lowrie, Swenson-Lowrie correspondence, Univ. of Minn. #38, Princeton #35.

[12]Ibid.

[13]Walter Lowrie, Swenson-Lowrie correspondence, Univ. of Minn. #45, Princeton #41.

stand is not this abstract capability but "man's concrete and rationalized consciousness of himself, of God, and of his own relationship to God."[14] Swenson and Lowrie here share common ground. Both of them know Kierkegaard, and in particular the classic passages of *Concluding Unscientific Postscript*, too well to think that he would advocate any kind of irrationalism.

To the other question, about the linguistic distinction between the terms *Forstand* and *Fornuft* in *Fragments*, Swenson answers simply that "I am not quite willing to say that there is no difference in meaning in Danish between *Forstand* and *Fornuft*, but merely that I know of none that is consistently and clearly a matter of accepted usage."[15] He says nothing, however, in reply to Lowrie's specific question about why, if the terms are equivalent, Kierkegaard so consistently uses only the one word *Forstand*.

Although this Swenson letter concludes the main interchange with Lowrie in the correspondence, Swenson as the translator of *Fragments* still retains the last word, and the next year, after fulfilling his word and translating *Forstand* in that book with the term "reason," he appends a note:

> The thoughtful reader will already have noted that "Reason," as used in this chapter and throughout, is not to be taken in any abstract-intellectual sense, but quite concretely, as the reflectively organized common sense of mankind, including as its essential core a sense of life's values. Over against the "Paradox" it is therefore the self-assurance and self-assertiveness of man's nature in its totality. To identify it with any abstract intellectual function, like the function of scientific cognition, or of general ideas, or of the a priori, or of self-consistency in thinking, etc., is wholly to misunderstand the exposition of the *Fragments*.[16]

With this analysis Swenson rejects specifically the Kantian distinction between reason and understanding, and he insists that his translation of the term *Forstand* should not be understood to imply

---

[14]Swenson, *Something about Kierkegaard*, 223. The original of this letter has been lost.

[15]Ibid., 222.

[16]Swenson, notes in Johannes Climacus [S. Kierkegaard], *Philosophical Fragments or a Fragment of Philosophy*, trans. with intro. and notes by David F. Swenson (Princeton: Princeton University Press, 1936) 99-100 =note to p. 39.

any distinction between those two faculties. This note was re-printed in the second edition of this translation and again in the notes for Kierkegaard's papers (JP, 3:907nn.).

In many ways the most remarkable thing about the correspon-dence is the good spirit and openness with which it was con-ducted. In the following years, the positions of each of the two shifted partly, and each seems to have given up a point. Lowrie remarks, in his foreword to Swenson's translation of *Concluding Unscientific Postscript*, that in the five-sixths of the manuscript that Swenson completed he was careful to use Swenson's terminology in preference to his own.[17] In fact, as Howard Hong notes, in the Swenson-Lowrie translation *Forstand* is commonly translated as "understanding"; very infrequently (such as on page 189) it is translated as "reason," and a few other times as "mind" or "wits" or "common sense" (JP, 3:906nn.). Lowrie concludes, therefore, that Swenson had had a change of mind on the topic, which he would have made clear if he had lived to write the preface to his trans-lation of *Postscript*.[18]

Recent commentators on *Fragments* are divided concerning the translation of the term *Forstand*, while standing with Swenson on the main interpretive issue. Writing before the Hong translation, Harry Nielsen follows Swenson's term "Reason" and also adopts Swenson's understanding of the term, as quoted by Niels Thul-strup in his 1962 commentary.[19] Robert Roberts, by contrast, adopts the term "understanding" used in the new Hong translation. In his analysis of this concept, however, he repeatedly interprets it through Swenson's expression "Common Sense," especially in the argument of the "Metaphysical Caprice."[20] C. Stephen Evans, in turn, translates *Forstand* interchangeably as "understanding" or

[17]Lowrie, editor's preface to *Kierkegaard's Concluding Unscientific Postscript*, trans. David Swenson, completed after his death by Walter Lowrie (Princeton: Princeton University Press, 1941) ix.

[18]Ibid., x.

[19]Niels Thulstrup, "Commentary" to *Philosophical Fragments or A Fragment of Philosophy by Johannes Climacus* (Princeton: Princeton University Press, 1962) 222-23; H. A. Nielsen, *Where the Passion Is: A Reading of Kierkegaard's Philosophical Fragments* (Tallahassee: University Presses of Florida, 1983) 54-55.

[20]Robert C. Roberts, *Faith, Reason, and History: Rethinking Kierkegaard's Philosophical Fragments* (Macon GA: Mercer University Press, 1986) chap. 3.

"reason," in order to signify his agreement with Swenson's interpretation of the concept.[21]

Like Swenson, Lowrie also abandons a point, and his move has been followed by later writers. Without giving up the concerns that led him to translate *Forstand* as "understanding," and retaining the reason/understanding distinction, he nonetheless accepts Swenson's analysis of the term *Forstand* as "the reflectively organized common sense of mankind," and this phrase has become the classic description of Kierkegaard's use of the concept.

Despite the way in which the Swenson and Lowrie positions move toward each other, they never completely converge. Part of their divergence may be due to deepseated differences in Kierkegaardian interpretation, while part may occur simply because they did not have sufficient time to agree before Swenson died. The next section discusses one of the differences in order in order to try to bring the two translators even closer together.

The Negative Case: The Absence of the Term Fornuft *and the Reason/Understanding Distinction*

One resolvable question that remains from the Swenson-Lowrie correspondence concerns the issue Lowrie raises near the end: if, as Swenson maintains, *Fragments* does not distinguish between the terms *Forstand* and *Fornuft*, why is it that the book, at least in the parts they are considering, uses only *Forstand* and not *Fornuft*? To this question Swenson provides no direct answer.

On one point Lowrie's position is well supported by the text, when he suggests that the book uses exclusively the term *Forstand* and not *Fornuft* in the passages he and Swenson are considering. The term *Fornuft* does not occur in the book at all.

In fact, the book is more painstaking in its use of that term *Forstand* than either Lowrie or Swenson seem to have noticed. The most common way the word *Forstand* is used in the book and in Kierkegaard's writings as a whole is as part of the expression "in the sense that" (*i Forstanden at*), or in related expressions, such as "in the . . . sense" (*i . . . Forstanden*). Because Kierkegaard is careful

---

[21]C. Stephen Evans, *Passionate Reason: Making Sense of Kierkegaard's* Philosophical Fragments (Bloomington: Indiana University Press, 1992) 188n.7.

to distinguish linguistic differences, this expression is common throughout his writings, and for much of *Fragments* he uses it in this way. When the book begins to approach the third chapter, the "Caprice," however, the use of the expressions "*i Forstanden at*" and "*i . . . Forstanden*" diminishes and then ceases until this section is past, when it increases again. Plainly Kierkegaard wants the reader to pay close attention to the concept of *Forstand*, and he is concerned that the other more common expression may get in the way. It is as if a writer in English were focusing on the concept of "sense," and therefore avoided the expression "in the sense that" in those sections of the essay where the reader might confuse the two.

On the key issue between Lowrie and Swenson, however, the data does not favor Lowrie's case. Lowrie argues that since *Fragments* is careful to use only the term *Forstand* it is evidently not using *Forstand* and *Fornuft* synonymously, and must therefore be making a distinction between the two terms, evidently along traditional lines. But a study of Kierkegaard's use of these terms, not just in *Fragments* but throughout his writings, shows a result unremarked upon by both Lowrie and Swenson. Far from the term *Fornuft* being a technical expression used by Kierkegaard to make a distinction with *Forstand*, as Lowrie thought, Kierkegaard does not even use the term in print regularly as part of his own working vocabulary during the period *Fragments* was written. Although Kierkegaard refers to the distinction and thus is aware of that to which Lowrie appeals, he clearly avoids making the distinction himself, evidently because he is using the term *Forstand* in ways that do not fit in with the philosophical tradition of his day.

The evidence for this result is easy to assemble. Fortunately the list of citations for the Danish term *Fornuft* in Kierkegaard's published writings is not very long, and many of them are clustered in the same passages. Checking this list shows that in most cases the word *Fornuft* is quoted or otherwise borrowed from other authors or from general contexts that are not distinctively his own. *The Concept of Irony*, for example, cites the word from Schlegel (CI, 292), *Concept of Anxiety* (CA, 142) puts the word in with a group of other words evidently from Hegel or his school, and *Postscript* builds on ideas from Plutarch (CUP, 1:161-62) and from an old Latin description of logic (CUP, 1:377; cf. CUP, 2:256n, n. 627). The reference in *Stages on Life's Way* (SLW, 480n) may derive from Börne; in any case the word is not being used in a technical sense.[22] Some references to the concept are even kept in the original language in quotations from a famous author. The term occurs in German (*Vernunft*) and French (*Raison*). On the title page of *Either/Or I* he translates the word from English as part of two lines in a poem by Edward Young, and he mentions this quotation again in a newspaper article about *Either/Or* in 1843.[23] Not all the references are from well-known sources, however. In his ironic 1834 defense of women's abilities he alludes to the French Revolution's cult of reason (*Fornuften*); in this festival the goddess of reason was represented by a prostitute (EPW, 4; cf. EPW, 229n.8, and JP, 4:4080). In another passage (CUP, 1:518n) the word *Fornuft* is in the bombastic refrain of a poem on a gravestone "Take comfort, reason, he lives!" which is signed "Hilarius, Executioner."

The passages in which *Fornuft* is Kierkegaard's own technical term occur long after *Fragments*, during the period of 1848–1850. *Works of Love* (1848) includes a passage (WL, 192) that speaks four times of the dangers of human reason (*Fornuft*). Another case is *Practice in Christianity* (1850), in which a passage closely parallel in sense to *Fragments*'s "Caprice" chapter uses *Fornuft* instead of *Forstand* five times (PC, 26). These are puzzling passages. Initially Hong translated the term *Fornuft* in *Works of Love* with "understanding" (see WL, 369 and 366, nn. 121 and 85). More recently, however, Hong has reversed that decision and said the term "should be translated 'reason'" (JP, 3:907n). Hong may well be right when he notes that each of the passages in *Works of Love* and *Practice in Christianity* "has Hegel in mind" (JP, 3:905n). Yet this can hardly be the reason Kierkegaard uses the term *Fornuft* in 1848 and 1850 but not earlier, since the anti-Hegelian bent is at least equally true of *Fragments*, which uses the term *Forstand*.

The easiest way to interpret the passages in *Works of Love* and *Practice in Christianity* is to suppose that Kierkegaard by 1848, but not earlier, was prepared on occasion to use *Fornuft* and *Forstand*

---

[22]In his translation, Walter Lowrie renders the term *Fornuft* here as "logic" (*Stages on Life's Way* [Princeton: Princeton University Press, 1940] 433n.).

[23]"Taksigelse til Hr. Professor Heiberg," *Fædrelandet*, #1168 (5 March 1843) in Søren Kierkegaard, *Samlede Værker* (Copenhagen: Gyldendal, 1962) 18:23.

synonymously. In fact, in one passage from this period, from *Three Discourses at the Communion on Fridays* (1849), the two terms are in apposition with each other (CD, 375). By this point in time Kierkegaard may have felt that the danger of a reader imagining there might be a "higher understanding" (that is, a *Fornuft*), for which the paradox of the incarnation was not offensive, had been sufficiently guarded against by the earlier works. Moreover, the use of the two terms *Fornuft* and *Forstand* interchangeably should by itself help prevent anyone from supposing that there is a distinction between them.[24]

The result of this survey of Kierkegaard's books is to show that the term *Fornuft* is simply not part of the working technical vocabulary of his published work during the early period when *Fragments* was written. Moreover, when he does begin to use it—late, in religious works, and rarely—it appears to be synonymous with *Forstand*.

The lack of the term *Fornuft* within Kierkegaard's main technical vocabulary, except sometimes as synonymous with *Forstand*, casts into question the supposed distinction between the *Fornuft* and the *Forstand* in his writings. Kierkegaard is perfectly aware that philosophers have used the distinction. Hong points out that he could have learned the Kantian version from lectures by Martensen in 1837–1838 (JP, 3:904n). Yet although Kierkegaard knows about the distinction he avoids using it in print. Nor does it seem likely that Kierkegaard fails to make use of this pair of terms merely because he lacks the occasion. The topics dealt with in several of his books, including *Fragments*, would have provided Kant or Hegel and some other thinkers of the time plenty of contexts for using the terms. The absence of the distinction throughout Kierkegaard's writings thus strongly suggests that he is aware of some major differences between his views and those of other thinkers and that he avoids using this paired set of terms to prevent anyone from confusing his position with one of theirs.

---

[24]Usage of the two terms synonymously can also be found in a note in Kierkegaard's unpublished papers from 1848, which says that one of the criteria for faith is that it "completely cuts across the grain of our reason and understanding" (JP, 2:1125).

This same reticence toward using the distinction is shown by Johannes Climacus, the pseudonymous author in whose name Kierkegaard writes *Fragments* and its *Postscript*. Intellectually Climacus is a different sort of person from the author who invented him, and Kierkegaard even sketches out a Climacus "biography" in 1842–1843 and occasionally puts Climacus's name on some unpublished papers, thereby giving him a life of his own;[25] but on the question of *Forstand* the two are of one mind. As with Kierkegaard, explicit reference to the Hegelian distinction between the *Forstand* and the *Fornuft* occurs only in unpublished papers (JC, 169n). In Climacus's published writings, *Fragments* and *Postscript*, the distinction is lacking.

That there is no *Forstand/Fornuft* distinction in the "Caprice" chapter of *Fragments* is not accidental. The text uses another vocabulary from Kant or Hegel and others because it differs from them fundamentally. The chapter is full of twists and turns and is often hard to follow, but on this point it is definite. As Swenson says in the correspondence with Lowrie, the Kantian distinction between reason and understanding is irrelevant, and the Hegelian distinction is formally repudiated.[26]

The survey of how the terms *Fornuft* and *Forstand* function in Kierkegaard's overall authorship confirms the situation in the *Fragment*'s "Caprice" chapter itself. Instead of making a distinction between the two terms, Kierkegaard typically uses in his works only *Forstand*, and in a distinctive way; while the "Caprice" chapter of *Fragments* flatly rejects one of the traditional understandings of the term. Moreover, this is the chapter in which, if anywhere, one would expect some form of the distinction to be drawn.

If someone were to insist on finding a parallel in Kant or Hegel for the "Caprice," the best place to begin might be, not in Hegel's *Phenomenology* or Kant's *Critique of Pure Reason*, but in Kant's *Critique of Practical Reason* and in his late ethical writings. Like Kierkegaard, Kant in these writings grounds the religious in the ethical life; and, somewhat like Climacus's *Forstand*, Kant's

---

[25]Andrew J. Burgess, "Kierkegaard's Climacus as Author," *Journal of Religious Studies* 7 (Fall 1979): 1-14.

[26]Swenson, *Something about Kierkegaard*, 218.

"practical reason" moves beyond limits and postulates the existence of God. Recently Ronald Green has identified several striking similarities between Kant and Kierkegaard, largely in the area of ethics and religion. In the end, however, Green acknowledges that, despite a partially similar starting point, Kant and Kierkegaard disagree on the nature of the ethical and the religious. Even when Kant in *Religion within the Limits of Reason Alone* concludes that there is a "radical evil" bringing infinite guilt to every human being, Kant still insists that human beings can somehow help to overcome their own infinite guilt. Kierkegaard, on the other hand, is more consistent, Green thinks. If human capacities have been corrupted by infinite guilt, there is no hope except from outside.[27]

On the basis of this premise the "Caprice" chapter has no need for a distinction, even on a moral or religious basis, between different kinds of intellectual capacities. All aspects of life are equally corruptible, including the intellectual aspects. *Fragments* thereby parts company with the Enlightenment confidence in unaided human intellectual powers that Kant still partly shares. The differences between Kant and Kierkegaard on this key point indicates that some apparent similarities of terminology and structure overlay deep disagreements. The similarities between the two thinkers merely highlight their basic divergence. Their disagreement is at bottom a religious one, between two competing "hypotheses," as *Fragments* calls them, and *Fragments* assumes that it cannot be resolved through philosophical analysis alone.

For the "Metaphysical Caprice" chapter in particular, general epistemological considerations are only ancillary to the main religious argument. Climacus's "hypothesis B" (Christianity) holds to the premise that human intellectual capacities, including the Kantian "faculties," are undermined by sin. Although Climacus recognizes that there are differences among these capacities, he has no immediate need to distinguish them in the "Caprice." For his purpose one term can identify them all: *Forstand*.

---

[27]Ronald M. Green, *Kierkegaard and Kant: The Hidden Debt* (Albany: State University of New York, 1992) 156-78.

The Positive Case: Forstand *as a Religious Category*

What is missing from the discussion between Swenson and Lowrie here is a substantial account of the rich religious background of the concept of *Forstand* found in *Fragments*. Once the reader has been freed from the task of finding a primarily philosophical source for the use of the term *Forstand*, the way is open to search in the obvious alternative area, within the religious tradition.

The best place to look for this tradition is in Kierkegaard's own religious writings. In the works he called the "upbuilding discourses," and in his other ethical and religious writings, Kierkegaard fashioned a subtly articulated technical vocabulary, whose precision may be overlooked because the works are sermonic. Among these terms is the word *Forstand*. The parallels in the ways the term is used in *Fragments*'s "Caprice" chapter and in the upbuilding discourses are often surprisingly close. The difference is that whereas the meaning of the term *Forstand* in *Fragments* is sometimes hard to pin down, because of the irony and indirection of that book, its sense in the upbuilding discourses may be as direct as a slap in the face.

A striking feature both in Kierkegaard's religious writings and also in *Fragments*'s "Caprice" chapter is the personification of the *Forstand*. In *Fragments*'s "Caprice" chapter the *Forstand* is treated as if it were a person: it tries to go beyond itself, it wills its own downfall (PF, 37), it collides with the unknown (PF, 39), and it surrenders itself to the paradox (PF, 54). The same literary device comes up in the religious writing, where the *Forstand* does things only a person can do.

The use of personification with the *Forstand* goes back to the early upbuilding discourses. In the first discourse on the text "Love Will Hide a Multitude of Sins" (1843), for example, shrewd, self-seeking *Forstand* is contrasted with love, which has its own way of knowing (EUD, 62). Or perhaps, he says, it is not a matter of intellect at all, but that the understanding simply lacks the courage to believe what love is bold to assert; "the understanding, after all, always makes a person only despondent and fainthearted, but love gives unbounded courage" (EUD, 65).

The same pattern for describing the *Forstand* carries through one religious writing after another. *Practice in Christianity* (1850) continues the theme:

> If I am to submit to a suffering, says the understanding [*Forstanden*], if I am to sacrifice something or in any way sacrifice myself, then I also want to be able to know what profit and advantage I can have from it—otherwise I would be lunatic to do it. (PC, 116)

Or *For Self-Examination* (1851): "The understanding [*Forstanden*] says, 'No, there is no hope'; you are, however, dead to your understanding and in that case it probably is silent" (FSE, 82). Or again, in *Judge for Yourself!* (published posthumously in 1856):

> The understanding [*Forstanden*] says: Too little and too much spoil everything; moderation, the middle way, and medium size, this is the truth. Therefore the understanding would certainly recommend dispensing with the star at the birth—that is too much, or so much is not required—but then it would also recommend being born in lawful wedlock and at least in a good, proper, well-to-do, middle-class family. (FSE, 161-62)

In all of these passages the *Forstand* acts like a person: it speaks, it is silent, it knows, it recommends prudence, it lacks courage.

What the passages have in common is more than the literary device of personification. As one passage succeeds another, the reader gradually gains an image of what this "person" *Forstand* is like: shrewd, self-important, cowardly, looking out only for itself. The *Forstand* is no mere philosophical abstraction here, nor a faculty in eighteenth-century psychology, but a possible total orientation of a human life.

The use of the concept *Forstand* in Kierkegaard's religious writings is not rooted in some modern philosophical theory but grows instead out of a much older and more varied tradition, best represented in sermons, plays, and other literature. The *Forstand* in Kierkegaard's religious writings reminds a person of nothing so much as a character in a medieval morality play—Worldly Wisdom, perhaps, or Intellectual Pride—that beckons Everyman to turn away from the path to the Celestial City.

This religious concept of *Forstand*, and not any Kantian or Hegelian version, is the main sense found in *Fragments*. The *Forstand* in the "Caprice," which arrogantly wills to go beyond its limits and thereby meets its downfall, only to surrender itself to the god which bestows itself, is the same *Forstand* that in the religious discourses dithers over calculations of self-interest until its self-important bubble is pricked. Only the abstractness of the context in *Fragments* masks the plain fit. As was the case with the shoe in the Cinderella story, the shape of the argument in the "Caprice" invites the reader first to try on the concept of *Forstand* with its obvious cognates in the imposing German philosophies of Kant and Hegel; but when the feet of these ugly older sisters fail, even when cut out of shape, why should one not try the shoe on the feet of the pious, stay-at-home youngest sister?

The reason for this parallel between *Fragments* and the religious writings is that according to *Fragments* itself the failure of the *Forstand* to grasp the Paradox (the incarnation) is brought about by a religious failure. It is not merely a mental lapse that may be remedied by more study. The failure is not caused by conceptual confusion, at least not alone, but by a twisted orientation in one's whole life, by sin. For this reason the *Forstand* is a religious concept, part of the network of more familiar religious concepts—rebirth, repentance, fullness of time, and the rest—the book *Fragments* begins to deduce, tongue-in-cheek, in the first chapter. Chapters 2 and 3 merely explore the implications of chapter 1's hypothesis B, the hypothesis of the divine teacher. That a religious concept in the third chapter of *Fragments* should fit in with the conceptual scheme of the upbuilding discourses is thus only to be expected.

According to *Fragments* the basic problem with the main current of Idealistic philosophy is a religious one. The drive to attain a purely autonomous reason, unlimited and self-certifying, has repeatedly generated conceptual tangles, but unsnarling these tangles is not enough. An endless philosophical "therapy" is called for as well. As in the late writings of Ludwig Wittgenstein, *Fragments* pushes the philosopher to check what it is that keeps generating the tangles in the first place. The book's diagnosis is that the cause is a kind of intellectual arrogance, that is to say, an extreme form of the *Forstand*.[28]

---

[28]Evans's characteristic expression "imperialistic reason" captures this aspect of *Forstand*. Evans interprets Climacus as a "sociologist of knowledge" who

This is why Kierkegaard can occasionally in his late religious writings use *Fornuft* interchangeably with *Forstand*. Some of the grandiose claims made for *Fornuft* by Idealistic philosophy are nothing but particularly outrageous variations of the *Forstand*.

At the same time as Climacus in *Fragments* is sounding the alarm against the extravagant claims the Enlightenment had made for autonomous Reason, he is also implicitly defining a modest but positive role for the *Forstand* within the religious life. The *Forstand* has a passion for a paradox, he says (PF, 37), and this passion can even point obscurely toward the supreme paradox of the incarnation. Within its limits the *Forstand* performs essential tasks; for example, according to *Postscript*, in identifying self-contradictory nonsense and preventing people from believing it (CUP, 1:568). The abuses that can arise from an unbridled exercise of *Forstand* should not blind anyone to the glory of its proper role.

But the primary function of *Fragments* is negative, probing for weak spots wherever they are. The thought project of *Fragments*, "to go beyond Socrates," is targeted at Martensen, the philosopher-theologian who promised to go beyond Hegel. *Fragments* exposes how self-defeating is Martensen's project to out-Hegel Hegel, not by mounting a counter case, but by carrying Martensen's own project out to the very end.

Nor is Martensen the book's only target. To the extent that *Forstand* means worldly prudence, self-seeking complacency, or academic pretentiousness, it also describes the intellectual life of much of the established church. In this sense the "Caprice" is not just going beyond Martensen, but also beyond Mynster, head of the state church of Denmark.

The Irony of Philosophical Fragments

Still, something is missing in the rather Swensonian tenor of the discussion thus far. Surely it is too simple merely to substitute the sense of *Forstand* from the religious writings into the philosophical context of the "Caprice." Why, if that is all there is at

---

exposes how the term "reason" often functions as an "instrument of control," through which those in power try to legitimate their ways of seeing and acting. See especially Evans, *Passionate Reason*, 118.

stake, does *Fragments* not just explicitly define the term *Forstand* as a religious concept rather than letting it be so easily misunderstood? The answer must lie in the ironical thrust of *Fragments*. Although the book presents itself as speculative philosophy, there are plenty of warnings against taking the argument at face value. The use of the pseudonym "Johannes Climacus" in both *Fragments* and *Postscript* should itself alert the reader that something strange is afoot.

In the massive *Concluding Unscientific Postscript* to the *Fragments* Climacus comments on the *Fragments*'s sole review, which sees it as a piece of doctrinizing. Exasperated, Climacus calls this "the most distorted impression of the book it is possible to have" (CUP, 1:275n). The whole book, he says, is a sustained parody, with the form of an exercise in speculative philosophy but the content of "old-fashioned orthodoxy." How could the reviewer miss the satire, which even "invents" Christianity, as if it were an extraordinary new version of speculative philosophy? The book is written for those who know too much and think they have "understood" Christianity as something easy. The irony is that they have not really understood it at all.

In a sense Lowrie and Swenson merely present two different aspects of the term *Forstand* in *Fragments*, each of which helps to make the "Caprice" a parody of speculative thought. Lowrie makes his case by drawing on the Kantian and Hegelian affinities of the term that get the speculative project going. Swenson brings out the distinctive sense the term has in other Kierkegaardian writings. Lowrie stresses the speculative form of the argument, Swenson its distinctive theological content. Both the form and the content have to be present for the parody to work. Only a person tempted to think as Lowrie does is enough of a speculative thinker to need the "Caprice."

Everything depends on reading *Fragments* from start to finish as a work of irony. That is why the pseudonymous author of the work must be "Johannes Climacus," the speculative thinker who sets out to storm heaven with his syllogisms. And that is why the translator dare not make things too easy for the reader. The reader who knows too much, as *Postscript* says, will not be helped by being given more knowledge. To feel the argument's ironical power the reader must first identify with Climacus's speculative enthusiasm and then learn from experience that the project will fail.

Yet the irony pervading *Fragments* is often elusive, and it is easy to lose one's way. For this reason readers can be grateful that the great translators of Kierkegaard into English—Swenson, Lowrie, and now the Hongs—not only grappled so hard with the twists and turns of the Danish but also took the trouble to share their deliberations with each other and, in some cases, with the scholarly world. Through this extra effort the translations gain an added dimension, and those who follow are in a position to use the disagreements for their own thinking and to look at the translations in a critical way.

7

The Lesson of Eternity:
Christ as Teacher in Kierkegaard and Hegel

Hugh S. Pyper

Imagine, if you will, a situation where a school board has decided that the children under their care are in need of special instruction. Naturally, they will consider carefully just what they want the children to learn before they begin to advertise for a teacher. They will want someone who can communicate to the children what they need to know, someone who can explain in language the children will understand the workings of a steam engine or the evolution of the pentadactyl limb. Not only that, however, the teacher will have to be able to show the children that they need to learn the subject in the first place. They will need to be persuaded that the knowledge is either useful or enjoyable, or at least that the consequences of not learning it will be rather uncomfortable.

It stands to reason, then, that the teacher must communicate with the children in their own language. Or does it? Take, for instance, the problem of learning a foreign language, say, French. The school might imaginatively decide that they will employ a teacher who speaks only French in the classroom. The children may never have met anyone who did not speak their native language before. At first, they will be baffled, but they will quickly learn that if they want to communicate with the teacher, they are going to have to adopt a whole new means of communication. Not only that, they will realize that what they had never questioned as a universal medium of communication, their own language, is in fact *a* language, one among many.

Of course, the success of the experiment depends entirely on the children's desire to communicate, on their decision to break out of the constraints of the language which, until then, they have seen as entirely sufficient. It may be very hard for the teacher, too, especially if she is bilingual and has to suffer the twin frustration of being unable to use the common language she shares with the children to express herself and of finding her beloved second language mangled and abused. She will also need to be willing to run the risk that she and her language may be rejected.

If the board decides to opt for this style of teaching despite these possibilities, then they may choose a candidate who paradoxically seems not to fulfil the fundamental condition of communicating with her pupils. Yet this is precisely because the children are being provoked to question the process of communication itself so as to expand their understanding.

Imagine, then, that instead of being exposed to merely another language the children are being asked to learn to exist. This seems an absurd proposition. Children who do exist can be enough of a handful to teach, and no doubt many a weary teacher has devoutly wished at times that her beloved pupils would cease to exist. These problems are insignificant, however, beside the practical problems of teaching a nonexistent class.

Yet this is the task which the pseudonym Johannes Climacus identifies for the Teacher in *Philosophical Fragments.* The whole book can be seen as an extended discussion paper of the qualifications required for a teacher of existence. The recommendation which is put forward has analogies to that of the language teacher who uses the language she is trying to teach as the medium of instruction. In order to teach people to exist, you have first to make them realize that they do not exist, and then hold out before them the actuality of existence in such a way that they grasp it as a realizable possibility for themselves.

Whatever the merits of this proposal, it still seems absurdly paradoxical to expect the teacher to address a nonexistent being (which can only even be spoken about in an oxymoron). The only entity that might persuade someone who thinks he exists that in fact he does not would be an entity that could not exist and yet does. This calls into question the whole understanding of what it might be to exist. Persuaded of this, the hearer might be brought to such a revolution of understanding that he or she comes to see that he or she *had not* existed, as *ex hypothese* nonexistent beings can no more comprehend their nonexistence than they can anything else. The category of nonexistence can only be dealt with in retrospect, yet it is one all of us do retrospectively come to grips with in the attempt to contemplate the world before our own birth.[1]

We should recall that, despite the seeming impossibility of this position, Kierkegaard had made considerable study in his youth of the writings of a man who was happy to declare that he had once been dead: the man who wrote "I was once alive apart from the law, but when the commandment came, sin revived and I died; the very commandment which promised life proved to be death to me. For sin, finding opportunity in the commandment, deceived me and by it killed me" (Rom. 7:9-11). In the letter to the Romans, Paul recalls to his readers the fact that they were all buried with Christ in their baptism, that they have all died to sin (Rom. 6:1-11), and by that same token that they have been given life in Christ. Again, in his letter to the Galatians, he writes: "For through the law I died to the law, that I might live to God. I have been crucified with Christ; it is no longer I who live, but Christ who lives in me" (Gal. 2:19-20).[2]

Paul writes out of an experience of a new birth, and part of the problem examined in *Philosophical Fragments* is the philosophical consequences of such a claim. What kind of understanding of the nature of human being does it imply? More particularly, the one capable of inducing such a change in the human subject has to accomplish an extraordinary act of communication. Paul offers a picture of Christ as the teacher who is a "stumbling block to the Jews and folly to the Gentiles" (1 Cor. 1:23). The gospels represent him as the teacher who tells parables in order that the people

---

[1]"In *the moment*, a person becomes aware that he was born, for his previous state, to which he is not to appeal, was indeed one of 'not to be' [*sic*]. In *the moment*, he becomes aware of the rebirth, for his previous state was indeed one of 'not to be.' If his previous state had been one of 'to be,' then under no circumstances would the moment have acquired distinctive significance for him, as explained above." (PF, 21)

[2]See also Col. 2:11-14; 3:3-4; and Eph. 2:1-7, though authorship is disputed.

should not understand.[3] Throughout the New Testament, then, Jesus is presented as a figure who prompts deep questions about the nature of communication.

The form of Climacus's argument, however, rather calls to mind that of St Anselm in his *Cur Deus Homo*. In that work, Anselm demonstrates the fitness of the incarnation by considering the problem of the satisfaction due to God for human sinfulness *remoto Christo*—as if Christ had not existed.[4] *Philosophical Fragments* can be read as a similar attempt to introduce the figure of the God-man by an exploration of the communicative problem between God and man. Instead of beginning with the figure of Christ and then seeking to explain his significance for the coming-to-be of the Christian, Climacus begins with the obstacles to the communication between the god and humankind. Given Climacus's account of this communicative problem, only the paradoxical figure of the God-man can effect any form of communication. In a very Anselmian formulation, Climacus writes: "Faith, then, must constantly cling to the teacher. But in order for the teacher to be able to give the condition, he must be the god, and in order to put the learner in possession of it, he must be man" (PF, 62).

Climacus is not simply producing his specification for the teacher in a vacuum. There are two formidable candidates for this post who set the parameters for the discussion in the *Philosophical Fragments*: the figure of Christ according to Hegel[5] and Kierkegaard's understanding of Christ as the God-man. Both of these are

---

[3]Mark 4:10-12; Matt. 13:10-13; and Luke 8:9-10; cf. Rom. 11:7-9.

[4]See the preface to *Cur Deus Homo*: "In accordance with the subject matter with which it deals I entitled [this work] *Why God became a man*; and I divided it into two short books. The first of these contains the answers of believers to the objections of unbelievers who repudiate the Christian faith because they regard it as incompatible with reason. And this book goes on to prove by rational necessity—Christ being removed from sight, as if there had never been anything known about Him—that no man can possibly be saved without Him." "Why God Became a Man," in *Anselm of Canterbury*, 3 vols., ed. and trans. Jasper Hopkins and Herbert Richardson (Toronto: Edwin Mellen Press, 1976) 3:43.

[5]Hegel's Christology is nowhere explicitly alluded to in *Philosophical Fragments*, but it is the purpose of this paper to show that (a) Hegel did have a concept of the Christ as teacher and (b) the distinctiveness of Kierkegaard's own account is seen in a sharper light when this hidden interlocutor is made visible.

set against another figure who might be thought to be an eminently suitable candidate: Socrates.

To carry our metaphor further, Climacus seeks to show why it is that Socrates not only does not fit the bill, but is wise enough not to apply. Socrates is a teacher of recollection, who brings people to a realization of what is already within them.[6] He is an occasion, a reminder, to those who do exist, but have forgotten it. That is a very different thing from bringing one's pupils into existence. Socrates, however, knows that this is the highest relation between human beings. One human being can serve as midwife to another, but it is for the god alone to give birth (PF, 9-11). Socrates took care never to claim authority. Christ, however, made explicit claims which both Hegel and Kierkegaard see as of primary importance in their discussion of his role.

Although the figure of Socrates is of great importance in the *Philosophical Fragments* as a foil to the Teacher, illuminating that role by contrast, I propose to focus on the two candidates who can be regarded as vying for the post. In particular, how do their claims reflect the perception of the communicative problem of their respective sponsors, Hegel and Kierkegaard?

To begin with, it is important to realize that there are basic areas where Hegel and Kierkegaard's accounts of Christ agree in the face of many of their contemporaries. Both of them insist that the being of the God-man, his ontological reality, is fundamental to coming to grips with Christianity. The concept of incarnation is the bedrock of both their accounts. Christianity is not simply a matter of a series of timeless moral teachings given by a respected prophet. It is a response to an event and a person. Where the two disagree is on the way in which that incarnation works as a strategy of communication between God and humanity, because they have fundamentally different views on the process of communication.

---

[6]In a note in *Concluding Unscientific Postscript* (CUP, 1:206-207), Kierkegaard acknowledges that a distinction should be made between Plato and Socrates on this point. However, in *Philosophical Fragments* Socrates represents a position, and indeed represents the Hegelian reading of Socrates, rather than offering a rigorous analysis of the Greek philosopher.

That difference can be obscured because Kierkegaard makes use of Hegel's terms and concepts to put forward a radically different view of the significance of Christ. It is not fair to represent this as demonstrating that Kierkegaard was ultimately dependent on Hegel. Kierkegaard himself accounts for the lack of Christian terminology in the *Philosophical Fragments* as an attempt to get away from a form of language which has been twisted by its incorporation into the Hegelian system[7]. He is trying to restate the truths of Christianity as he interprets it within a context where the very tools of argument have been appropriated by his opponents. Hegel and the Hegelians purport to have established the meaning of words such as Spirit and reconciliation in a way that finally does justice to the insights contained in them. Rather than abandon this terminology to the Hegelians, Kierkegaard runs the risk of being interpreted as a parasite on their discourse in the attempt to rescue the language that Hegel has, in Kierkegaard's opinion, misappropriated. Kierkegaard's own situation parallels that of the Teacher in some respects, although it is crucially different in others. He is addressing problems of communication, but has to do this within a system which has already been set up on what he is arguing are fundamentally false principles.

Let us then begin by looking at Hegel's account of Christ, concentrating particularly on the issue of Christ as communicator or teacher, in order to draw out some of the principles in question.

Hegel's Account of Christ as Teacher

For Hegel the incarnation is the necessary concrete demonstration of the process of reconciliation which constitutes the being of God and defines the meaning of love, a demonstration which brings humankind to the awareness of the eternal truth that this constitutes the nature of humanity as well.[8] It holds up a mirror in

---

[7]"Just as an old man who has lost his teeth now munches with the help of the stumps, so the modern Christian language about Christianity has lost the power of the energetic terminology to bite—and the whole thing is toothless 'maundering'." (CUP, 1:363)

[8]This account of Hegel's teaching draws mainly on his *Lectures on the Philosophy of Religion* in the edition edited by P. C. Hodgson, 3 vols. (Berkeley:

which the human individual can finally recognize himself or herself.

By taking on human nature, the Christ demonstrates finally that the divine and human natures are one and the same. For Hegel, God *is* the process of postulating another and reconciling it to oneself through love, an eternal dynamic which Hegel relates to the church's doctrine of the trinity. But humanity is not merely an accidental adjunct to this process. As absolute self-consciousness, God postulates finite consciousness in order that he can both know and be known. As Hegel puts it in the 1831 version of his *Lectures on the Philosophy of Religion*:

> *Absolute* self-consciousness is found only to the extent that it is also [finite] consciousness; it thus splits into two, on the one side the subject remaining wholly and simply present to itself, on the other also subject, but differentiated as finite. Thus God knows himself in humanity, and human beings, to the extent that they know themselves as spirit and in their truth, know themselves as God. (LPR, 1:465)

But the problem is that humanity is finite and therefore unaware of its infinite capacity. And yet, humankind does have a consciousness of its falling short, a sense of its finiteness which gives an entrée to the idea of the infinite. There is an anguish which, Hegel claims, results from the awareness of the radical evil of the human being and the infinite demand of the good. What might otherwise be construed as an exoneration of human evil, the human lack of ability to will the good, is in itself the index of just how radical the problem of evil is.

Redemption consists in bringing this tension to the highest pitch to allow for a sublation, and ultimately a recognition that precisely this sublation is the determination of the idea of God. The "otherness" of the human can be subsumed in the reality of

---

University of California Press, 1985). Hereafter, this work is referred to as LPR. This is not a claim that Kierkegaard was directly influenced by these lectures, but rather an attempt to set Kierkegaard's account in the context of an approach that has fundamental differences and yet intriguing similarities to his own, and that, at whatever level of direct or mediated influence, was a powerful force in the theological climate in which he worked.

God because God is the process of the sublating of otherness, or, in other words, love.

But how is this synthesis to be made apparent to humanity so that this sublation may occur? Somehow God must reveal himself[9] to humanity. That he will do so is, for Hegel, inevitable. It is a necessary consequence of God's being. As God is love, he is *ipso facto* self-revelatory. This is constitutive of the idea of God as Spirit:

> A spirit that is not revelatory is not spirit. It is said that God created the world and has revealed himself. This is spoken of as something he did once, that will not happen again, and as being the sort of event that may either occur or not occur: God could have revealed himself, he could have created the world or not; his doing so is one of his capricious contingent characteristics, so to speak, and does not belong to the concept of God himself. But it is the essence of God as spirit *to be for another*; i.e. to *reveal* himself. He does not create the world once and for all, but is the eternal creator, the eternal act of self-revelation. This *actus* is what he is: this is his concept, his definition. . . . (LPR, 3:170)

> What indeed does God reveal other than that he is this process of self-revelation? (LPR, 3:22)

Yet how is this revelation to be effected? How is humanity to be made aware of its true nature as essentially divine when it labors under the consciousness of its finitude? The truth, according to Hegel, has to appear as certainty, as something that is before us, something immediate and sensible which can be experienced before it is thought. It has to be presented as a brute fact, of the order of the existence of the sun, something that "has to be put up with because it is there" (LPR, 3:336).

For Hegel, this immediate communication can only be through the appearance of a concrete human being in the flesh. This appearance, the incarnation, is a necessary corollary of the nature of the spirit.

------

[9]In using the male pronoun here and elsewhere to refer to God, I am following the usage of Hegel and Kierkegaard as I attempt to expound their thought. Rightly or wrongly, the gender they both assign to God is not without significance for their argument. Where I write of God outside the framework of their discussions I have sought to use gender-neutral language.

The success of the communication requires that "a human being appears to consciousness as God, and God appears to it as a human being" (LPR, 3:313). Hegel insists on the importance of this appearance as a concrete and specific human individual. He characterizes as "revolting arrogance" and "sentimentality" (LPR, 3:134) any attempt to decry the need for this sensible presence in the interests of a supposedly higher abstract thought. It may be true that humanity in the universal sense is implicitly to be defined as the unity of God and humanity, but this is not immediately available to consciousness. Hegel calls the concept of the God-man a "monstrous compound" but concedes its usefulness in making it clear that the otherness, the finitude, of human nature does not damage the fundamental unity of the human and the divine.

Christ, then, appears as an ordinary human being, but a human being whose sole concern is the proclamation of the truth. His office as Teacher is central to this. Hegel takes pains to differentiate Christ's own teaching as recorded in the Gospels from the later doctrine of the church. Christ's teaching is immediate, appealing to the sensible consciousness through intuition, unlike doctrine which is conceptual and mediated through language and the historical reflection of the community. It is a teaching which negates the present world, demanding that the whole attention of the hearer is directed to the infinite interest. In its extravagant claims which demand the severance of natural bonds of affection and family loyalty and its bold assertion of the imperative necessity of love and of the search for truth, it has a sweep and an authority which mark it as divine. This teaching is not mediated: "nothing is said about any mediation through which this elevation [of soul] may come to pass for humanity; rather what is spoken of is this immediate being, this immediate self-transportation into the truth, the kingdom of God" (LPR, 3:319).

Hegel summarizes the demand made by this teaching as the need to "cast oneself upon the truth" (LPR, 3:320). Such a demand throws attention onto the one who makes it. What is his authority for issuing such a summons? It is clear that Christ here speaks as a prophet rather than as a teacher. "He is the one who, because his demand is immediate, expresses it immediately from God, and God speaks it through him" (LPR, 3:320). Yet he is essentially human, so that he becomes the revelation of God's divine presence as "essentially identical with this human being."

At this point one might ask what is unique in this. What about other great prophetic teachers who have presented their hearers with the immediate demand for personal commitment to the truth? For Hegel, the final determinant of Christ's singular significance is his death and resurrection.[10] In his 1831 lectures, Hegel makes explicit how this is in contrast to Socrates, whose career he sees as similar to Christ's until the point of death.

He grants that there is nothing unique in the fact that Christ dies, nor in the manner of his death as an innocent man cruelly executed. Indeed, Hegel argues that it is precisely the fact that death is the universal demonstration of the finitude of humanity that gives Christ's death its unique significance. Christ's death is the proof that this finitude is to be found in God:

> God has died, God is dead—this is the most frightful of all thoughts, that everything eternal and true is not, that negation itself is found in God. The deepest anguish, the feeling of complete irre-trievability, the annulling of everything that is elevated, are bound up with this thought. (LPR, 3:323)

Out of infinite love, God has taken upon himself this ultimately alien finitude. Yet even here there is a sublation and it is in the light of this that God's involvement with Christ and so with humanity is made manifest. God maintains himself through death and rises again. In this God has demonstrated his reconciliation with the world. It is not a reconciliation that has to be effected in some specific transaction between God and a world that has alienated itself through sin. God is eternally this reconciliation of the other. By the concrete example which Christ's resurrection affords, God has shown that "even the human is not something alien to him, but rather that this otherness, this self-distinguishing finitude as it is expressed, is a moment in God himself, albeit a

---

[10]"The history of [Christ's] teaching, life, death, and resurrection [has] taken place; thus this history exists for the community, and it is *strictly adequate to the idea*. ([It is] not just teaching, a [merely] intellectual foundation.) This is the crucial point on which everything depends, this is the verification, the absolute proof." (LPR, 3:145)

disappearing moment" (LPR, 3:327). Christ has made explicit what is implicit in the ontology of every human being, and in the teaching of every religious system. He has demonstrated the essential identity of the human and the divine, in which human individuality becomes a "disappearing moment" in the wider identity of God.

Hegel makes it clear, however, that this understanding of the death of Christ is only accessible to those who are brought into the community of the Spirit. In this context, "Spirit" is yet another term for that which manifests its being in the process of reconciliation and mediation. The Spirit itself is characterized by its work of bringing humankind into community. It is in the community that the consciousness of the reconciling work of Christ can arise. This community, which becomes the church, sustains itself by offering those who wish to come to the truth a presupposition of the certainty of reconciliation. This presupposition becomes enshrined in the church's *doctrine*.

As a result, we can distinguish between three groups of learners in Hegel's account:

1. The contemporaries: those who encounter Christ *before* his resurrection, who have a presentiment of the reconciling power of God through the direct teaching of Christ.

2. The disciples of the first generation: those who experience the emergence of the Spirit in the formation of the postresurrection community, and who thus come to a certainty about the nature of Christ as God-man, the representation of the reconciliation of the divine and human.

3. The disciples of the second generation: those who come to know the truth of reconciliation through the teaching of the church. The church presents them with religious truth as an external certainty with which they must come to terms, which they must appropriate to themselves.

In all these cases, however, what Christ's hearers must realize is something that has always been true about their own nature. It is, in Kierkegaardian terms, a matter of recollection rather than repetition. Ultimately, the teacher's task is to prompt the learners to realize a truth which has always been accessible to them, to look again at an aspect of their being which they have never truly understood. The teacher is the unarguable, pellucid, immediate demonstration of this truth.

Kierkegaard's Account of Christ as Teacher in Relation to Hegel

The depiction of the Teacher in *Philosophical Fragments* stands in opposition to the Hegelian account. Fundamental to this opposition is the radically different view of the communicative transaction involved. Where Hegel sees the figure of Christ as the crucial immediate communication of a truth intrinsic to the human condition, the Teacher of *Philosophical Fragments* is the occasion for scandal and misunderstanding which may bring about the new birth of the individual. The God-man does not make anything clearer, but is himself the Absolute Paradox.

For Kierkegaard, the implications of God's loving concern for those who cannot understand him are quite the opposite to those set out by Hegel. God's love is what *prevents* him from communicating directly with those who are incapable of understanding him. Climacus uses the parable of the king who loves the servant girl to make his point (PF, 26-29). The king cannot communicate his love directly to her because the difference in rank and understanding between them will cloud the girl's apprehension both of her own worth and of the king as a man. Such a difference is the case between the god and the human learner; knowing that the learner has fallen into untruth by his own fault, the god still loves him. Although it is an option, the god will not abandon the learner because of his love for him, which yearns to be reciprocated, yet the god cannot directly communicate with the learner who has no faculty to understand the god. Through love, the god must restrain his impulse to declare himself, and that restraint is a source of grief. Climacus sums this up as follows: "Who grasps the contradiction of this sorrow: not to disclose itself is the death of love; to disclose itself is the death of the beloved" (PF, 30).

The only answer to this contradiction is for the lover to become the equal of the beloved, not by appearing in disguise, but by truly taking on the condition of the lowliest. Otherwise, the lover will deceive the beloved by glossing over the beloved's lack of understanding. Either he will surreptitiously remove the veil over the beloved's eyes in such a way that the beloved is never conscious that such a veil existed, or else, he will allow the beloved to fool herself into thinking that her distorted vision of their relationship represents the true depth of love which should exist between them.

The nature of this communication and its causes and consequences are spelled out in *Practice in Christianity*, in particular in the section on "The Categories of *Offense*" (PC, 123-44). Here Kierkegaard writing as Anti-Climacus clarifies the concept of indirect communication as it applies to Christ. Far from being the immediate physical manifestation of the self-revealing God, Christ's human appearance serves in fact as an incognito which ensures his unrecognizability. The spectacle of a human being, indistinguishable from his fellows, who announces himself to be God is one calculated to provoke scandal and offense rather than the immediate acceptance of his claims as the key to human self-understanding. Although the communication may be direct, it contradicts the person of the bearer of that communication who is seen to be human. Such a mismatch between the communication and the communicator faces the hearer with the choice between offense or belief.

This is all in complete contrast to Hegel's account. Kierkegaard insists that there is no possibility of direct communication between the god and a human being in the grip of deception, or, in other words, of sin. While Hegel's Christ comes as the inevitable revelation of a self-revealing God in immediate and concrete form to provide a basis of certainty to human self-understanding, Kierkegaard's God-man comes as the representative of a loving God unable to communicate his love to a sin-deadened human being, and thus resorting to a paradoxical communication which may bring the dead to life by revealing the deadly nature of sin.

Yet this leaves us wondering what exactly sin can be if it has so devastating an effect on the communication between God and humanity. Climacus does not specify this in *Philosophical Fragments*. For a fuller exposition of Kierkegaard's understanding of sin, we can turn to his *The Sickness unto Death*, where he defines it as "before God or with the conception of God, in despair not to will to be oneself, or in despair to will to be oneself" (SUD, 77). But what is the root of this despair, and how might it act as a barrier to communication?

Kierkegaard relates despair to the notions of possibility and necessity.[11] Both are essential for the actualization of the self. By refusing to acknowledge its necessity, the self can lose itself in a realm of abstract, unrealized, and ultimately unrealizable possibility. On the other hand, the self can also lose its actuality by refusing to acknowledge the transforming power of possibility. Insofar as it loses its grip on one or the other pole of this dialectic, then the self can be said to lose its actuality, or in plain language, not to be.[12]

The relationship between possibility, necessity and actuality is also discussed in the Interlude in *Philosophical Fragments*. Here again we find a radically different account from that found in Hegel. For Hegel, actuality and possibility interact to constitute necessity. By possibility he means what he defines as "*real* possibility": the totality of conditions presupposed by a certain actuality. If all these conditions are fulfilled, then the actuality itself will be instanced. The inevitability of this outcome constitutes necessity, but is also the essence of freedom, in that freedom is the untrammelled outworking of the relations of coimplication.

Kierkegaard, on the contrary, regards this as the negation of freedom. He reorients the whole dialectic.[13] Far from necessity

---

[11]See here esp. SUD, 35-42.

[12]The well-known opening paragraph of *The Sickness unto Death* where Kierkegaard concludes that the human self is not yet a self illustrates this paradox. Insofar as the self is not yet itself, it does not exist.

[13]He takes issue with Aristotle's discussion of the interrelationship of these three terms in his *De Interpretatione* (see *The Works of Aristotle*, vol. 1, ed W. D. Ross [Oxford: Clarendon Press, 1926]) on the grounds that Aristotle makes a fundamental error in describing what is necessary as possible. Aristotle's argument is that if what is necessary has happened, that shows that it must have been possible that it would happen. This, however, involves him in distinguishing different senses of the concept "possible." If we mean by describing an event as *possible* that it could have happened or not, then, by definition, this cannot apply to necessary events. Necessary events could not fail to occur. Hence Aristotle adopts a definition of possibility that lies behind Hegel's discussion: what is possible for a subject depends on what it has the intrinsic capacity to become. Kierkegaard, however, refuses this argument. The necessary is just that—necessary; talk of possibility and actuality has no meaning in this context as the necessary is absolutely different from both the possible and the actual (PF, 74-75).

being the union of actuality and possibility, he sees actuality as "the unity of possibility and necessity" (SUD, 55). His definition of the possible is very different from Hegel's. Rather than possibility preceding actuality in the guise of necessary conditions, possibility is infinite, and to be identified with the future, not the past. *The Sickness unto Death* makes explicit a further implication: "since everything is possible for God, then God is this—that everything is possible" (SUD, 40). Hegel's God is free because he can manifest his necessity; Kierkegaard's is free because he has infinite possibility.

The role of the teacher, then, is to point to the realizability of possibility in the learner's life. Paradoxically, it is the *impossibility* of the God-man which is the source of his salvific role. As the concrete instance of the impossible actualized, he bursts the bonds of the necessity that masquerades as possibility in the Hegelian account. As Kierkegaard remarks in *Judge for Yourselves!*, considered as mere possibility, Christianity seems easy, attracting the plaudits of the crowd. What an illusion, however, if someone imagines that instantiating this possibility would draw even greater acclaim (FSE, 116-17). Actuality is the occasion of offense, not a means of ensuring capitulation to the irresistible evidence of God's nature.

This in turn means that Kierkegaard can regard everyone as standing in an equal relation to the communicator, regardless of the temporal distance between them. Unlike Hegel, with his three classes of believers, Kierkegaard sees everyone as standing in an equal relationship of possible offense at a paradox which is absurd in a way that has no relationship to the historical context in which it occurs, rather as the square root of two is an irrational number. Whether a contemporary or a follower at any remove, it is the hearer's reaction of offense or faith to the paradox embodied in Jesus Christ that is important.

Kierkegaard protests vehemently at the idea that for subsequent generations Christianity becomes a doctrine which must be agreed to. He agrees with Hegel that this idea arises as an inevitable development given the human condition, but unlike Hegel, he sees it as one to be deplored and resisted at every level. If the content of Christianity is reduced to a body of knowledge which can be assented to, then the essential recreative movement of faith has been lost. What is more, the person of the teacher loses its significance; knowledge is knowledge, independent of its source.

Rather than confronting the problem of existence, this attitude compounds it, by assimilating the paradox of the God-man to the etiolated life of illusion which passes for existence. It is as if the teacher of a foreign language were to assimilate its pronunciation and its cultural references entirely to his own, through coming to his knowledge of it not from the immediate circumstance of communication, but by memorizing a grammar book. Perhaps such a teacher can persuade children to parrot the phrases of the language, but will not expand their possibilities of communication, and so the parameters of their own existence.

To find an account of how Kierkegaard conceives the educative process, we can turn to an astonishing passage in *Practice in Christianity* (PC, 174-79). Here Anti-Climacus explains how to introduce the story of Christ to a child "who is not warped by having learnt by rote a simple school assignment about Jesus Christ's suffering and death" (PC, 174). Anti-Climacus envisages showing the child a picture book which contains among other pictures of heroes an illustration of a crucified man. He traces the child's reaction from discomfort to indignation at God's permitting it to happen, and then to a desire to avenge this death. But as the child matures, it becomes a desire to share in that suffering.

It is the concrete image of the crucified Christ placed in the context of the triumphs of human heroes that is the key to this process, not rote learning of catechisms and creeds. Nor is it the glorious outcome of the resurrection from which Kierkegaard starts, as that can only have meaning in the light of being seized by the innocent suffering of the figure on the cross. The child is confronted with an impossible possibility, the cruelty inflicted on the best of men, the paradox of suffering, and the alarming confession of the child's confidant: "At that moment, the adult stands there as an accuser who accuses himself and the whole human race!" (PC, 176)

It is in this sense that the summary of the message that Climacus provides as all that would have been necessary for the contemporary generation to relay has its power: "We have believed that in such and such a year the god appeared in the humble form of a servant, lived and taught as a servant and then died" (PF, 104). This is the impossible possibility in its starkest form. It is the paradox that cannot even be engaged with as it stands; it can only *have been* engaged with. It is only in retrospect that the learner can grasp that he or she has been seized by this paradox.

To ask then what the teacher can do for me is, to return to our initial scenario, as if the pupil were to persist in asking the teacher in English for an explanation of what she is doing speaking this gibberish. Explanations can only be given if the child enters into the world of this new language, tentatively exploring and building a capability. In itself, as this is confirmed by the encouragement of the teacher, it becomes its own explanation. By entering into the process, the benefits of entering upon it make themselves manifest in the expansion of the world through the increased possibilities of communication, possibilities which may allow the pupil to change, to "come to be," to grasp the lesson of eternity.

8

Revelation, Knowledge, and Proof

J. Heywood Thomas

Kierkegaard is so often quoted as an example of a nonmetaphysical Christianity that it is instructive to look again at *Fragments* to see what light it throws on this view. Though a related theme, this description of Kierkegaard is different from the surprisingly long-living myth that Kierkegaard is an irrationalist. While there have been numerous attempts to lay that ghost, what has not been attempted is a clarification of the issue by locating Kierkegaard's endeavor in the history of nineteenth-century philosophy of religion. If it is appreciated that the nature of nineteenth-century philosophy of religion was determined by the double legacy of Kant's rationalism and his pietism, one can instantly grasp how there can be a very close relation between Kierkegaard and Kant. One form of expression that could be given such appreciation is the argument that what Kierkegaard did was to push Kant's *rational* (that is, logical) critique of speculative theology to the point of destroying any possibility of a metaphysical understanding of Christianity. This is very suggestive and a very attractive view, but it seems to me that such an argument is a classic example of wrong conclusions being drawn from correct premises. What I want to argue here is that in *Fragments*, Kierkegaard was calling philosophy of religion back to Kant in order to build upon the critical philosophy a much better metaphysic than that which historically had followed, namely, Hegelianism.

To see how this is a useful and illuminating way of reading *Fragments* we need to treat two kinds of issues—philosophical and thought-historical. There was a time when Kierkegaard was read as if the history of philosophy was the account of a meeting of the

Aristotelian Society at which Hegel read the first paper and Kierkegaard was the critical reply. Now we are very much aware of the complexity of nineteenth-century idealism and the equally complex relation between Kierkegaard and the various European philosophers of whom he had heard. The more research that is done on his background the clearer it becomes that his perception of the starting point of philosophical theology is Kant's critique of metaphysics and rational theology. This is not a simple matter. The crucial problem for the interpreter of Kierkegaard's thought is, first, to clarify Kierkegaard's problems so that the relation between them and Kant's is identified and, second, to demonstrate the way he uses the Kantian legacy both to clarify the problems of idealist theology and to offer his *correction* of it.

Beginning with the historical analysis of *Fragments* we can take it as incontestable that the intention and the theme of the work are clear. As Billeskov Jansen pointed out,[1] Kierkegaard's general method was to propose a single main problem for each of his works, matching form to content with a remarkable skill. The form of *Fragments* has been aptly described by the late Niels Thulstrup as "at once like a classical drama in five acts, with an interlude interpolated between the last two acts . . . suggestive of the 'passage of time' . . . and a Platonic dialogue which has as its purpose the internal clarification of concepts and categories and their distinction from others."[2] We know too, as Thulstrup has shown,[3] that both the title page and the preface were originally cast in first-person language so that it is proper to infer that the issues were of decisively personal import. That is, of course, significant when we want to map Kierkegaard's development; but it is also important for an analysis of his relation to the development of philosophical

---

[1]See F. J. Billeskov Jansen, *Studier i Søren Kierkegaards litterære Kunst* (Copenhagen: Rosenkild and Bagger, 1951).

[2]Kierkegaard, *Philosophical Fragments or A Fragment of Philosophy by Johannes Climacus*, trans. and intro. by David Swenson, new intro. and commentary by Niels Thulstrup, and trans. revised and commentary trans. by Howard V. Hong (Princeton: Princeton University Press, 1962) lxvii-lxviii).

[3]Ibid., 149-51 and 152-54. It is worth noting that the classical introduction by Swenson and the very important scholarly commentary of Thulstrup are not to be found in the 1985 Hong edition.

debate on these issues. The problem is Lessing's "ugly ditch" and it was brought to Kierkegaard's attention by his reading of Brøchner's translation of Strauss's *Die Christliche Glaubenslehre*.

In his *Fragments* commentary, Thulstrup points out that the conflict of references (Kierkegaard following Strauss's reference to volume 6 of Lessing's work when the relevant passage in the edition he owned is found in volume 5) suggests that it was only after reading Strauss that Kierkegaard purchased Lessing's work and made the close study that is evident in *Postscript*. This seems to me of more than trivial significance in that it could be argued that the problem of *Fragments* is precisely that—a problem. Kierkegaard is not here continuing some polemic against Hegelianism, as one tends to think of the progression of the *oeuvre*. He is in a very real sense working from within that tradition to face what he sees to be *the* problem. Exactly as Kant had not set out to criticize or repudiate rationalism in *The Critique of Pure Reason* but worked out the problems of rationalism until he "found" that he "had to make room for faith," so Kierkegaard here works out the idealist problems. My contention has to do with *Fragments*, not with the position Kierkegaard held in 1844. To confuse these two would be to forget the indirect communication exemplified in it, a work by Johannes Climacus for which Kierkegaard himself takes only the responsibility of publication. The argument that I have tried to develop seems to be confirmed by the language of the original preface: "My intention in that undertaking is not at all polemical, to defend something or to attack something."[4]

Once again I would emphasize that this in no way alters the nature or the effect of the argument in *Fragments* which is the clear demonstration of the contradiction between Christianity and idealism. If, then, it is important to remember that Strauss is the context of the problem as formulated, it will be useful to look at the features of that context. Strauss's two-volume dogmatics was the companion work to the *Life of Jesus* which strangely enough Kierkegaard seems not to have possessed and to which he makes no reference. The work represented Strauss's rejection of any

---

[4]*Søren Kierkegaards Papirer*, VB 24 udg. af P.A. Heiberg og V. Kuhr (Copenhagen: Gyldendal, 1909–1948).

biblically based theology. It is indeed a dogmatics which "attacked theism from every side" and openly used pantheistic language.[5] Influenced though it is by Schleiermacher, it is essentially Strauss's attempt to revivify Daub's Hegelian dogmatics.[6] Strauss begins his apologetic section by contrasting "two classes of human society in the intellectual and the people, that is, the nonphilosophically minded of the higher as well as the lower classes." This is an unbridgeable gulf in his view, and it has the peculiar consequence of an intolerant attitude towards the intellectual.[7]

There is no need to concern ourselves with the details of the doctrine expounded beyond saying that since God is not conceived as personal or even as universal personality, the Christology is essentially metaphysical. The person of Jesus is irrelevant to the truth of the doctrine that has to do with the applicability of divine predicates to humanity. Discussing Strauss's achievement and influence, Horton Harris describes him as an antitheologian and neatly characterizes his dogmatics as "simply a negative criticism of the Christian doctrine, the work of a critical philosopher" and says that he began not with "the supernatural presupposition of orthodoxy" but with "those of Hegelian philosophy" where a personal God was replaced by an impersonal "Idee."[8]

It might be thought that this historical investigation has either come to a dead end or that it was an unnecessary task. Either it yields nothing about the background of *Fragments* or it points us merely to the Hegelian background which we knew well enough anyway. However, my reason for pointing out the historical effect of that quotation from Lessing is simply to indicate the significance of the adjective "eternal" when it is used to modify "consciousness" and "happiness." Any of these expressions—but especially the phrase "necessary truths of reason" quoted by Strauss from Lessing—brings us into the domain of metaphysical theology. And so I wonder whether there is an echo here of Fichte's insistence

---

[5]Letter to Adolf Rapp of 27 February 1840 in Strauss's *Ausgewählte Briefe*, ed. Zeller (1895) 90, as quoted in H. Harris, *David Friedrich Strauss and His Theology* (Cambridge: Cambridge University Press, 1973) 134.

[6]See Harris, *David Friedrich Strauss*, 135.

[7]*Glaubenslehre*, 1:355; cited by Harris, *David Friedrich Strauss*, 137.

[8]Harris, *David Friedrich Strauss*, 276-77.

that only the metaphysical saves; for it should not be forgotten that Fichte had sought to elaborate the first distinctively postcritical theology, one founded squarely on the next stage of Kant's metaphysical theology, but one which at the same time corrects Kant. Certainly what Kierkegaard is doing with Strauss and the Christology of the left-wing Hegelians is bringing them back to the issue of Christology as that emerges in Fichte.

It is important to remember that while the very idea of a special divine revelation presented difficulty for the skeptical rationalism of the eighteenth century, the effect of Kant's philosophy of religion was to shift the understanding of revelation beyond the traditional notion of the provision of transcendent truths. Kierkegaard's contention is thus that these modern theologians on whom he comments have elaborated a theory that has distorted the very function of the theory. Instead of offering an answer to the question "Who or what is Jesus Christ?" it substitutes itself for that very historical anchoring of faith in the person. This will be clearer if a brief sketch of Fichte's development of Kant is attempted.

Fichte had set out as a disciple and the heir of Kant and his *Critique of all Revelation* is a deliberate spelling out of the consequences of the notion of Kant's view of religion as essentially morality. "God," for Fichte, "is to be thought of in accordance with the postulates of reason, as that being who determines nature in conformity with the moral law. The entire world is for us a supernatural effect of God."[9] The concept of God is thus not something that is derived a posteriori, but something that *precedes* religion. There are two features of Fichte's argument that are relevant to the historical development I am mapping: his distinction between religion and revelation, and his acceptance of Kant's emphasis on radical evil. Fichte did not view religion as some abstract scheme of ideas but understood that the theological idea only becomes religion when we make those critical postulates the policies of our behavior. In a very Kantian fashion Fichte sees the notion of right as God's commandment to be that extra dimension that transforms

---

[9]J. G. Fichte, *Attempt at a Critique of all Revelation,* trans. Garret Green (Cambridge: Cambridge University Press, 1978) 119-20.

morality into religion, "religion in its *most proper* meaning."[10] Such an understanding of religion yields, Fichte argues, the twofold classification of religion as natural and revealed. The latter presupposes "a fact in the world of sense, whose causality we would posit *forthwith* . . . in a supernatural being."[11] If such a revelation is a rational possibility, Fichte agrees with Kant that there is a radical tendency in man towards sin. The concept of revelation presupposes this "empirical datum," he says, that "there could be moral beings in which the moral law loses its causality *for ever*, or only *in certain cases*." This he establishes.[12]

It is true that just as Fichte was less emphatic than Kant on the radical evil in man, so too his view of revelation is that it is really necessary only for sensuous beings rather than human beings in general.[13] One concludes one's reading of Fichte's *Critique* with a sense of confusion as well as disappointment. It is disappointing to find something so crucial to our understanding of morality and religion as the fact of evil being treated as if in the end it is not a disease but a peculiar and rather limited aberration. And if revelation is after all not a matter of *general* importance but merely the strong medicine that is needed by these few, or many, but certainly limited number of cases, then the assertion of its meaningfulness and rationality must be said to be confusing.

I have deliberately avoided complicating the matter further, but I am well aware that there is a missing actor in my account of the drama of nineteenth-century philosophy, namely, Schelling. The reason I do not mention him here is that it seems to me that he did not contribute to the peculiar force that Lessing's affirmation of his "ugly ditch" had for Kierkegaard as he read those words in Strauss. Still it may well be that Schelling was important for some of the metaphysical discussion in Kierkegaard's argument in the "Interlude." The obvious influence of Trendelenburg and Aristotle should not blind us to the relevance of Schelling's recent discussions of potentiality and reality. Yet Kierkegaard's more epistemo-

---

[10]Ibid., 76.

[11]Ibid., 79.

[12]Ibid., 100-102; §8 is entitled "The Possibility of the Empirical Datum Presupposed."

[13]See ibid., 144.

logical discussion of revelation is surely pitched in a very clearly Kantian key. As Kant and Fichte had said, revelation does need a fact in the sensible world and it presupposes an empirical datum of radical evil. That idealism was prepared to make such an admission did not, however, alter what seemed to Kierkegaard to be its hollow optimism. It ends up by offering a travesty of a logical analysis of the basic concepts of Christian faith. Providing such an analysis and sketching its proper epistemology constitute the basic critical concern of *Fragments*. What critical philosophy had made clear about revelation was the relation to the two very different concerns of public history and the human moral need.

Interestingly enough, Fichte's *Critique* represents a step from critical philosophy to idealism because it abandoned the Kantian dualism of the phenomenon and the noumenon and made that very move the key to our solution of the problem of relating the theoretical and the practical. *Fragments*, I contend, should be seen as taking up that issue, especially as it relates to the problem of the presupposition of revelation. It does so moreover *as* a problem of idealism because that is what the critical philosophy of religion has become. Furthermore, it does this very much in Kant's manner— not least because it poses the problem as one that is raised by the implication of idealism. Perhaps Kierkegaard was reminded of his dissertation and its treatment of Socrates which bears the imprint of his reading of Hegel. However, it seems to me that he had understood both that the vital thought in idealism had been grasped by Plato and that the great contribution of Christianity to the history of philosophy was that it stood Platonism on its head. Hence, Kierkegaard neatly begins his book with Socrates because this point of departure will raise those two problems of history and human need. In the remainder of this paper I want to discuss the significance of the book's argument for the elucidation of the concepts of revelation and transcendence in the epistemological and metaphysical discussion of the complex notion we call Christian faith.

What has been said of *Fragments* already—quite apart from its pseudonymous authorship—makes it impossible for me to suggest any simple connection between it and the Kantian philosophy of religion. However, it will also be clear that in Fichte's estimate of the significance of revelation we have reached a point not very far from Hegel's. Moreover, even the ethical emphasis in Kant does not remove religion from the sphere of the rational. My suggestion about *Fragments* is that in the analysis of what is meant by "learning the truth" which opens the work, we are not far removed from that double legacy of the Kantian philosophy of religion which we have just uncovered. That there should have been a moment of concrete revelation was a matter of indifference to both Kant and Fichte. However, the other "empirical datum" was of greater significance especially to Kant. This is surely the point on which Kierkegaard insists as the first feature of what is implied by our making the moment in time of decisive significance, that the learner is in error (PF, 13-16). That is, the achievement of Kierkegaard is that he was able to restore the problem of revelation to the kind of context it had in the philosophical discussion of the Fathers. Modern philosophy had separated the issue of historicity from that of salvation which was the answer to the question about the "why" of a historical revelation. But by linking the two sides of Kant's legacy Kierkegaard had shown the complexity of the Christian language. For the next step is to illustrate what is involved in such an ethicoreligious development—that it is a matter of the Teacher giving the condition of learning as well as the Truth, and secondly, that there must be a change, a conversion, a departure by the disciple from his former state. This is what *Fragments* asserts in the opening chapter, and this is meant to show that the kind of theory that idealism was offering could be shown to be false from within its own tradition.

There is almost a reactionary quality in the argument in the sense that Kierkegaard seems to be saying that the Hegelians should turn the clock back. "You would not talk the nonsense you do" he might say, "if you realized how the Kantian legacy has been distorted. Get back to the honest appreciation of the tragic element in human history." Chapters 3 and 4 again take up distinctly Kantian motifs. Though there is not the slightest evidence to suggest that Kant's Antinomies were the inspiration of the theme of the Absolute Paradox yet there are two ways in which the whole discussion is undeniably Kantian. First, the problem is described as a "metaphysical crotchet" and, second, it is seen by the author as a sine qua non of a real philosophy. Undeniably, Kantian themes prevail the basic problem of chapter

4 with its distinction between faith and any form of knowledge (PF, 59) which is perhaps the clearest indication of the importance of the fundamental epistemological problem of the first Critique. The necessity of making room for faith in any account of knowledge is thus an obvious concern which Kant and Kierkegaard had in common.

Finally, what is so forcibly reminiscent of Kant's *Critique of Pure Reason* is the way Kierkegaard inserts into his discussion of the Absolute Paradox the little excursus on theistic proof (PF, 38-44). Just as Kant need not have offered any specific argument to demonstrate the invalidity of the traditional proofs, so too Kierkegaard has made it abundantly clear here that the Unknown cannot be a matter of deductive or inductive inference. Yet out of the same conviction that he has something worthwhile to say he gives the subtle argument about the proofs and the nature of proof. This is more than the kind of outright rejection of speculative theology that had characterized Lutheran pietism. It must be said that this section of *Fragments* is extremely difficult to interpret, more so indeed than the analogous section of *Critique of Pure Reason*.[14] This is partly because the argument is so cryptically brief and partly because it relates to logical discussions in particular that are more fully conducted elsewhere.

Even so, these comments on the philosophical problem of theistic proof are haunting suggestions of a metaphysic and not merely powerful negative criticism. In much the same way, Kant's thoroughgoing demolition of the proofs can end up by saying not only that rejection of the notion of a "first cause" brings us to an abyss, but also that the teleological argument is the oldest and best suited to reason. In his *Kant and the Transcendental Object*, J. N. Findlay argued that Kant was a latter-day Platonist who agreed with Plato both that human life is lived in a realm of phenomena and that there is a better "noumenal" world outside it.[15] The difference between them is simply one of the connection between them or rather the epistemological manifestation of the transcendent. For

---

[14]Immanuel Kant, *Critique of Pure Reason*, trans. Kemp Smith (London: Macmillan, 1953) 500-31.

[15]J. N. Findlay, *Kant and the Transcendental Object* (Oxford: Clarendon Press, 1981).

on this view the transcendent is not a mere notion but an evident fact. Seen in that light, Jacobi's well-known criticism and apophthegm is perhaps an apt description of Kierkegaard's view of Kant's account of the transcendent: "without the thing-in-itself, no entry into the *Critique of Pure Reason;* with the thing-in-itself no staying in it." Though Kierkegaard did not want to stay in it he did think that there was no way forward except through the *Critique.* That said, we tend to forget that with regard to his sharp distinction between theoretical and practical reason Kant took the view that it is the latter that has "primacy." This is what motivates Kierkegaard's understanding of how the situation of the learner must be viewed as he contrasts the two presentations of it in *Fragments.* On the other hand, the Socratic position has an entirely noetic approach to the truth while, on the other hand, for the Christian position the whole process of learning has to be seen as the effort of a moral agent who is "in the wrong." It is not fanciful to find an echo of that "edifying" thought here. Viewed in this way the distance between Kierkegaard's position in *Fragments* and Kant's in his *Critique of Pure Reason* is perhaps less than we might think.

Let us for a moment reflect on that essential starting point of philosophy that is indicated in the early pages of *Fragments*—a knowledge of what man is. For both Kierkegaard and Kant, men are not just inquirers but moral agents. As Kant had often spoken as if the whole of ethics consisted in our being honest to ourselves, so Kierkegaard here suggests that the entire weakness of contemporary philosophy was that it lacked the honesty of Socrates. Instead of recognizing that the discussion could not begin unless we knew what a man was, the philosopher pretended that we could begin our metaphysical investigation without any presuppositions. The moral nature of man as a free will gives rise to the conception of what Kant called the Kingdom of Ends; but how free action is possible remained for him a mystery. As Cassirer puts it,

A sphere of the "in itself" is indeed pointed to and defined by freedom in contrast to the world of appearances, the objective reality of which is manifested in the moral law "just as through a fact" but we can approach it only in action; we grasp it only in the form of a goal and a task, not in the form of a "thing."[16]

What this amounts to is that for Kant man's moral nature and his moral life lead us to a larger view of life than a scientific rationalism but it adds nothing to our knowledge. Cassirer argues that in the *Critique of Judgement* the discussion of aesthetic judgement shows that the gulf between freedom and nature can be bridged, imagination and understanding being harmonized.

> Here, in the free play of the powers of the mind, nature appears to us as if it were a work of freedom, as if it were shaped in accordance with an indwelling finality and were formed from the inside out—while on the other hand the free erection, the work of artistic genius, delights us as . . . a creation of nature.[17]

This might be thought more reminiscent of Schelling than of Kant; but that will serve as a reminder of the way *Fragments* is raising the Kantian question from *within* its idealist expression. For what is so thoroughly Kantian is the awareness that the transcendent is not visible in the world, not something we can read in the face of nature. Here is in fact one reason for saying that there is no echo of the Antinomies in the Absolute Paradox. Another is that this Kantian theme seems to me to play a more fundamental role in Kierkegaard's epistemology here.

It is time to illustrate my thesis by an analysis of *Fragments* itself and in so doing I want to try to avoid useless discussion of misleading debates regarding this "exercise of thought." In his introduction to his commentary on *Fragments*, Thulstrup gives "a summary sketch" of the various arguments by Drachmann, Bohlin, Hirsch, and Holm in support of the view that Kierkegaard's view of Christianity is a flawed version of faith because it reflects the influence of the very idealism it opposed.[18] Now, Thulstrup is right enough in his clear rejection of this view,[19] but it is also true that historical analysis does not really tackle the central problem of

---

[16]Ernst Cassirer, *Kant's Life and Thought* (New Haven: Yale University Press, 1982) 256.

[17]Ibid., 333.

[18]Thulstrup, *Philosophical Fragments* (see above, n. 2) lxxxixff.

[19]See my *Subjectivity and Paradox* (Oxford: Blackwell, 1957) 103-15.

interpretation. That is a matter of classifying a philosophical attitude, and my view of the matter is that Kierkegaard's philosophical method anticipates logical analysis. If that is the case then we
should approach the discussion in *Fragments* as less an attempt at
doctrinal definition than an exercise in grammar.

The particular problem is the logical grammar of the notion of
"revelation," asking the question of its use in relation to the relationship between revealer and believer, how far the Platonic model
of learning the truth which idealism adopted could accommodate
both the transcendent reference of "an eternal consciousness" and
the concern for "an eternal happiness" and the historical anchoring
of anything that could be called revelation. This explains why Kierkegaard describes his task as "a project of thought" and "an essay
of the imagination": it is not a description or analysis of defined
faith but a more formal undertaking that only serves to give
greater force to the conclusion of the book's argument that idealism is inconsistent with Christianity. It is thus beside the point to
complain that the notion of paradox is a philosophical conception.
It is like complaining that when we purchase a pound of apples
arguing about the number of apples or their weight is too mathematical and not sufficiently dietary or whatever. It is perhaps relevant to recall just what "eternal happiness" means. The phrase is
an example of what I. T. Ramsey called the model-qualifier[20] structure of religious and theological language with "eternal" reminding us of the way in which the "story" about "happiness"
needs to be developed so that the proper illumination dawns. In
his study of this concept Abrahim H. Khan offers the following
summary:

> Kierkegaard understands *Salighed* as an ethicoreligious good. It
> is ethical because of its bearing on human behavior and
> character. It is religious because it nurtures the kind of human
> character that will make a person become sensitive to his
> spiritual needs, to his inner stirrings, or to the yearning of his
> soul. However, *Salighed* is never acquired completely in this life,
> for it is a reality that is essentially in the future and is of the
> spirit rather than of the flesh and senses. This does not mean that
> it has no significance for an earthly human existence. In fact, for

---

[20]I. T. Ramsey, *Religious Language* (London: SCM Press, 1957).

Kierkegaard, the means through which life constitutes and reveals itself as properly developed and genuine is through the wish for, the concern for, the expectation of *Salighed* as a good and a future reality. But *Salighed* provides meaning for a life only through an individual's inner striving rather than through his abstract thinking.[21]

This makes clear both the way in which *en evig Salighed* (an eternal happiness) is indeed reminiscent of Kant's "summum bonum" *and* the way in which it cannot be contained within such a conception; for it is clearly a much more multifarious concept—concern for salvation, hope for an ideal existence, and a striving for perfection.

As I have said, it seems to me important to appreciate that Kierkegaard's discussion in *Fragments* is of a "problem." Thulstrup reminded us of Clausen's revulsion against the excessive domination of the student mind by Martensen. He wrote of "Hegel's terrorizing the spiritual life and of the fanaticism of his followers."[22] The viewpoint Kierkegaard himself described as "a positional philosophy,"[23] and this very choice of words throws into higher relief the different mood and character of his own work as a "fragment of philosophy." Nevertheless the point of departure is Hegel's own formulation of Socratic or Platonic epistemology. The emphasis is not only on the interiority of knowledge but on the spiritual nature of the inward. Knowledge only seems to be received but is in reality nothing but recollection. "The spirit of man contains reality in itself and in order to learn what is divine he must develop it out of himself."[24] This is why I register a slight dissatisfaction with the way Thulstrup expounds the nature of *Fragments*'s problems. He reminds us of the formulation in the first

---

[21]Abrahim H. Khan, *Salighed as Happiness? Kierkegaard on the Concept Salighed* (Waterloo, Ontario: Wilfrid Laurier University Press, 1985) 38-39.

[22]Thulstrup, *Philosophical Fragments* (see above, n. 2) 157-58. The reference is to H. N. Clausen's memoirs, *Optegnelser om mit Levneds og min Tids Historie* (Copenhagen: G. E. C. Gad, 1877) 210ff.

[23]*Papirer* X2A 155, p. 117.

[24]Hegel, *Lectures on the History of Philosophy* 2:32; quoted by Thulstrup, *Philosophical Fragments* (see above, n. 2) 168. Thulstrup discusses Kierkegaard's knowledge and understanding of Plato at some length in 164-72. He points out (170) that Kierkegaard's critique is not simply of Hegelianism but of every possible form of idealistic philosophy.

draft (JP 3:2370) where its reference to Lessing is a further explanation of the formulation. This seems to me to limit what is indeed Thulstrup's own proper perception of the real nature of the argument, namely, that it examines the adequacy of *any* idealist analysis of revealed religion.

This insistence that the argument of *Fragments* works from within idealism enables one to make better sense of what Kierkegaard says about Plato in his journal entry of 10 July 1840:

> It is a thought just as beautiful as profound and sound which Plato expresses when he says that all knowledge is a recollection, for how sad it would be if that which should bring peace to a human being, that in which he can really find rest, were external to him and would always be external to him, and if the only means of consecration were, through the busy, clamorous noise of that external science (*sit senia verbo*), to drown out the inward need, which would never be satisfied. This point of view reminds one of that which in modern philosophy has found expression in the observation that all philosophizing is a self-reflection of what already is given in consciousness, only that this view is more speculative and Plato's view more pious and therefore even a little mystical. (JP, 2:2274)

What the journal entries of 1840 show is that Kierkegaard was far from having abandoned the world of idealism and yet was aware of the problem that Christianity posed for such an epistemology. Thus he says, "All this big talk about having experience in contrast to the a priori is all very well" but it can lead to ludicrous nonsense (JP 2:2275), and then—presumably later in the same year—he defined his own philosophical, indeed speculative, position under the heading of the Pauline declaration "Everything is New in Christ":

> This will be my position for a speculative Christian epistemology. (New not merely in so far as it is different but also as the relationship of the renewed, the rejuvenated, to the obsolescent, the obsolete.) This position will be simultaneously polemical and ironical. It will also show that Christianity is not a construction around a particular object, around a particular normal disposition. (JP, 2:2277)

This latter entry is a lengthy one and goes on to contrast "the idea of mediation, the watchword of modern philosophy" with the Christian position. His conclusion is that it is necessary both to deny that Christianity arises in any man's thought and to affirm its naturalness because it is something that God creates. There seems to me little doubt that the Kantian philosophy of religion is a motive force here. Kierkegaard's quest is for a new speculative Christian epistemology. His stance is the paradoxical insistence on the transcendence necessitated by the human situation and the kind of immanence implied by the Kantian conviction that knowledge is a transcendental possibility.

The philosophical problem of *Fragments*, then, is precisely that of revelation, which had been first queried and then ignored by Kant but reexamined by Fichte. Kierkegaard seems then to take up the latter's analysis that shows how a knowledge of the truth is in fact achieved. Earlier I compared the total undertaking with Kant's in *Critique of Pure Reason* where, despite the fact that the general thesis makes certain discussions such as that of theistic proof unnecessary, nevertheless these are pursued. So far is *Fragments* from coming up with "no results at all," as Louis Mackey says,[25] that these are the extra results over and above the basic thrust forward from the understanding of revelation to which Kant had been brought in idealism. There is a very fundamental sense in which *Fragments* is an appeal to idealism to go back to Kant and that is the distinctly ethical tone. As Kant had often spoken as if the whole of ethics consisted in being honest to ourselves so Kierkegaard here suggests that the entire weakness of contemporary idealism was its lack of a Socratic honesty. Instead of recognizing our fundamental ignorance and agnostic situation, the idealist philosopher pretended that we could undertake the task of metaphysical inquiry without any presupposition, confident of the presence of knowledge within us already.

It cannot be emphasized too often that what Kierkegaard was in fact doing in this work was not rejecting metaphysics but seeking an alternative metaphysical theology. Too often his polemic against idealist theology is taken literally and indeed is even overstated. Thus Josiah Thompson would have us view any philosophi-

---

[25]Louis Mackey, *Kierkegaard: A Kind of Poet* (Philadelphia: University of Pennsylvania Press, 1971) 68. Climacus, he says, makes light of everything in *Fragments* and "reneges the conclusions he implies and comes up with no results at all."

cal exposition of a work such as *Fragments* as misguided and "missing the point" about all the pseudonymous works—"that ultimately they seek to show the vacuity of all philosophy and metaphysics."[26] It was precisely because that metaphysic was illustrated by the discussion of theistic proof that this was included in *Fragments*.

A very interesting feature of this discussion is that it follows Kierkegaard's very clear contention that in knowing its limit reason is aware of something. That is, there is a revelation in the very awareness of the limits of reason. It is not the passive nature of knowledge that is of importance for the moment but the simple fact of some kind of knowledge. And however un-Kantian he was in identifying a something that is transcendent, Kierkegaard is now very Kantian in his anxiety to distinguish between such knowledge and a logical proof. As is often the case, Kierkegaard's argument is very convoluted and one sometimes feels he is being just a little too clever. First, he makes the point that calling the unknown something the God is no more than assigning a name to it (PF, 41-42); and what exactly he means by this is not at all clear. Probably he wants to call attention to the discontinuity between any such logical construct and the Revealer. If so, then it is quite the opposite of how Barth thinks of the Name of God in his account of the ontological proof.[27]

The next step is a quite different point—that a proof of God's existence is irrational. "For if the God does not exist it would of course be impossible to prove it; and if he does exist it would be folly to attempt it." The first alternative is clear enough since if X is not the case then no proof that it is the case can be valid. However, why is it "folly" to try to prove that something that exists does exist? One's first reaction is that if this were so then no detective story could be written. In a murder case that seems an accident, the solution that concludes the story is the maneuvering of the puzzle that establishes the fact that there is a murderer—and in all the best detective stories he or she is there all along. Two things seem to be in play in Kierkegaard's argument: one the ever-

---

[26]Josiah Thompson, *Kierkegaard* (New York: Alfred Knopf, 1973) 146.
[27]Karl Barth, *Anselm*, trans. Ian W. Robertson (London: SCM Press, 1960) 73-89.

lively fascination of theistic proof and especially the Ontological Argument and the Kantian appreciation of the synthetic nature of existential assertions. Thulstrup calls attention to Kierkegaard's notes of Martensen's lecture given in 1837 *(Prolegomena til den Speculative Dogmatik)* where he comments:

> It is remarkable that the above proofs [cosmological and theological] were known in the ancient world; whereas this one [ontological] first appeared in the Christian world. . . . This was later advanced by Leibnitz . . . and by Wolff . . . *cuius essentia existentia.*[28]

Thulstrup refers to Kierkegaard's minimal knowledge of Spinoza, and though he relates the argument of this passage to the thought of Kant, Hegel, and Schelling, he sees little of note in this discussion.

Once again, though I applaud and agree with Thulstrup's scholarly account, I feel he does not go far enough. He is quite right to reject any sort of connection between Kierkegaard's argument here and the argument of Schelling that God's existence cannot be proved. To imagine that similarity of position implies a historical connection is the easiest and the most disastrous of mistakes in the history of philosophy. Thulstrup does not seem to appreciate either the full significance of the ontological argument in the development of the *Fragments* or the logical problems with existential claims. Kierkegaard puts to good use the lessons he learned from Trendelenburg about the logical weakness of the Hegelian system; and it is also important that the use to which he puts Trendelenburg's insights is a religious one. Kant's subtle critique of speculative theology and his declared aim of limiting knowledge to make room for faith are the same kind of exercise. There are one or two things that Thulstrup thus misses.

In the first place, there is a very revealing mistake in Kierkegaard's formulation of Anselm's ontological argument. He sees clearly enough that it is no simple argument from thought to being and regards the ontological argument as indicating the necessity of thinking God because "the thought of God is in me." This is much more like Bonaventura than Anselm; but what is

---

[28]*Papirer* II C 22 336; as quoted by Thulstrup, *Philosophical Fragments* (see above, n. 2) 213.

perhaps more significant is the recognition that thinking God is a very different matter from thinking other things. Is Kierkegaard not here pointing out that anyone who seeks to prove the existence of God will be faced with the difficulty of laying hold of this idea? The reference to the contrast between the proofs known to the ancient world and the one that emerged only in the context of Christian thought is surely more than an idle observation of history. Both the ancient proofs were a posteriori proofs—and this is what makes the connection of this argument of Kierkegaard's with Schelling's critique of the ontological argument quite unlikely. It seems to me that what Kierkegaard is saying is that if our purpose is to outline the grammar of Christian talk of God's existence then we must grasp the way in which that has a very distinctly a priori character. That the thought of God is in oneself is the Augustinian recognition that God is to be conceived as Revealer. If so, then the story of our discovery is the very opposite of the detective story mentioned above. This is why it is nonsense to talk of proof here. Moreover, the other half of the argument is a logical point that shows that the only kind of proof that can be offered of an existential statement is a posteriori so that an a priori proof is indeed nonsense. It is worth returning to the issue of Schelling's influence the better to grasp this point about the nature of God's existence.

The significance of Schelling is primarily that in his positive philosophy he was attempting to express the religious attitude of a return to the living God. Thus Tilliette in his definitive study of Schelling points out more than once that the connection between Kierkegaard and Schelling though studied by several scholars has not been exhaustively treated. He also speaks of the way in which, though they form a common front against Hegel's panlogism, the allusive language of *Fragments* shows that Schelling does not escape Kierkegaard's criticism.[29] Even so, Tilliette says, in *Fragments* Kierkegaard has selected what he wanted to retain of the "Bore" of Berlin[30]. From his ambivalent relation toward Schelling

---

[29]Xavier Tilliette, *Schelling une philosophie en devenir*, 2 vols. (Paris: Vrin, 1970) 2:238n.18.

[30]Ibid., 2:336, 86n., 238n.18, 466n.

one sees most clearly what I have described as the difficulty of interpreting Kierkegaard's purpose and attitude toward idealism in *Fragments*. It is clear that Hirsch was wrong to see it as continuing some kind of idealism but it is equally clear that Schelling occupies a special place in his struggle with idealism. The point I have tried to argue is that the theological problem posed by post-Kantian idealism constitutes the framework of the argument of *Fragments*. For all the echoes of Schelling in the talk about time and eternity, the irony of nature, subjectivity and existence, the form of the servant and the importance of freedom—all these are in fact involved in the issue of the possibility of salvation and revelation. That is to say, it is the problem that is important and once again the particular idiom is that of Kant, which was so faithfully and effectively echoed by Fichte. That Kierkegaard is elaborating the Kantian perception that the idea of God is both unique and elusive seems to me to gain credibility from the next stage of the argument. The point about existential statements being synthetic is obvious enough; but more significant, I feel, is the Kantian tone of the argument about "developing the content of a conception" and the passion of reason to which I called attention in an earlier paper.[31] Not only do I remain very convinced of this but I see the same perception of the gap between faith and empirical knowledge in Kierkegaard as that displayed by Kant. This development of a concept is a nice example of what Kierkegaard sees as the interplay of transcendence and immanence.

As we have seen, one thing is quite clear to Kierkegaard as a matter of logic: proofs cannot yield existential statements. Yet in that same spirit of thoroughness Kierkegaard, like Kant, wants to look at what *kind* of knowledge we seek from these theistic proofs. So he considers the analogical case of proving Napoleon's existence from his works. We face, he says, the problem that these works could be someone else's—*unless* we have "already understood the word 'his' so as thereby to have assumed his existence" (PF, 40). There is a weakness in the causal-type argument for Napoleon's existence that the theistic proof lacks. There is "no absolute rela-

---

[31]See "Paradox," *Bibliotheca Kierkegaardiana* 3 (1980) *Concept and Alternatives in Kierkegaard*, 203.

tionship between him and his deeds." God's works, by contrast, are his and his alone. Then comes his coup de grace: "Just so, but where then are the works of God?" Kierkegaard conflates here the cosmological and teleological proofs; and that makes clear the lesson he had learned well from Kant. In his seminal paper on Kant's philosophy of religion, Donald M. MacKinnon reminds us of the impact that the Lisbon earthquake of 1755 made on the intellectual world to which Kant belonged.

> It was not only the crude metaphysics of those who argued this to be the "best of all possible worlds" that received a heavy blow from this disaster. The circumstances in which men and women met their deaths reminded such a philosopher as Kant that if indeed "ought implies can," he must reckon with the seeming total indifference of the environment in which men and women lived towards the sort of moral self-discipline, the sort of strenuous struggling after honesty, on which he laid such emphasis. Questions were raised concerning the relation of the "realm of nature" to the "realm of ends" to which theoretical answers were already ruled out as inconceivable.[32]

Kierkegaard's rhetorical question indicates his own intellectual struggle with the question of natural teleology. The starting point of this discussion was the assertion that Kierkegaard's use of his Kantian legacy was a more subtle philosophical development than a simple rejection of metaphysics.

This has been an attempt to contextualize this critique in the tradition of the metaphysical discussion of Christianity. More than once Kierkegaard's position has been characterized as Kantian. That description is something more than a historical or chronological point. It is not simply that one cannot ignore the way in which Kant's critique of metaphysics and speculative theology was already part of the history of thought. Rather what is significant is that Kierkegaard recognized and approved of what Kant had done—especially Kant's attitude. It is telling that in 1847 in an undated journal entry the adjective Kierkegaard applies to Kant is "honest" (JP 2:2236, 3:3558). Even more significant is a comment

---

[32]Donald M. MacKinnon, *Themes in Theology: The Threefold Cord* (Edinburgh: T.&.T. Clark, 1987) 26.

recorded two years earlier on the inadequacy of immanence being made clear by the relation between Kant and Hegel on radical evil (JP, 3:3089). Several times in the *Papers* Kierkegaard makes clear his dissatisfaction with Kant, and what seems to me most significant is his impatience with Kant's view of the *ding an sich* as a limit of thought that excludes this entire sphere from human consciousness (JP, 2:2252). The contradiction of Kant's philosophy is that it recognizes a sphere of the ethical as essentially real and yet wants to make the *ding an sich* a limit. In short, Kierkegaard feels that Kant did not press far enough ahead with his own recognition that the error of rationalism was its failure to recognize that reason too had its *interests*. Consequently, though he praises him for not pretending that his notion of radical evil was "a speculative comprehension of the Christian problem" (JP, 3:3093), Kierkegaard takes Kant to task for not establishing that this "inexplicable is a category" (JP, 3:3089).

This long-standing dissatisfaction with a solution to what Kierkegaard regards as the real problem of a philosophical treatment of Christianity is, I have argued, the background to the way the discussion proceeds in *Fragments*. Kierkegaard was considering the latest solution that was in fact more unsatisfactory than had been Kant's own—and this is precisely because idealism had failed to appreciate the very clarification of the problem that had been achieved in the idealist tradition by Fichte. I have specifically *not* claimed that Kierkegaard is in any way dependent on Fichte but simply that his question and mode of attack are formed by the same Kantian outlook of a transcendental idealism. If this argument is right, then *Fragments* must be seen as continuing the critique of a transcendent metaphysics while also effecting a critique of the critical limitation of the range of meaningful discourse.

Kierkegaard's great achievement was to show how Kant's argument is essentially a metaphysical one, and that it is a paradoxical recognition of the dimension of reality of which we have no knowledge but still attempt to grasp by mere thought. Looking at such an argument and not merely the random reflections of the *Papers* that relate to this argument of *Fragments*, I am constantly struck by the way cleverness and confusion seem often to go together in Kierkegaard's thinking. Thus it seems clear that there is in *Fragments* a very strong sense of the critical outlook in philosophy that is developed in the final section into a radical skepticism with regard to historical knowledge.

The same mood had characterized both the discussion of what I called the "grammar" of the words "God" and "revelation" and is indeed most obvious in the very concern with what is said about proof. Yet it is the same Kantian concern with the conditions of knowing the transcendent and with a recognition of the fact of sin that animates Kierkegaard's rejection of both the critical philosophy and idealism. As Kant failed to articulate the way in which the transcendent infringes on our experience and forces upon thought the facts we neglect, so Hegel had reduced the notions of the transcendent to a mere immanence, emptying Christianity at once of the very presence that brings joy and of the objectivity of that joy.

It would be foolish to suggest that *Fragments* has delineated that new speculative epistemology that was mentioned earlier; but if anything is established by this examination of its argument and the context of its composition it is that this epistemological purpose is the nerve of its argument. This means then that it will not do simply to lump Kierkegaard with Kant and see his enterprise as some accessory to Kant's alleged "murder" of metaphysics. What Kierkegaard sought to do was in a sense something more profound than the composition of a piece of philosophy. One of the illuminating features of Thulstrup's comparison with classical drama is precisely that reading *Fragments* is like reading John's Gospel or a Greek or Shakespearean tragedy. Here is a philosopher who has, like the poet, plumbed the depths of the human psyche and seen man's sinfulness illumined by the presence of God. His thesis is that we can only understand the grammar of "God" and "revelation" when we resist the temptation to apply the wrong models of knowledge and proof and pay attention to that radical evil that Kant and Fichte had indeed recognized as part and parcel of the talk of "revelation."

9

Kierkegaard's Philosophical Fragments: *A Kantian Commentary*

Ronald M. Green

Philosophical Fragments is one of Kierkegaard's most philosophically informed and preoccupied works. Its pages abound with references to a host of well- and lesser-known philosophers, among them Socrates, Plato, Aristotle, Democritus, Epicurus, Lactantius, Descartes, Spinoza, Leibniz, Jacobi, and Hegel. Curiously missing from this list is the name of Kant, something usually explained in terms of Kierkegaard's tendency to perceive Kant as part of an undifferentiated tradition of philosophical idealism reaching back from Hegel to Plato and Socrates.[1] In the remarks that follow, I offer a very different view. Kant, I will contend, is a lurking presence in the *Fragments*. His specific writings on epistemology and philosophy of religion provided Kierkegaard the major stimulus for its composition. Implicit references to Kant's ideas abound in the text, and, in at least several important instances, Kant's words are picked up by Kierkegaard. If Kant is not singled out for mention in the *Fragments* it is partly because his presence is everywhere.

To defend this claim fully would require a thorough review of Kant's philosophy and its relationship to Kierkegaard's authorship.

---

[1]E.g., Hegel dominates Niels Thulstrup's "Commentary" in the Swenson translation of the *Fragments*. After a few remarks relating Kierkegaard's discussion to Kant, Thulstrup immediately turns his attention to Hegel. See *Philosophical Fragments*, trans. David F. Swenson (Princeton NJ: Princeton University Press, 1962) 213ff.

This review would begin with an examination of Kant's epistemology in the *Critique of Pure Reason* (1781), would proceed
through the complex development of his ethics in *The Foundations
of the Metaphysics of Morals* (1785) and the first part of the *Critique
of Practical Reason* (1788), and would conclude with an examination
of his philosophy of religion in the second half of this *Critique*, the
Religion within the Limits of Reason Alone (1793), and his essay *The
Conflict of the Faculties* (1798).[2] This examination would then serve
as background for coming to terms with the complex encounter
with Kant that Kierkegaard begins in his earliest pseudonymous
writings and vigorously continues in the *Fragments* and the *Postscript*. Succinctly stated, after appropriating key elements of Kant's
epistemology and ethics (including Kant's polemic against traditional metaphysics and ethical eudaimonism) and, after deeply
learning from Kant's development of the ideas of freedom and
radical evil in the *Religion*, Kierkegaard dramatically parts ways
with Kant over the issue of our need for a revealed, historical
redeemer. Kierkegaard defends an orthodox perspective while
Kant, despite his virtually Augustinian understanding of the depth
and totality of human sin, continues to adhere to a rationalist
"moral faith," with Christ an exemplary figure rather than efficacious savior. It can be argued, however, that Kierkegaard's orthodox Christian position is actually more consistent with themes in
Kant's mature philosophy of religion than is Kant's own moralistic
Christology. To the extent this is true, Kierkegaard was thus able
to turn Kant against himself by using Kant's doctrine of sin to
develop the orthodox Christian conclusions that Kant, ever the
Enlightenment thinker, shied away from.[3]

---

[2]Mary J. Gregor maintains that the section of *The Conflict of the Faculties*
dealing with "The Conflict of the Philosophical Faculty with the Theology
Faculty" was written between June and October 1794. Hence it follows soon on
the writing and publication of the *Religion*. See her "Translator's Introduction" in
The Conflict of the Faculties: Der Streit der Fackultäten (New York: Abaris Books,
1979) xvi. Henceforth all references to this work are to this German-English, side-
by-side edition.

[3]For a recent discussion of the equivocations in Kant's philosophy of religion,
see Gordon A. Michalson, *Fallen Freedom* (Cambridge: Cambridge University
Press, 1990).

I do not intend to develop these points here. Though I will occasionally touch on them in what follows, I have already done so at greater length in my book, *Kierkegaard and Kant: The Hidden Debt*.[4] My aim here is more limited. I propose merely to marshall evidence to show that although Kant is not once mentioned in the *Fragments*, his thinking is virtually omnipresent there. The most effective way of doing this, I believe, is to offer an abbreviated commentary on the *Fragments* in the manner of those developed by scholars like Niels Thulstrup and Howard and Edna Hong, whose own annotated treatments of the *Fragments* barely mention Kant. This Kantian commentary is motivated throughout by a very specific question: to what extent are particular ideas, terms, or passages in the *Fragments* reasonably linked to Kant? Although this approach may not enhance our appreciation of the full extent or lines of Kierkegaard's relationship with Kant, it does establish a background for the claim that this relationship is among the most important in Kierkegaard's authorship.

Chapter 1. Thought-Project

The problem explored in this opening chapter, the question of whether religious and moral truth is resident within us or must be learned from without, is rightly placed by Kierkegaard (Johannes Climacus) in a tradition going back to Socrates. Nevertheless, in the decades preceding Kierkegaard's authorship, this problem had been raised anew by Lessing[5] and it was exhaustively studied by Kant. As early as the *Foundations of the Metaphysics of Morals*, for example, Kant rejected any role for Christ in human moral redemption beyond that of serving as an example of moral purity confirmed to us by our own rational moral concepts.[6] In the wake of his mature development of the idea of sin in the *Religion*, Kant expanded this notion to include a view of Christ as an indwelling

---

[4]Albany: State University of New York Press, 1992.

[5]For a discussion of Lessing and his influence, see Gordon Michalson, *Lessing's "Ugly Ditch": A Study of Theology and History* (University Park PA: Pennsylvania State University Press, 1985) 17.

[6]*Grundlegung zur Metaphysik der Sitten*, edition of the Preussischen Akademie der Wissenschaften, vol. 4, 409.

"archtype" both of the suffering transition each of us makes as we repent for sin and of the form of a redeemed humanity well pleasing to God. By drawing on the possibility and encouragement provided by this inner conceptual archtype, what Kant here terms God's "only-begotten Son,"[7] human beings are rationally able to renew a dedication to the moral law that has become weakened by our own freely incurred—and seemingly inescapable—susceptibility to moral wrongdoing. However, despite new emphases on the redeemer's role resulting from Kant's deepened appreciation of the problem of sin, in the *Religion* Christ remains a concept only, whose presence in history is unimportant. Indeed, in an important footnote in the *Religion*, Kant explicitly rejects the understandable human impulse to "schematize" religious concepts of this sort by rendering rational ideas in temporal or spatial terms. Kant acknowledges that schematization in general may serve as a useful aid to our thinking about intelligible objects, but he vehemently rejects any inference from this that these religious objects actually have the sensory qualities attributed to them. "On the contrary," Kant says:

> between the relation of a schema to its concept and the relation of this same schema of a concept to the objective fact itself there is no analogy, but rather a mighty leap [*ein gewaltiger Sprung*] (μετάβασις εἰς ἄλλο γένος), which leads at once to anthropomorphism.[8]

We will return to this footnote remark later, when we look more closely at Kierkegaard's own use of the term "leap" and his employment of μετάβασις εἰς ἄλλο γένος, Aristotle's phrase for a transition from one genus to another and, hence, an illegitimate confusion of categories of thought.[9] For now, it is enough to observe that in the *Religion*, Kant gives attention to Kierkegaard's question in the *Fragments* of the relationship between "an eternal

---

[7]*Religion within the Limits of Reason Alone*, trans. Theodore M. Greene and Hoyt H. Hudson (New York: Harper & Row, 1963) 54. Henceforth, unless otherwise indicated, all references are to this translation.

[8]*Die Religion innerhalb der Grenzen der blossen Vernunft*, GS VI, s. 65n. The translation here is my own since Greene and Hudson's translation (*Religion*, 59n) misses the explicit use of the noun "leap" (*Sprung*).

[9]*Posterior Analytics*, bk 1, chap. 7.

consciousness" and "a historical point of departure." His conclusion there, however, is that history is essentially unimportant for religious-moral salvation. At the same time, this concern with history is an abiding feature of Kant's mature work and, as we'll see in a moment, moves even more to the fore in his 1794 essay *The Conflict of the Faculties*.

The Teacher as "Occasion": PF, 11 lines 5-7; 14 line 4; 15 lines 24-25; 16 line 6; 23 lines 13-14; 24 lines 3-4

For the Socratic viewpoint, Kierkegaard-Climacus tells us, the truth is resident within us. As a result, the moment of learning is accidental and the teacher is only the "occasion" for the student's learning. Were the student deeply in error, in untruth, all this would be different. The moment of learning would be decisive and the teacher would, as *savior*, provide the unique condition of truth. By this development of presuppositions, Kierkegaard-Climacus reinvents Christianity.

In developing this contrast, Kierkegaard employs the term *Anledning*, "occasion" (Formal: *Foranledning*), more than forty times, nearly twenty times in conjunction with the "teacher" and as many times in relation to the historical "moment." The idea that the "teacher" is only an "occasion" for the student's learning is explicitly attributed by Kierkegaard-Climacus to Socrates, whom he presents as introducing it in the *Meno*.[10] It is noteworthy, however, that although a pedagogical relationship is assumed in the famous portion of the Meno where the young slave is made to "recollect" the truths of geometry, few uses of the term "teacher" are made there and the term "occasion" is never used. Similarly, this conjunction of terms is not found elsewhere in Plato's writings nor in any of the rationalistic philosophers preceding Kierkegaard—except for Kant.

Kant explicitly joins these terms in an important passage of *The Conflict of the Faculties*. We know Kierkegaard was intimately familiar with this work. Among other things, he took pains to copy out a witty passage from it into his notebooks (JP, 2: 2239). As

---

[10]Kierkegaard cites the passage as "80, near the end." The explicit discussion of this matter actually extends from 82-86.

we'll see shortly, Kant's critical treatment of Abraham there must also have provoked Kierkegaard's interest in the essay. The *Conflict* is Kant's effort to define the roles of the philosophical and theological faculties of the university, and hence, the respective roles of philosophical reflection and historical religious revelation in the religious-moral life. Among the essay's features is a remarkable degree of concession by Kant to the possible role of divine grace in reforming the corrupted human will and an explicit (but very Kantian) agnosticism concerning our *theoretical* determination of the role of human versus divine causation in the process of our moral redemption.[11] Although Kant fully concedes the importance of our assuming divine support for the completion of our moral efforts, he nevertheless urges us to put aside any kind of speculation on *how* this support operates in relationship to our own moral striving and free will. He further insists that we put aside all such questions as we singlemindedly rededicate ourselves to moral purity. As in the *Religion*, Kant persists in his Enlightenment standpoint by refusing to allow any kind of reliance on revealed grace, however minimal, to take the place of active moral striving in our efforts at moral reform. He also rejects any role for historical revelation in the process of moral-religious redemption, apart from its usefulness in presenting us with independently deducible rational ideas. Long sections of the first part of the essay (dealing with "the conflict between the philosophy with the theology faculty") are devoted to the matter of history. Kant sums up his position near the close of this part when he observes that "it is superstition (*Aberglaube*) to hold that historical belief is a duty and essential to salvation."[12]

In a key passage at the center of Kant's discussion of revelation and reason, Kant also rejects any reliance on revelation as a guide to the *knowledge* of our religious and moral duties. The italics in this passage are my own and represent an effort to bring out Kant's distinctive way of stating the issue:

> The biblical theologian says: "Search the Scriptures, where you think you find eternal life." But since our moral improvement is

---

[11]See, e.g., Kant, *The Conflict of the Faculties*, 76-77.
[12]*The Conflict of the Faculties*, 119.

the sole condition of eternal life, the only way we can find eternal life in any Scripture whatsoever is by putting it there. For the concepts and principles required for eternal life cannot really be learned from anyone else: *the teacher's exposition is only the occasion [Veranlassung] for him to develop them out of his own reason.*[13]

The German term *Veranlassung* Kant employs here is cognate to the Danish *Anledning* (*Foranledning*) which Kierkegaard repeatedly uses in the *Fragments*. Given the centrality of the issue of historical redemption for Kant in *The Conflict of the Faculties* and his explicit use of this term in connection with it, I think it is reasonable to suppose that from the outset, Kierkegaard's thought experiment in the *Fragments* was stimulated by Kant's argument. It may also be supposed that the Socratic viewpoint presented in the *Fragments* is modeled on the rationalist position in *The Conflict of the Faculties* which Kant, despite his otherwise important concessions there to Christian orthodoxy, continues to defend. If we keep in mind that in the "Preface" of the second edition of the first *Critique*, Kant boldly and explicitly likens his entire intellectual project to that of Socrates,[14] and that in the *Religion*, Kant's preferred term for Christ is "the Teacher," there is reason to think that the Socratic position developed in the *Fragments* has its more proximate representation in Kantian philosophy.[15]

---

[13]" . . . weil die dazu erforderlichen Begriffe und Grundsätze eigentlich nicht von irgend einem andern gelernt, sondern nur bei Veranlassung eines Vortrages aus der eigenen Vernunft des Lehrers entwickelt werden müssen." —Kant, *The Conflict of the Faculties*, 62-63. Kant also uses the term "occasion" in a similar fashion on 127 of *The Conflict of the Faculties* and he uses the term "pupil" (*Lehrling*) in this connection on 121.

[14]Speaking of the purpose of his project of showing the limits of knowledge, Kant states, "But, above all, there is the inestimable benefit, that all objections to morality and religion will be forever silenced, and this in Socratic fashion, namely, by the clearest proof of the ignorance of the objectors." —KRV B xxxi: *Immanuel Kant's Critique of Pure Reason*, trans. Norman Kemp Smith (New York: St. Martin's Press, 1929) 30. Henceforth, all references to this *Critique* are, first, to the corresponding page numbers in the standard edition of the Preussischen Akademie der Wissenschaften and, second, to this translation.

[15]Kierkegaard's tendency to identify Kant with Socrates may have been stimulated by Kierkegaard's great reliance on Wilhelm Gottlieb Tennemann's eleven-volume *Geschichte der Philosophie* (Leipzig, 1798–1819). Tennemann's history is written from a thoroughly Kantian perspective and includes a view of Socrates

The Nature and Status of Historical Knowledge:
PF, 12 line 8 to 13 line 4

Further developing the "Socratic" viewpoint, Kierkegaard-Climacus here makes a distinction between historically acquired, external information and internally developed, religious-ethical truth. My relation to teachers like Socrates or Prodicus, he observes, is of no concern to me "with regard to my eternal happiness" because the truth that bears on such matters "was in me and emerged from me" and is "truth that I had from the beginning without knowing it." To believe that a historical teacher can give us truth of this sort is like thinking that it is the coachman's whipping that pulls a wagon's load. At best, the questions asked by a teacher like Socrates serve only to alert the student that he "must himself possess the truth and acquire it by himself."

Near the very end of Kant's *Critique of Pure Reason* we find a passage in which a similar set of ideas is expressed. This passage is worth quoting in its entirety because it represents Kant's only foray in this lengthy volume into the issue of historical knowledge. Furthermore, it contains ideas that may assist our understanding of Kierkegaard's subsequent argument in the *Fragments* and elsewhere. The passage itself is preceded by a statement by Kant dividing our knowledge into two contrasting "stems": the rational and the empirical. Kant then continues:

> If I abstract from all the content of knowledge, objectively re-garded, then all knowledge, subjectively regarded, is either his-torical or rational. Historical knowledge is *cognitio ex datis*; rational knowledge is *cognitio ex principiis*. However a mode of knowledge may originally be given, it is still, in relation to the individual who possess it, simply historical, if he knows only so much of it as has been given to him from outside (and this in the form in which it has been given to him), whether through im-mediate experience or narration, or (as in the case of general knowledge) through instruction. Anyone, therefore, who has

---

as an opponent of ethical eudaimonism and speculative metaphysics who anticipates Kant's great achievements centuries later. The Tennemann history appears in the catalogue of books in Kierkegaard's library at the time of his death (*Auktionsprotokol*) as Ktl. 815-26.

learnt (in the strict sense of that term) a system of philosophy, such as that of Wolff, although he may have all its principles, explanations, and proofs, together with the formal divisions of the whole body of doctrine, in his head, and, so to speak, at his fingers' ends, has no more than a complete *historical* knowledge of the Wolffian philosophy. He knows and judges only what has been given him. If we dispute a definition, he does not know whence to obtain another. He has formed his mind on another's, and the imitative faculty is not itself productive. In other words, his knowledge has not in him arisen *out* of reason, and although objectively considered, it is indeed knowledge due to reason, it is yet, in its subjective character, merely historical. He has grasped and kept; that is, he has learnt well, and is merely a plaster-cast of a living man. Modes of rational knowledge which are rational objectively (that is, which can have their first origin solely in human reason) can be so entitled subjectively also, only when they have been derived from universal sources of reason, that is, from principles.[16]

Kant's dismissal here of the importance of externally (and, hence also, historically) acquired knowledge surely parallels the "Socratic" position sketched by Kierkegaard at this point in the *Fragments*. This passage is also important, however, because in it, Kant firmly links historical information with the empirical side of cognition. Knowledge is empirical, Kant tells us, if it is acquired from without "whether through immediate experience or narration, or . . . instruction" and, as such, it stands in contrast to knowledge developed in and through rational principles.

Kant's equation here of historical and empirical knowledge has two important implications for our understanding of the *Fragments*. First, it may help explain the curious interweaving of historical and epistemological argumentation found in Kierkegaard's work. It is apparent that in several sections of the *Fragments*, especially the third chapter and the Interlude, Kierkegaard seeks to employ key epistemological concepts like actuality and existence, possibility and necessity to form an understanding of historical knowledge. When we turn to the Interlude, I shall try to indicate how much Kierkegaard relies on Kant's treatment of existence and necessity in the first *Critique*. In view of this, we can see Kant's comment on

---

[16]Kant, KRV A 836 B 864: NKS 655-56.

history near the end of this *Critique* as a stimulus for Kierkegaard's own effort to explore the relationship between the kinds of epistemological issues developed in preceding sections of the *Critique* and the cognitive status of historical knowledge.

A second interesting implication of Kant's remarks relates to Kant's linking of immediate experience, historical narration and external instruction, and his subordination of all these, as forms of empirical knowledge, to inner rational truth. This calls to mind the *Fragments'* treatment of "the contemporary follower" and "the follower at second hand." Kierkegaard-Climacus's insistence that being a contemporary offers no decisive advantage in matters of faith parallels Kant's dismissal of all outer experience, whether direct or narrated, as merely empirical and as inferior to rational "inner" knowledge based on inwardly developed principles. Of course, like Socrates, Kant's rational knowledge (and the religious faith he bases on it) remains essentially self-developed, while Kierkegaard's "faith" is traceable to a divinely bestowed "condition." Despite this important difference, however, and apart from his insistence on the actual fact of Christ's life and death, Kierkegaard shares Kant's belief that there is no real role for external empirical or historical information in the process of salvation.

Finally, before leaving Kant's passage, it is also worth noting his emphasis on the distinction between the the objective and subjective evaluation of an individual's knowledge. Knowledge is essentially worthless, Kant tells us, if it is merely learned from without and not personally appropriated through the exercise of one's reason. Although Kierkegaard's idea of "becoming subjective" has many sources, including some found elsewhere in the corpus of Kant's writings, it is intriguing to think that this brief and unusual passage near the end of the first *Critique* may have stimulated Kierkegaard not only to offer a reformulation of the issue of historical knowledge and faith (the project of the *Fragments*) but also to develop in the *Postscript* his own defense of "subjectivity" in the religious-ethical life.

The Passion of Thought: PF, 37 lines 10-19

Every passion wills its own downfall, Kierkegaard-Climacus tells us, and correspondingly "the ultimate paradox of thought" is "to want to discover something that thought itself cannot think" (PF, 37). Kant would not call thought a "passion"—although he does frequently speak of the "interest" of reason[17]—but Kierkegaard's confident assumption that human knowing drives itself to and beyond its limits again has its counterpart in Kant, whose project in the first *Critique* essentially involves probing the limits of human cognition and exploring the ways in which its inner dynamics lead almost unavoidably to repeated metaphysical violations of these limits. In a passage that could well be superimposed on Kierkegaard's remarks here and that appears at the very beginning of the Preface to the first edition of the *Critique*, Kant signals his focus on reason's impossible drive to completion:

> Human reason has this peculiar fate that in one species of its knowledge it is burdened by questions which, as prescribed by the very nature of reason itself, it is not able to ignore, but which, as transcending all its powers, it is also not able to answer.[18]

Kierkegaard's perhaps implicit reference to this central Kantian idea is a fitting beginning for a portion of the *Fragments* (the third chapter through the Interlude) that makes intensive use of Kant's epistemology.

The Epistemological Status of Existence: PF, 39 line 23 to 42 line 21

This section develops at length Kierkegaard-Climacus's contention that one cannot rationally demonstrate the existence of God or any existing thing. "[W]hether I am moving in the world of sensate palpability or in the world of thought, I never reason in conclusion to existence, but I reason in conclusion from existence" (PF, 40). Kierkegaard's unacknowledged reference to Kant in this section has already been noted by Thulstrup.[19] In the portion of the

---

[17]Kant, *Kritik der Praktischen Vernunft*, Preussischen Akademie der Wissenschaften (Berlin: Georg Reimer, 1907) 120-21, henceforth referred to as KPV; *Critique of Practical Reason*, trans. Lewis White Beck (Indianapolis: Bobbs-Merrill, 1956) 125. All subsequent references to this *Critique* are, first, to corresponding page numbers in the the standard edition of the Preussischen Akademie der Wissenschaften and, second, to this translation.

[18]Kant, KRV A vii: NKS 7.

[19]"Commentary," 213.

first *Critique* entitled "The Impossibility of an Ontological Proof of the Existence of God,"[20] Kant contends that the defenders of this proof erred in believing that *'being'* or existence is a predicate that might be added to the concept of an object. This error, in turn, led them to reason that *'being'* is naturally predicable of the most perfect entity we can conceive, i. e. God, since the omission of a predicate would render this concept less perfect. The mistake here, said Kant, consists in introducing existence into the concept of a thing whose logical possibility is in question. A concept is logically possible, according to Kant, if it is not self-contradictory, but something exists, has *'being'*, only if its object is also given to us in experience. *'Being'*, says Kant, is not a predicate that can be added to the concept of a thing. Rather, it is "the copula of a judgment" that tells us whether a concept, with all its predicates, is or is not given to us in experience. "A hundred real thalers do not contain the least coin more than a hundred possible thalers," Kant observes in a famous remark. "My financial position is, however, affected very differently by a hundred real thalers than it is by the mere concept of them." It follows from this that *'being'* adds nothing at all to the object of a concept:

> If we think in a thing every feature of reality except one, the missing reality is not added by my saying the defective thing exists. On the contrary, it exists with the same defect with which I have thought it, since otherwise what exists would be something different from what I thought [*sonst würde etwas anderes, als ich dachte, existiren*].[21]

This series of ideas and other related elements of Kant's discussion underlie a number of Kierkegaard's remarks in this section of the *Fragments*. Kierkegaard's distinctions between "ideal being" and "factual being," "essence" and "being," and "concept existence" and "real existence" all parallel Kant's distinction between the logical possibility of the object and its real existence. Like Kant, Kierkegaard has no objection in principle to any logically possible elaboration of the concept of God, to what he variously terms developing "the definition of a concept" or "the ideality I have

---

[20]Kant, KRV A 597 B 625-A 600 B 628; NKS 503-505.
[21]Kant, KRV A 600 B 628; NKS 505.

presupposed." But like Kant he objects to the movement from the elaboration of this merely possible concept to the conclusion that God actually exists. Kant's insistence that a judgment of something's existence cannot be logically proven but proceeds from the givenness of the thing in our experience relates closely to Kierkegaard-Climacus's observation that "I never reason in conclusion to existence, but I reason in conclusion from existence." Finally, for Kierkegaard, as for Kant, existence is an all or nothing attribute, not a predicate added to the concept of an object. In a lengthy footnote in this section, Kierkegaard-Climacus tells us that "the Hamlet dialectic, to be or not to be, applies to factual being." And in a remark in this same footnote reminiscent of Kant's jest about the 100 dollars,[22] and Kant's observation that a judgment of existence includes the object with all its defects, Kierkegaard-Climacus tells us that "A fly, when it is, has just as much being as the god."

This last remark merits special attention because it illustrates the subtle, ironic and covert nature of Kierkegaard's relationship to Kant in the *Fragments*. Immediately following his comparison of "the god's" being with a fly's, Kierkegaard-Climacus adds, "with regard to factual being, the stupid comment [*dumme Bemærkning*] I write here has just as much being as Spinoza's profundity." To understand this comment better, it helps to keep in mind that Hegel, in his *Enzyklopädie* (§51), had disputed Kant's argument against the ontological proof on the grounds that, while necessary existence was not logically predicable of ordinary entities, it could be predicated of a perfect entity like God. Hegel then further dismissed as "a barbarism" [*eine Barbarei*] Kant's comparison of God with a mundane hundred dollars. We can be certain that Kierkegaard was aware of this particular intellectual exchange. In the *Postscript*, he playfully appears to agree with Hegel's criticism by terming the Kantian argument "a foolish attack" (*taabeligt Angreb*) on the philosophical thesis of the identity of thinking and being" (CUP, 1: 329). Within the space of a few sentences, however, he then clearly rejects Hegel's view at least where human existence is concerned and ends effectively by upholding Kant's argument.

---

[22]Kierkegaard makes repeated reference to this jest by Kant. See JP, 1:649, 650; 3:3558.

Against this background, we can now appreciate Kierkegaard's subtle irony in this footnote. If Kant would defeat the ontological proof by means of a "foolish" comparison of God to a hundred dollars, he (Kierkegaard-Climacus) would go one step further and "stupidly" compare God with a fly. He would then compound his audacity by declaring that insofar as factual being is concerned his own "stupid" comment has just as much factual being (real weight?) as Spinoza's (Hegel's?) profundity. Within the space of several sentences, in other words, Kierkegaard joins the list on Kant's side against Hegel and, like Kant, uses wit and irony to demolish his opponent.

Finally, any doubt that Kant is a powerful, albeit hidden presence in this section of the *Fragments*, should be put to rest by Kierkegaard-Climacus's use here of the term *accessorium* to describe existence. Although Kant is not connected with this term in the existing text of the *Fragments*, the term is explicitly attributed to him in a draft of this section appearing in Kierkegaard's *Papers* and published in the "Supplement" (PF, 190). Interestingly, as editors have repeatedly observed, Kant seems not to use this term in the first *Critique*, although the idea that existence is something "added on" to a concept with all its predicates is surely contained in his idea that '*being*' is "the copula of a judgment" indicating that the object of a concept is given to us in experience.

However, while Kant does not use the term *accessorium* in the first *Critique*, it does appear in two places in his writings, once in *The Metaphysics of Morals*[23] in connection with a discussion of property rights, and once in a passage in *The Conflict of the Faculties*,[24] a work we know Kierkegaard studied closely. The first passage has little to do with Kierkegaard's concerns, but the passage in *The Conflict of the Faculties* has an intriguing relevance. It follows immediately on Kant's stinging rebuke of Abraham for having placed obedience to an alleged divine command to sacrifice his son over the clear prohibition of such slaughter issuing from rational conscience. Continuing this discussion, Kant then distinguishes the

---

[23]Kant, *Die Metaphysik der Sitten* (1797), Preussischen Akademie der Wissenschaften, VI, 268.
[24]Kant, *The Conflict of the Faculties*, 117.

universal and essential element of biblical teaching, its rational moral content, from what is merely secondary and associated with it, the historically revealed statutory precepts. These secondary elements he calls an *accessorium*.[25] Hence, this employment of the term *accessorium* occurs within a network of ideas at the very center of Kierkegaard's engagement with Kant on the matters of sin, faith and human beings' need for a positive act of historical redemption. Kant's dismissal of the *accessorium* of faith corresponds directly to his indifference to the need for a living, existing historical redeemer. It is worth noting here that this same Kant had shown in the first *Critique* that there is a vast difference between the *concept* of God's existence and his *real* existence, and that in the *Religion* and *The Conflict of the Faculties* Kant had also developed the depth, totality, and inescapability of human sinfulness. Kierkegaard-Climacus's employment of the term *accessorium* in this context, therefore, seems related to his effort in the *Fragments* to turn aspects of Kant's epistemology and philosophy of religion against Kant's impoverished rationalist Christology. In any event, Kierkegaard-Climacus's use of the term *accessorium* connects Kant's epistemology with Kant's treatments of historical faith and strongly suggests that the *Fragments* is in conversation both with the epistemology of the first *Critique* and Kant's focus on historical revelation in *The Conflict of the Faculties*.

The Leap of Faith: PF, 43 line 27

In any effort to demonstrate the existence of God, Kierkegaard-Climacus tells us here, "the existence itself emerges from the demonstration by a leap." The concept of the "leap of faith" is, of course, one of the hallmarks of Kierkegaard's thought. In view of Kierkegaard's remarks in the *Postscript*, his employment of this term and the idea are often seen to have been decisively shaped by Lessing's treatment of the leap (*Sprung*) in his essay "On the Proof

---

[25]In the *Postscript*, Kierkegaard uses the term *accessorium* in just this way to object to the Hegelians excessive involvement with the accidental details of history at the expense of ethical seriousness (CUP, 1:135).

of the Spirit and The Power."[26] Lessing's influence is undoubted, but totally missed by commentators is the fact that Kant himself employs this term in several places in his writings that were surely of interest to Kierkegaard. We have already seen one of these in the *Religion*, a passage where Kant rejects as illegitimate anthropomorphism the "schematization" of God's only begotten son in sensory (temporal-spatial) terms. Kant declares this to be "a mighty [but impermissible] leap" of thought, a confusion of appropriate categories of thought, a μετάβασις εἰς ἄλλο γένος.

Kierkegaard uses both these terms in a passage in the *Postscript* in connection with his specific treatment of Lessing (CUP, 1: 98). Since this side-by-side conjunction of terms, leap (*Sprung*) and the Aristotelian phrase μετάβασις εἰς ἄλλο γένος, also appears in Lessing's essay, there is no special reason to think that Kierkegaard was influenced by Kant's discussion in the *Religion*. However, it becomes less easy to dismiss the impact of Kant on Kierkegaard's employment of these terms if we consider that in the first *Critique* Kant also employs both terms in a powerful passage in the fourth "antinomy of reason" in connection with his effort to refute the cosmological proof of the existence of God.[27] Kant argues in this passage that the cosmological proof goes wrong because those who employ it typically follow an "ascending series of empirical conditions" (causally connected events in time and space) and infer from these the existence of an absolutely necessary first cause outside of time and space. Such a move in Kant's view involves an impermissible "cognitive" leap (he uses the Latin term *saltus*), a μετάβασις εἰς ἄλλο γένος, whereby a category suitable only for empirical knowledge (causality) is illegitimately applied to nonempirical reality.

It is not hard to see that the issue Kant is dealing with in this section of the *Critique*, the effort to demonstrate existence by means of concepts, exactly parallels Kierkegaard's concern in this passage of the *Fragments* and helps explain his assertion that existence can

---

[26]*Gotthold Ephraim Lessings Sämtliche Werke*, 23 vols., ed. Karl Lachmann and Franz Muncker (Leipzig: G. J. Göschen'sche Verlagshandlung, 1886–1924) B. 13, 7; *Lessing's Theological Writings*, ed. and trans. Henry Chadwick (Stanford: Stanford University Press, 1957) 53-55.

[27]Kant, KRV A 457ff. B 485ff.: NKS 418-20.

emerge from these efforts only by a leap. If we keep in mind that Lessing's use of the term leap deals only with historical knowledge and does not touch on the kinds of epistemological issues surrounding existence that interest both Kierkegaard and Kant, we have good reason for believing that it is Kant's discussion of the leap in the first *Critique* that underlies Kierkegaard's use of the term here. This suspicion is reinforced by two other considerations. One is the fact that this section of the *Fragments* is permeated with Kantian themes derived from the first *Critique*. A second is the fact that in the Interlude ahead Kierkegaard uses the Aristotelian phrase μετάβασις εἰς ἄλλο γένος again in Kantian fashion in connection with the epistemological issue of necessary versus contingent existence. Elsewhere, I have argued that Kierkegaard's concept of the leap is more profoundly influenced by Kant's development of this idea than Lessing's.[28] The evidence of the *Fragments* lends support to this view.

Before leaving this section of the *Fragments*, it is perhaps worth noting that Kierkegaard-Climacus's repeated insistence that it makes no sense to "demonstrate" the existence of God may also to some extent be influenced by Kant. In the portion of the first *Critique* entitled "The Discipline of Pure Reason in its Dogmatic Employment," Kant tries to provide a comprehensive discussion of the role of definitions, axioms and demonstrations in mathematics in order to show that none of these tools may appropriately be used in philosophy to generate knowledge of

---

[28]"The Leap of Faith: Kierkegaard's Debt to Kant," *Philosophy and Theology* 3/4 (Summer 1989): 385-421. It is noteworthy that in a footnote in his *Biographia Literaria* (London: J. M. Dent, 1906) 106, Samuel Taylor Coleridge raises the issue of antinomies and uses the phrase μετάβασις εἰς ἄλλο γένος to illustrate the fallacies involved in metaphysical arguments for the existence of God. (Somewhat earlier in his discussion, Coleridge also introduces the topic of the leap, though not in a religious context.) The influence of Kant here—as elsewhere in Coleridge's writings—is clear, but Coleridge's employment of this phrase suggests that Kant's use of it was provocative enough to catch one close reader's eye, as it must have caught Kierkegaard's. In her *Transforming Vision: Imagination and Will in Kierke-gaardian Faith* (Oxford: Clarendon Press, 1991) 147, M. Jamie Ferreira notes the intriguing parallelism between Coleridge and Johannes Climacus's use of this phrase (in the *Postscript*), but she makes no mention of their common Kantian inspiration.

metaphysical realities.[29] A demonstration, according to Kant, is a necessary (apodeictic) proof that involves the construction of mental objects (e.g. geometrical figures) out of *a priori* intuitions in accordance with concepts. Since, as Kant says here, empirical reality may never be said to be necessary, no empirical grounds of proof can ever be called a "demonstration."[30] Whether Kierkegaard-Climacus's repeated use of this term in this section of the *Fragments* is influenced by Kant's discussion at this point in the *Critique* remains uncertain, but the terminological and conceptual parallel is noteworthy.

Physicoteleology: PF, 44 lines 4-6

Kierkegaard-Climacus here credits Socrates with advancing "the physicoteleological demonstration for the existence of God." The phrase "physicoteleological" brings to mind Kant's own preferred term for this proof of God's existence. In the first *Critique* Kant calls this the "physicotheological" proof.[31] He does so as well in the *Critique of Judgment*, although here he also frequently refers to this proof as the *physical teleological* proof.[32]

The Unknown as Frontier: PF, 44 line 17 to 45 line 14

Kierkegaard-Climacus's treatment here of the "unknown" as "the absolutely different" that "cannot be thought" calls to mind two related treatments by Kant of religious speculation at the frontier of knowledge. We find one in a key section of Kant's *Critique of Practical Reason*;[33] the other in *The Conflict of the Faculties*. The

---

[29]Kant, KRV A712 B740-A738 B766: NKS 576-93.

[30]Kant, KRV A 734 B 702: NKS 590.

[31]Kant, KRVA 620 B 648: NKS 518.

[32]Kant, *Kritik der Urteilskraft*, §§85-87; *The Critique of Judgement*, trans. J. H. Bernard (New York: Hafner Press, 1951) 285-304.

[33]Kant's *Critique of Practical Reason* is not among the books listed in the *Auktionsprotokol*. Nevertheless, one of the important questions on Kierkegaard's *Attestats*, his degree examination, concerned how Kant made the transition from ethics to religion. (The questions for this examination are found in LD, 10-16.) This transition is rigorously developed only in one place in Kant's writings, the section of the second *Critique* we are now discussing.

first of these, the passage in the second *Critique*, is immediately preceded by Kant's development of our rational need to "postulate" the existence of God as a concomitant to dedicated moral striving. Kant then explores the conflict this creates between our theoretical reason's ordinary interest in seeing to it that we not transcend the limits of possible experience and our moral or practical-rational "interest" in a postulate of this sort. In view of the conflict, Kant asks which of these interests is primary. This particular transgression of the boundaries of knowledge is allowable, he maintains, "because every interest is ultimately practical," but he quickly adds that such transgression is permitted only for the strictest of moral reasons and, even then, only in ways that minimize the transgression into a realm otherwise inaccessible to reason or experience:

> In fact, so long as practical reason is pathologically conditioned, i.e., as merely regulating the interest of the inclinations by the sensuous principle of happiness, this demand [that theoretical reason should yield primacy to practical reason] could not be made on the speculative reason. Mohammed's paradise or the fusion of the deity of the theosophists and mystics, according to the taste of each, would press their monstrosities [*Ungeheuer*] on reason, and it would as well to have no reason at all as to surrender it in such a manner to all sorts of dreams.[34]

The second passage appears in *The Conflict of the Faculties* at the center of the section dealing with historical revelation versus rational religious knowledge. Here Kant rebuts the charge that rational interpretation of scripture leads to mysticism:

> [T]he sole means of avoiding mysticism (such as Swedenborg's) is for philosophy to be on the lookout for a moral meaning in scriptural texts and even to impose it on them. For unless the supersensible (the thought of which is essential to anything called religion) is anchored to determinate concepts of reason, such as those of morality, fantasy inevitably gets lost in the transcendent, where religious matters are concerned, and leads to an Illuminism in which everyone has his private, inner revelations, and there is no longer any public touchstone of truth.[35]

---

[34]Kant, KPV 120f.: Beck 125.
[35]Kant, *The Conflict of the Faculties*, 81.

Both these remarks find their counterpart in Kierkegaard-Climacus's insistence here that unless the "unknown" (the God) is treated as solely a "frontier" then the one idea about the different will be confused with many such ideas. "The unknown is then in διασπορά [dispersion], and the understanding has an attractive selection from among what is available and what fantasy can think of (the prodigious, the ridiculous, etc.)" (45 lines 8-14).

Faith and Knowledge, PF, 62 lines 1-13

"Faith is not knowledge, for all knowledge is either knowledge of the eternal, which excludes the temporal and the historical as inconsequential, or it is purely historical knowledge, and no knowledge can have as its object this absurdity that the eternal is the historical." Kierkegaard-Climacus's mention here of eternal versus temporal-historical knowledge again recalls the bifurcation of knowledge into the rational and historical-empirical found in Kant's sole treatment of historical knowledge near the end of the first Critique (quoted above). Like the related Kantian passage, this passage goes on to emphasize the philosophical (as opposed to faithful) nature of the learning process, and points out rational knowledge's stress on the inward apprehension of a teaching, not on any attachment to the teacher's person. Of course, Kierkegaard-Climacus here concludes by arguing for the paradox of historical-temporal faith and the teacher-devoted side of religious learning, as Kant does not, but the categories he uses are Kantian.

Without developing the point here, it is worth signalling that the sharp contrast between faith and knowledge offered in this paragraph has a profound resonance in Kantian philosophy. Kant's self-proclaimed objective in the first Critique, as he stated it in the preface to the second edition, is "to deny knowledge, in order to make room for faith."[36] However, it may be objected that the specific basis offered here by Kierkegaard-Climacus for the distinction between faith and knowledge, that faith has as its object the historical existence of the savior-teacher, is decidedly unKantian, since Kant precisely rejects such a role for the historical in religious

---

[36]Kant, KRV B xxx: NKS 29.

salvation. Indeed, in a later passage (87 lines 16-21) Kierkegaard-Climacus goes so far as to say that a nonhistorically apprehended god is not the object of faith but knowledge:

> One does not have *faith* that the god exists [*er til*], eternally understood, even though one assumes that the god exists. That is improper use of language. Socrates did not have faith that the god existed. What he knew about the god he attained by recollection, and for him the existence of the god was by no means something historical.

This view would run directly counter to Kant's particular understanding of the faith-knowledge distinction. Kant believed that any *knowledge* of God is impossible and must involve *faith* since God transcends the temporal and spatial realm to which all our knowledge pertains. Remarkably, however, in a later unused "Note" for *The Book on Adler*, Kierkegaard corrects his statement in the *Fragments*:

> Reminiscent of *Fragments*, in which I said that I do not believe that God exists [*er til* eternally is], but know it; whereas I *believe* that God has existed [*har været til* (the historical)]. At that time I simply put the two formulations together in order to make the contrast clear and did not emphasize that even from the Greek point of view the eternal truth, by being for an existing person, becomes an object of faith and a paradox. But it by no means follows that this faith is the Christian faith as I have now presented it. (JP, 3:3085; PF, 222)

Once again, Greek philosophy may be a stalking horse for Kantianism. Although Socrates and Plato both assumed that religious objects pertain to a timeless realm, it is not clear that within the corpus of their writings we find anything like the very clear distinctions between faith and knowledge developed by Kant in the first *Critique* and elsewhere. For Kant, the "timeless" quality of intelligible realities like God, freedom and immortality necessarily locates them in a noumenal realm beyond the reach of our (temporal-spatial) knowledge, a realm approachable only in faith.[37] In view of this, I think it is reasonable to suppose that in these

---

[37]Kant devotes a lengthy section of the first *Critique* to these epistemological distinctions. See §3 of "The Canon of Pure Reason" entitled "Opining, Knowing, and Believing," A 820 B 848-A 830 B B858: NKS 645-52.

passages in the *Fragments* as elsewhere, Kant is very much on Kierkegaard's mind. Although Kierkegaard clearly wants to distinguish his—the Christian—view from Kant's nonhistorical perspective on faith, he is honest enough to the Kantian standpoint ultimately to acknowledge that it, too, has a faith component and is alert to the distinction between faith and knowledge.

The Nonperceptibility of God: PF, 63 lines 9-14

Kierkegaard-Climacus asks rhetorically whether the contemporary who goes to observe the teacher dares to believe that he is a follower. "Not at all," he replies, "for if he believes his eyes, he is in fact deceived, for the god cannot be known directly." This claim that God cannot be perceived with the senses is an ancient one, but is also a strict consequence of Kant's philosophy of religion. For Kant, God is a "transcendental idea" who, like the related transcendental ideas of freedom and the immortal soul, "cannot be an object of experience."[38] Indeed, Kant insists that because God's cognition exists outside of the phenomenal realm, not only can God "never be an object of intuition to us but [he] cannot be an object of sensible intuition even to himself."[39] Gordon Michalson sums up the parallels between Kant's understanding of God and Kierkegaard's view of the follower's relation to God when he observes that, "Within Kierkegaard's scheme, the divine presence in history is protected by something like Kant's noumenal shield; indeed, Kierkegaard's position is thoroughly Kantian."[40]

This Kantian background also makes clear why the object of faith for Kierkegaard is "the paradox" or "the absurd." If, within the framework of Kant's epistemology, God cannot be thought to have a sensible intuition of things and we cannot "think" the eternal or anything outside the sphere of time-space experience, how much less can we cognize Kierkegaard-Climacus's paradoxical object of faith, the "eternalizing of the historical or the historicizing of the eternal" (61 lines 34-35). It would take me far afield to develop the claim that Kant's epistemology does not necessarily

---

[38]Kant, KRV A 580 B 608: NKS 493; B xxx: NKS 29.
[39]Kant, KRV B 70: NKS 89-90.
[40]*Lessing's "Ugly Ditch,"* 17.

rule out such a paradoxical object, and Kierkegaard may recognize this when he observes in the remark (quoted above) that "from the Greek point of view the eternal truth, by being for an existing person, becomes an object of faith and paradox." The objects of faith that Kant does allow, intelligible causalities like God and freedom that somehow interact with phenomena, similarly relate the eternal and the temporal and are, strictly speaking, "unthinkable" for us, although it is just the point of Kant's epistemology to show that our not being able to "think" something does not mean that it cannot be. It is true that Kant does reject the idea of a historical savior, but on moral, not epistemological grounds. In both the *Religion* and *The Conflict of the Faculties* he concedes the possibility of a "supernaturally begotten" individual who is the example of a man well pleasing to God, but he adds that if we regard this individual as fundamentally different from us, he loses his value as an example of what human beings can become.[41] This returns us to the basic disagreement between Kierkegaard and Kant over the depth of human sin and the remedies it requires. But, as is true elsewhere, this soteriological disagreement seems to be played out on Kantian epistemological terrain.

Before leaving this passage, it is important to note that the idea that human beings are unable sensorily to perceive God is also given vivid expression in *The Conflict of the Faculties* in the context of a discussion that should interest all students of Kierkegaard. This is the portion of *The Conflict* where Kant openly criticizes Abraham for heeding God's command to sacrifice his son. Kant is led into this discussion by his epistemological point and makes a transition to its moral and biblical implications:

> For if God should really speak to man, man could still never *know* that it was God speaking. It is quite impossible for man to apprehend the infinite by his senses, distinguish it from sensible beings, and *recognize* it as such. But in some cases man can be sure that the voice he hears is *not* God's; for if the voice commands him to do something contrary to the moral law, then no matter how majestic the apparition may be, and no matter how

---

[41]Kant, *Religion*, 57; Kant, *The Conflict of the Faculties*, 67.

it may seem to surpass the whole of nature, he must consider it an illusion.[42]

A footnote in the text here introduces the matter of Abraham's conduct as reported in Genesis 22. Although in the *Religion* Kant had questioned whether the historical reports of this episode are to be believed, here he criticizes Abraham directly, faulting him for not openly questioning the validity of the "supposedly divine voice" in view of its inducement to a violation of morality.

This passage in *The Conflict* immediately precedes Kant's introduction of the term *accessorium*. A few pages further on, Kant makes the link between Abraham and Christ by alluding to Christians' use of the sacrifice of Isaac as a "symbol of the world-savior's own sacrifice."[43] It view of the multiple links here to Kierkegaard's authorship and concerns, including Kierkegaard's own strong defense of Abraham in *Fear and Trembling*, we have ample reason to believe that these passages in *The Conflict* were a major stimulus for Kierkegaard's discussion of God, history, and the role of a historical savior in the *Fragments* as well. Indeed, in view of Kierkegaard's deep commitment to Christ's role in our salvation, it must have been a red flag for him to read the summary remark by Kant I quoted earlier: that it is "superstition" (*Aberglaube*, the opposite of faith, *Glaube*) "to hold that historical belief is a duty and essential to salvation."[44]

Interlude

If, as Thulstrup observes, this is "among the most difficult parts of Kierkegaard's writings,"[45] it is so, in part, because once again we have a whole series of references to a complex section of Kant's first *Critique* with the key that might assist us in understanding these references—open citation of Kant's arguments—missing. Some of the specific items found here also have alternative sources elsewhere in the philosophical tradition, and Kierkegaard openly cites many of these. However, most also receive

---

[42]Kant, *The Conflict of the Faculties*, 115.
[43]Ibid., 121n.
[44]Ibid., 119.
[45]"Commentary," 232.

strong expression in the first *Critique,* particularly in those adjacent sections of the *Critique* where Kant rejects the leading metaphysical proofs of God's existence. The structural and substantive parallels between the discussions in the *Fragments* and the *Critique* suggests the degree of Kant's influence on Kierkegaard's work.

Coming into Existence: PF, 73 lines 12-21

Kierkegaard-Climacus here seeks to develop the idea of historical existence and to identify the characteristics of things that come into existence in history. His principal contention is that nothing that comes into existence is necessary since necessity excludes the possibility of change, while all coming into existence involves a change from possibility to actuality.

In the course of developing this idea, Kierkegaard-Climacus insists that the transformation involved in coming into existence entails no change in the *essence* of that which comes into being: "[I]f that which comes into existence does not itself remain unchanged . . . then the coming into existence is not *this* coming into existence." This, of course, reiterates Kant's contention in his refutation of the ontological proof that "[b]y whatever and by however many predicates we may think a thing . . . we do not make the least addition to the thing when we further declare that this thing *is*."[46] Kant immediately follows this remark with the observation: *"Otherwise, it would not be exactly the same thing that exists,* but something more than we had thought in the concept [*Denn sonst würde nicht eben dasselbe, sondern mehr existiren, als ich im Begriffe gedacht hatte*]." In a remark quoted more fully above, he then says that a missing feature of a thing is not added by saying that the thing exists, *"otherwise what exists would be something different from what I thought* [*sonst würde etwas anderes, als ich dachte, existiren*]."

I have italicized parts of Kant's observations here to draw attention to their intriguing parallelism with a sentence a bit further along in Kierkegaard's discussion in the *Fragments* that contains a quoted remark. After observing that the nonbeing abandoned by that which comes into existence must also exist, Kierkegaard-Climacus adds (the italics, again, are my own), "for *otherwise*

---

[46]Kant, KRV A 600 B 628: NKS 505.

'*that which comes into existence would not remain unchanged in coming
into existence*' [*thi ellers 'forblev det Tilblivende ikke uforandret i
Tilblivelsens'*]." In their notes to this passage, the Hongs indicate
that they are unable to locate the source of Kierkegaard-Climacus's
quotation here. They speculate that it may refer to his own
statement earlier in the paragraph "for if that which comes into
existence does not in itself remain unchanged in the change of
coming into existence [*thi dersom det Tilblivende ikke i sig selv
forbliver uforandret i Tilblivelsens Forandring*]." This is certainly a
reasonable supposition. However, the ideas and phrasing are also
close enough to Kant's to strongly recommend him as its original
source. Is it possible that a reference to Kant's writings was
intended by Kierkegaard in some earlier draft of this section but
that ultimately the citation was removed, just as we know was
done with the use of the term *accessorium* in his discussion of "The
Absolute Paradox" in chapter three of the *Fragments*? This would
perhaps explain Kierkegaard-Climacus's reiteration of the idea and
terminology and the sense that the idea is significant enough to
distinguish it with quotation marks. This hypothesis is somewhat
reinforced by the appearance right here, in an epistemological
connection, of the phrase μετάβασις εἰς ἄλλο γένος. I have already
said that Kierkegaard seems to have taken note of Kant's use of
this phrase, and there is evidence elsewhere in the corpus of
Kierkegaard's writings that he associated it at least as much with
Kant's arguments in the first *Critique* as with Lessing.[47]

Annihilating Existence in Thought: PF, 74 lines 8-19

This paragraph, with its insistence that the necessary cannot
"come into existence" because "all coming into existence is a
change" plays an important—even central—role in Kierkegaard-
Climacus's ensuing argument and in his thinking as a whole. The
idea is not a new one. In his *Monadology*, Leibniz articulates it
when he observes, "There are two kinds of truths: those of

---

[47]Kierkegaard employs this phrase twice in the draft of the *Book on Adler* in
references that appears in the *Papirer* at VII[2] B 235, 7 and 81. Lowrie employs only
the latter in his translation (OAR, 61). In both instances the phrase is used to
suggest logical error and is used in tandem with the Kantian term "paralogisms."

reasoning [and] those of *fact*. Truths of reasoning are necessary and their opposite is impossible: truths of fact are contingent and their opposite is possible."[48] The contingency of nonnecessary truth is picked up in Kierkegaard-Climacus's observation here that possibility can be "annihilated" (*tilintetgjort*) in two ways: by the fact that it may be excluded from coming into existence, and by the coming into existence that converts possibility into its opposite, actuality.

Once again, however, Kant's writings appear to offer a more proximate source for Kierkegaard's ideas here. In a passage of the first *Critique* directed against the "cosmological proof" Kant observes:

> [I]f I take the concept of anything, no matter what, I find that the existence of this thing can never be represented by me as absolutely necessary, and that, whatever it may be that exists, nothing prevents me from thinking its non-existence. Thus while I may be obliged to assume something necessary as a condition of the existent in general, I cannot think any particular thing as in itself necessary.

Kant goes on to argue that absolute necessity cannot be found in things but only in our cognitive activity as we seek to unify the world of phenomena. This activity prompts us to locate the ground of things outside the world of causal determination, and erroneously to ascribe real existence to such a ground. The ancients did this, says Kant when they viewed *matter* as the substratum of phenomena and as having absolutely necessary existence. They were mistaken in doing this, Kant observes,

> For there is nothing which absolutely binds reason to accept such an existence; on the contrary, it can always annihilate it in thought [*in Gedanken aufheben*], without contradiction; absolute necessity is a necessity that is to be found in thought alone.[49]

Here and elsewhere, Kant goes beyond Leibniz in providing a specific cognitive test of the contingent nature of existing things: the fact that any such thing can without contradiction be "annuled" or "annihilated" in our thought. This is the very same

---

[48]*Monadology*, §33.
[49]Kant, KRV A 615, 617 B643, 645: NKS 15-16.

concept and terminology that Kierkegaard-Climacus employs to describe what actuality does to possibility as proof of its nonnecessity. Kierkegaard-Climacus's repeated employment of this terminology and idea (e.g. PF, 81 lines 29-30; 83 line 18; 86 lines 4-6) points to Kant's discussion. Indeed, in two of these uses (86 lines 4-6) Kierkegaard-Climacus employs the term *ophævede*, the cognate form of Kant's term *aufheben*.

It is true, of course, that Kierkegaard-Climacus's treatment here of existence and necessity contains features not present in Kant. Kant does not speak of "coming into existence" as a suffering. Nor does he argue that actuality annihilates possibility, although this idea follows from his understanding that possible but nonnecessary things can be thought either to exist or not exist. This idea also follows, as we'll see in a moment, from Kant's conception of the categories of the understanding. But the general lines of Kant's discussion and its proximity to other matters we have seen to be relevant to Kierkegaard again suggest its influence on his thinking.

Possibility and Necessity, PF, 74 lines 20-22; also 75 lines 7-8

Kierkegaard-Climacus here rejects at least two ways previous philosophers have sought to relate possibility and necessity: Hegel's contention that necessity is a unity of possibility and actuality and Aristotle's view that everything necessary is possible.[50] The issues here are complex, but it is worth noting that Kierkegaard-Climacus's position most closely approximates the one established by Kant in connection with the "pure concepts of the understanding" listed in his "Table of Categories."[51] Within the category of "modality," Kant lists three conceptual pairs: Possibility/Impossibility;Existence/Nonexistence;Necessity/Contingency. For Kant these are three different kinds of judgments which are applied, in binary fashion, to exclusive domains of thought. When I make a judgment of existence or nonexistence (actuality or non-actuality), for example, I am synthesizing elements of experience and neither the categories of possibility or necessity apply.

---

[50]For the appropriate references, see PF, 299-300.
[51]Kant, KRV A 80 B 106: NKS 113.

Similarly, the judgment of possibility/nonpossibility applies to concepts capable or incapable of being synthesized in thought and is distinct both from the sphere of necessary ideas (that cannot be thought otherwise) and from actually existing things. Kierkegaard's rejection of Hegel's and Aristotle's views, therefore, seems to draw upon Kant's understanding of the categories. It is well known that Kierkegaard was fascinated with the idea of a "category." Stephen N. Dunning also points out that the three chapter titles in the first part of Kierkegaard's dissertation *The Concept of Irony* exhibit the employment of Kant's three categories of modality.[52] These titles are "The Conception Made Possible," "The Conception Made Actual," and "The Conception Made Necessary." In view of this, it seems reasonable to suppose that Kierkegaard is once again involved here in a Kantian position taking in opposition to his Hegelian foes.

Simultaneity: PF, 75 line 32 to 76 line 6

We have already discussed Kant's bifurcation of knowledge into two opposing "stems" the rational and the empirical, with the latter encompassing historical as well as immediately experienced knowledge. It is now worth adding, however, that Kant's understanding of causality, with its implication of succession in time, also applies to simultaneously occurring but causally related events, such as the impression made in a soft cushion by a ball. Discussing simultaneous occurrence in the first *Critique* as posing a "difficulty" for the idea that causality involves succession, Kant removes the problem by stating that it is the "order" of events in time, not the lapse between them, that is relevant to our determination of causality. A is the cause of B if it is necessarily thought of as present at the occurrence of B, whatever the time lapse between them. "The time between the causality of the cause and its immediate effect may be [a] vanishing [quantity], and they may thus be simultaneous," Kant says, "but the relation of the one to the other will always still remain determinable in time."[53]

---

[52]*Kierkegaard's Dialectic of Inwardness* (Princeton: Princeton University Press, 1985) 13.

[53]Kant, KRV A 203 B 248: NKS 228.

Against this background we can better understand Kierkegaard-Climacus's observation here that even "something whose
coming into existence is a simultaneous coming into existence
(*Nebeneinander* [side-by-side], space) [and] has no other history
than this" belongs to nature and, like nature, "does have a history." This, I would argue, merely carries forth Kant's contention
that simultaneity can involve causality, that all causally conditioned events are sequentially located in time and, that, as Kant
explicitly says at the end of the first *Critique*, that all causal occur-
rences belong to the sphere of the empirical/historical. In their
notes to this passage, the Hongs suggest that Kierkegaard's use of
the German *Nebeneinander* may be a reference either to Hegel or to
the Romantic philosophy of nature found in Heinrich Steffens or
Schelling (PF, 303), even though the term is actually used by Hegel
in a quite different context.[54] Since Kant does not use the term
Nebeneinander in this way, the Hongs may be right about a non-
Kantian influence here. Nevertheless, the basic idea is thoroughly
Kantian.

The Source of Illusion: PF, 81 line 14 to 83 line 10

This passage and those following develop a series of ideas,
some of which are explicitly attributed to the sceptics, to Plato,
Aristotle and Descartes. The leading one of these is the idea that
"immediate sensation and cognition cannot deceive." Kierkegaard-
Climacus explicitly finds this idea in the sceptics, who traced error
not to sensation but to the conclusions we draw from it. He also
mentions its presence in Plato and Aristotle and, at somewhat
greater length, Descartes, who locates error in the will's haste in
drawing conclusions. Kant is not mentioned here in any way,
although he makes the same point very clearly in a passage at the
beginning of the second main division of the first *Critique*, the
"Transcendental Dialectic":

> truth or illusion is not in the object, insofar as it is [sensibly]
> intuited, but in the judgment about it, insofar as it is thought. It
> is therefore correct to say that the senses do not err—not because
> they always judge rightly but because they do not judge at all.

---

[54]*Enzyklopädie* §254.

> Truth and error, therefore, and consequently also illusion as leading to error, are to be found in the judgment, *i.e.* only in the relation of the object to our understanding.[55]

Kierkegaard-Climacus's argument in the passage at hand is that historical events have an elusive quality not present in immediate sensory experience. This suggests to him that the understanding of these events derives from the activity of an "organ" which he here terms belief (*Tro*). Further on, he is clear to add that he uses a "direct and ordinary meaning" of this term and not its "eminent sense" as religious faith (87: lines 12-14). If we keep in mind that for Kant, empirical relationships of cause and effect require the exercise of the faculty of judgment, we can see similarities and differences in the two thinker's positions at this point. Kant, for example, does not typically emphasize the unsureness of our empirical causal knowledge, and he does not really discuss the volitional element in such knowledge in the way this is emphasized here by Kierkegaard-Climacus (who is perhaps influenced in this by Descartes's emphasis on the role of volition in such determinations[56]). Nevertheless, none of these ideas is opposed to Kant's understanding of judgment, and Kierkegaard's broad insistence that any conclusion about the meaning or causes of a sequence of events in time requires a nonsensory conceptual act of decision conforms to Kant's thinking. Kant also anticipates Kierkegaard in applying these ideas to historical religious judgments. In the *Foundations of the Metaphysics of Morals* and the *Religion*, as I said earlier, Kant refuses to give any determinative significance to the example provided by Jesus in history precisely because he is convinced that finding a universal moral meaning in historical persons or events involves a judgment that begins with the independent exercise of our own moral reason. (The exercise of judgement, for Kant, always involves the bringing of single instances under universal rules[57]). Kierkegaard would, of course, reject Kant's insistence on the self-initiated feature of such acts of religious judgment (belief in the "eminent" sense). God provides

---

[55]Kant, KRV A 293 B 350: NKS 297.
[56]Selections from Descartes's writings on this subject appear in PF, 338-39.
[57]Kant, *Kritik der Urteilskraft*, 179; *Critique of Judgement*, 15.

the condition for the proper exercise of this organ-faculty. But once this condition is bestowed, as he says, "everything is again structured Socratically" (PF, 65 lines 33-34), the appropriate judgment emerges from within us, and is not compelled by external, sensory events.

The Desirability of God's Nonpresence:, PF, 105 lines 5-9 and 25-28

Immediate contemporaneity with the god, Kierkegaard-Climacus argues here, is of no real advantage in matters of faith. It provides merely an occasion for receiving (or not receiving) the condition for learning bestowed by the god and it is always confronted by the paradoxical nature of what must be learned. Consequently, if the devoted follower really understood himself, he would eschew outward evidences of the god and would have to wish that his contemporaneity "would be terminated by the departure of the god from the earth."

This is a fitting passage to end our review of Kierkegaard's (possible) employments of Kant's thought, since the idea expressed here has a central place in both Kant's and Kierkegaard's writings. Kierkegaard-Climacus's devaluation of contemporaneity to the point where the devoted follower might be expected to wish the God out of his sight anticipates, of course, the profound presentation of the concept of truth—and faith—in the *Postscript* as "an objective uncertainty, held fast through appropriation with the most passionate inwardness" (CUP, 1:203).

Ordinarily, we do not associate Kant with a view of this sort, but at the end of the second *Critique* Kant introduces a very similar understanding of religious faith. Kant had previously developed the notion of faith in God as a desperate but necessary presupposition (or postulate) of our commitment to morality. Because this faith lacks grounding in objective experience, it is never entirely certain, although its important relationship to moral commitment and its nonempirical content also render it immune to refutation. As a result, says Kant, this faith "can therefore often waver even in the well disposed but can never fall into unbelief."[58] One might think that the limited certainty of this practical faith is

---

[58]Kant, KPV, 146: Beck, 151.

an unfortunate obstacle to the ambitions of practical reason. But in a closing series of remarks, Kant says that it is good that the objects of practical faith remain distant and uncertain. For what would happen if the opposite were true? Then, Kant observes,

> instead of the conflict which now the moral disposition has to wage with the inclinations and in which, after some defeats, moral strength of mind may be gradually won, God and eternity in their awful majesty would stand unceasingly before our eyes. . . . Thus most actions conforming to the law would be done from fear, few would be done from hope, none from duty.[59]

Kant does not say that the genuinely moral religious person wishes that God would depart from sight, but the thought is the same and his idea may be closer to Kierkegaard's than the source which Kierkegaard-Climacus openly attributes. At this point in the *Fragments*, Kierkegaard-Climacus has an unnamed interlocutor observe that the author has again chosen to "mix in" a phrase from someone else, in this case from the Gospel of John (16:7). But the idea in John, that the disciples are fortunate to have Christ depart so that they may receive the "comforter," is only loosely related to Kierkegaard-Climacus's discussion. Once again, despite this playful excursion into the matter of sources and attribution—a theme repeated throughout the *Fragments*—no mention is made of Kant.

These last perhaps implicit borrowings from Kant in the *Fragments* (81 line 14 to 83 line 10; 105 lines 5-9 and 25-28) epitomize Kierkegaard's relationship to the theological-philosophical tradition and to Kant. Kierkegaard draws freely on this tradition and on Kant's philosophy while turning both to his purposes. An important difference, however, is that while other sources are named or have phrases from or paraphrases of their arguments inserted into the text, Kant goes entirely unnamed. So effaced is Kant from the *Fragments*, in fact, that with only one or two small exceptions, the editorial tradition represented by Thulstrup and the Hongs has

---

[59]Kant, KPV 147: Beck 152. Cf. Kant's *Lectures on Philosophical Theology*, trans. Allen W. Wood and Gertrude M Clark (Ithaca NY: Cornell University Press, 1978) 123.

picked up none of the parallels or possible borrowings we have noted.

I shall not try to speculate on the reasons for Kierkegaard's failure to cite Kant here and in other key places in his writings. (Elsewhere, I partly attribute this to Kierkegaard's complex effort to critique Hegelian philosophy while remaining aloof from the philosophical controversies of the day and while remaining un-identified with a philosopher, Kant, widely regarded by the smug Hegelians as passé.[60]) Nor shall I try at the close of this brief essay to undertake the larger conceptual task of relating Kierkegaard's specific thought-project, his defense of the idea of a historical redeemer, to Kant's own tortured wrestling with this question in the *Religion* or *The Conflict of the Faculties*. As I said at the outset, the greatest interest of the *Fragments* lies in the way Kierkegaard turns the whole of Kant's philosophy of religion against him: using Kant's notions of freedom, ethics, sin, and his understanding of the nature and limits of human knowledge precisely to "reinvent" the historically rooted faith that Kant rejects.

My purpose here has been more limited. I have tried to show that although Kant is not once mentioned, the argument of the *Fragments* unfolds in intense conversation with his philosophy. I may be wrong about this but I hope I have marshalled enough evidence at least to stimulate the reader to do what Kant and Kierke-gaard would surely recommend: return to the texts and judge for yourself.

---

[60]See the conclusion to my *Kierkegaard and Kant: The Hidden Debt*.

10

The Illusory Grandeur of Doubt: *The Dialectic of Subjectivity in* Johannes Climacus

Stephen N. Dunning

As our contemporary age gropes its way through the maze of poststructuralist texts-within-texts and texts-about-texts, no doubt Kierkegaard is gazing upon us with a gently ironic smile. For no one today is a more artful Daedalus than that nineteenth-century Danish creator of a pseudonymous literary labyrinth. And no subject illustrates the skill with which Kierkegaard develops—or better, unveils—the full dimensions of a problem through a number of various and contrary voices than a topic which is sacred to every deconstructor: doubt. In the literary and philosophical marketplace of the present age, hardly a transaction can occur that has not been conceived in and confirmed by a skeptical posture.

The insightful comments on doubt by Kierkegaard's pseudonyms initially applaud its attractions, then explore its conundrums, and finally expose its pretensions. In the caustic wit of A in the first part of *Either/Or*, we find an expression of Faustian doubt that makes even the most radical contemporary skeptic seem healthy and humdrum. In his rebuttal to A, Judge William, as is his wont, affirms the letter but not the spirit of what A has said. The earnest Judge writes that "the grandeur of doubt" is its intellectual and impersonal character, but then he goes on to describe it in pallid terms that would surely draw mockery if not horror from A. It is typical of the Judge that, in the process of attempting to correct A, he apparently stumbles over a profound truth—this one concerns the relation of doubt to personality—that he does not (cannot?)

develop but that other pseudonyms will. *Fear and Trembling,* attributed to Johannes de Silentio, opens with a brief meditation on the authenticity of Descartes's method of doubt. But it is Johannes Climacus, alone among the pseudonymous authors, who is portrayed as one obsessed with the problem of doubt. In his posthumously published manuscript entitled *Johannes Climacus, or De omnibus dubitandum est,* Kierkegaard describes young Climacus as a person who probes dialectically the possibility of grounding philosophy in doubt. Analysis of the text of *Johannes Climacus* reveals a position quite at odds with that of Judge William, namely, that doubt, however intellectual and impersonal it may seem to be, is in fact a volitional and personal matter. In his own literary productions—*Philosophical Fragments* and *Concluding Unscientific Postscript*—Climacus presupposes this result and develops some of its ramifications. The one Kierkegaardian pseudonym for whom it might be claimed that he actually achieves closure with regard to doubt is Anti-Climacus. A brief look at *The Sickness unto Death* will show, in conclusion, that the path beyond doubt leads through despair and ultimately to faith.[1]

The Grandeur of Doubt

Given its imaginative literary power, it is hardly surprising that *Either/Or* is Kierkegaard's most widely appreciated work. Religious themes, which dominate most of his other works, are present only at the margins of part 1, a collection of essays by the pseudonymous A in which the aesthetic doctrines of Romanticism are parodied with merciless wit. Part 2 constitutes an ethical criticism of the presuppositions and implications of A's aesthetic position. There religious language moves closer to the center, but always in fundamental continuity with the central ethical concepts. At no point in part 2 does Judge William either recognize or affirm the

---

[1]An early version of this paper was presented to the New Haven Theology Group in March 1992. I am grateful for the comments I received there, and especially for additional suggestions made later by Stephen Crites. Thanks also to Ed Drott for his helpful responses.

tension between the ethical and the religious that Kierkegaard presents so starkly in *Fear and Trembling*.[2]

To convey succinctly the primary message of the two large and multilayered volumes of *Either/Or* is not easy, but the task can be broached by a brief reflection upon their title. "Either/Or" is a phrase that is often heard from the Judge, for whom the primary task in life is that of choosing to be ethically responsible for oneself: "The Either/Or I have advanced is, therefore, in a certain sense absolute, for it is between choosing and not choosing. But since the choice is an absolute choice [to be ethical and to exclude the aesthetic], the Either/Or is absolute" (EO, 2:177-78). A is predictably reticent on the subject of ethical choice, yet one of his introductory "Diapsalmata" is entitled "Either/Or," and it encapsulates his view of the whole matter: "Whether you marry or you do not marry, you will regret it either way" (EO, 1:38). This pearl of skeptical wisdom should provoke even the most jaded imagination. Nothing can be trusted: no other person, no relationship, no decision or action, not even one's self in a thoroughly solitary state. The subsequent essays illustrate this view, portraying in turn persons who deceive, relationships that end in sorrow, and individuals who seek contentment by denying or dissimulating their actual desire. In his refusal to enter authentically into the fabric of human relationships, A portrays and personifies the subtle brutality of aesthetic negativity.

Judge William opposes this jaundiced view with all the ethical passion and dialectical ingenuity he can muster. In a long plea to A to choose to be the person he is, even if it means choosing his own despair, the Judge devotes two very suggestive pages to the contrast between doubt and despair. He has, he writes, often reflected on the difference between the claim of modern philosophy

---

[2]*Either/Or* part 2 concludes with a sermon entitled "The Upbuilding That Lies in the Thought That in Relation to God We Are Always in the Wrong." This sentiment certainly stresses the tension between the ethical and the religious. Moreover, Judge William introduces the sermon as an "Ultimatum" that states precisely what he, the Judge, means to say. Despite this claim, the sermon is very difficult to reconcile with the Judge's reiterated belief that each individual can and must choose to be an ethical self, a choice that will, he seems to assume, fulfill the demands of the religious.

to begin all speculation with doubt and the actual experience of despair. Then he recounts the fruit of these reflections:

> Doubt is thought's despair; despair is personality's doubt. That is why I cling so firmly to the defining characteristic "to choose"; it is my watchword, the nerve in my life-view, and that I do have, even if I can in no way presume to have a system. Doubt is the inner movement in thought itself, and in my doubt I conduct myself as impersonally as possible. I assume that thought, when doubt is carried through, finds the absolute and rests therein; therefore, it rests therein not pursuant to a choice but pursuant to the same necessity pursuant to which it doubted, for doubt itself is a qualification of necessity, and likewise rest.
>
> This is the grandeur of doubt; this is why it so often has been recommended and promoted by people who hardly understood what they were saying. But its being a qualification of necessity indicates that the whole personality is not involved in the movement. (EO, 2:211-12)

The fundamental difference between doubt and despair, according to Judge William, is that doubt is impersonal whereas despair is profoundly personal.[3] Doubt is an operation of thought that remains obedient to the law of necessity, which governs all logical thought, and that ends by resting in the dialectical "absolute" in which subject and object are fully adequate to one another. This is, the Judge avers, its grandeur. In contrast, despair is a free choice. Therefore it constitutes "an expression of the total personality" and implicitly includes a fair measure of anguish (in contrast to the restful harmony that rewards doubt). Yet the grandeur of doubt is also its "imperfection," for it is an expression "only of thought." Thus the "supposed objectivity" of doubt is undermined by the fact that it requires "a natural aptitude" (EO, 2:212), presumably an aptitude for thinking. Despair, however, requires no aptitude whatsoever. Anyone can despair, including the philosopher who has struggled with and finally conquered all

---

[3]Niels Thulstrup is one of the few scholars who takes note of this connection between doubt and despair. See *Kierkegaard's Relation to Hegel*, trans. George L. Strengren (Princeton: Princeton University Press, 1980) 332. Thulstrup also offers an unusually extensive discussion of *Johannes Climacus*, most of which he devotes to defending his thesis that Kierkegaard had nothing in common with Hegel (296-310).

doubt! A doubter need not be in despair, however, for doubt is an expression of only a part—the impersonal part—of the personality. All that doubt requires is intellectual talent and an acceptance of logical necessity, but despair demands passion (not the Judge's term) and an embrace of the freedom to choose (EO, 2:213).

A word of caution is necessary concerning the Judge's use of language in this analysis of doubt and despair. To say that "doubt is thought's despair" and "despair is personality's doubt" could be taken to imply a continuity between them, as though doubt were a merely intellectual form of despair as such, and, conversely, despair were an all-encompassing intensification of doubt.[4] However, as the Judge's discussion makes clear, it is the *contrast* between doubt and despair that preoccupies him. Doubt is merely intellectual, whereas despair involves the total personality. Doubt does not necessarily involve despair, nor must every despairing person engage in intellectual doubt. According to Judge William's formula: doubt is to thought as despair is to personality. That is the extent of his claim. Each relation can help us to understand the other, but neither doubt nor despair presupposes or promotes the other.

It is also significant that the "supposed objectivity" of doubt is never seriously questioned by the Judge. His reservation about this "imperfection" results from its merely intellectual nature and the inevitable distinctions it will create among people, for some are certainly more gifted intellectually than others. But doubt remains, for the Judge, an activity in which "I conduct myself as impersonally as possible" (EO, 2:211). This means that doubt is object-oriented thought, and that self-doubt would equally be a thought in which the self views itself as an object. Despair, however, is an action of the total personality: it is fundamentally a subjective state of being. To paraphrase the Judge's characterization of doubt, in despair "I conduct myself as personally as possible." We can infer

---

[4]It has often been remarked that the Danish for "doubt" and "despair" connect the two concepts in a way that is impossible in English. In short, "despair" (*Fortvivelse*) is linguistically represented as an intensification of "doubt" (*Tvivl*), just as the German *Verzweiflung* ("despair") intensifies *Zweifel* ("doubt"). Other words that exploit the root *tvi* or "two" (as in *two*-mindedness) are *tvetydighed* ("ambiguity") and *tvivlesyg* ("skepticism"). On the dichotomous nature of doubt, see *Johannes Climacus*, 169.

from this that despair focuses upon the self even more intensively than self-doubt, for it penetrates the self-as-subject, whereas self-doubt merely analyses the self-as-object. Indeed, the Judge implies that part of the grandeur of doubt is the capacity to direct its energy towards any object whatsoever (*qua* object), while despair occurs when a "total personality" is caught in a dialectical loop embracing other objects only in their relation to the self.

The importance of doubt's orientation toward objects is brought home by the tribute that Johannes de Silentio pays to Descartes in the preface to *Fear and Trembling* (FT, 5-6). Ever eager to subvert Hegelianism,[5] Kierkegaard has de Silentio criticize contemporary philosophy by eulogizing Descartes as one who "did what he said and said what he did." More to the point, Descartes "did not doubt with respect to faith," even when reason suggested it; nor did he "make it obligatory for everyone to doubt." In other words, doubt should neither be directed toward objects that are inappropriate for a merely intellectual and impersonal approach, nor be expanded into a moral imperative without which knowledge cannot be validated. Doubt has its place, but must also be kept in its place. De Silentio closes this brief discussion with the observation that the ancient Greeks assumed that doubt, like faith, is "a task for a whole lifetime, because proficiency in doubting is not acquired in days and weeks," a clear contrast with the doubt with which "everyone begins in our age" (FT 6-7).[6]

Like Judge William, Johannes de Silentio affirms doubt as impersonal thought. Rather than criticize this fundamental principle

---

[5]According to Gregor Malantschuk, the primary "Hegelian" target of Kierke-gaard's discussion of doubt in *Johannes Climacus* is H. L. Martensen, who "excelled in the interpretation of Descartes's *De omnibus dubitandum est*." See *Kierkegaard's Thought*, ed. and trans. Howard V. Hong and Edna H. Hong (Princeton: Princeton University Press, 1971) 208. No doubt these remarks in *Fear and Trembling* are also directed toward Martensen. For a fuller account of the career of Denmark's leading "(modified) Hegelian," see Bruce H. Kirmmse, *Kierkegaard in Golden Age Denmark* (Bloomington: Indiana University Press, 1990) 169-97.

[6]In *For Self-Examination*, Kierkegaard carries his ridicule ever further: "And while one doubted everything, there was still one thing beyond all doubt—namely, that by means of this ('One must have doubted everything'), one guaranteed oneself an anything-but-doubtful, indeed, an utterly solid position in society, as well as great honor and prestige among men" (FSE, 68).

of modern philosophy, they both understand doubt as a valid and vital—but never more than partial—aspect of the personality. However, it is precisely this qualified embrace of doubt as a legitimately *im*personal "grandeur of thought" that Johannes Climacus questions and finally rejects.

Doubting Doubt

We come now to Kierkegaard's primary text on the subject of doubt, *Johannes Climacus, or De omnibus dubitandum est*. Kierkegaard never published this work, nor did he attribute it either to himself or to a pseudonym, so it inhabits, as it were, a limbo of anonymity.[7] Be that as it may, Climacus is presented as a young man who attempts to think through the meaning of the philosophical injunction "de omnibus dubitandum est," which the Hongs translate "everything must be doubted" (JC, 131n.).

The narrative introductions to *Johannes Climacus* and its pars prima relate the life and character of Johannes Climacus in a style that demonstrates Kierkegaard's skill in merging philosophical argument with ironical fiction. At the end of the second of these introductions, it is reported that Climacus has heard three principal statements concerning the relation between the *de omnibus dubitandum est* thesis and philosophy: "(1) *philosophy begins with doubt*; (2) *in order to philosophize, one must have doubted*; (3) *modern philosophy begins with doubt*" (JC, 132). Each of the three chapters of the pars prima is devoted to one of those statements in thesis form. It is in these three chapters that the issue of doubt is explored in depth.

The strategy employed in *Johannes Climacus* resembles that found in *Philosophical Fragments*. Both texts exploit the concept of history to undermine the assumption that belief in philosophical truths is as objective and eternal as the purported truths themselves. Although the oft-cited aphorism, "truth is subjectivity," will

---

[7]The Hongs assume that it is *by* Johannes Climacus as well as a third-person narrative *about* him (JC, xv-xvi). But, in a note on the title page of pars secunda (JC, 161), the author writes of his "solicitude" for the young Climacus, and thereby clearly establishes an authorial voice distinct from that of Climacus (certainly for pars secunda and probably for the entire book).

not appear until *Concluding Unscientific Postscript*, the doctrine itself is already implied in both of the earlier Climacus texts.

Chapter 1 takes up the third thesis first on the basis that it appears to be an historical claim, whereas the first and second theses seem philosophical in nature. The historical element in the proposition that "modern philosophy begins with doubt" is, of course, the implication that philosophy has somehow changed in the modern period, so that it now begins with doubt in a sense that was not true in the premodern period. Several of the Hongs' notes to the introduction helpfully provide texts which reflect the extent to which Hegel and Martensen subscribed to this view, thereby demonstrating its *prima facie* plausibility: Descartes's *De omnibus dubitandum est* was enthusiastically affirmed and generalized as an "absolute beginning" by Hegel, who in turn was echoed by Martensen in the claim that "doubt is the beginning of wisdom." Even more relevant to Kierkegaard's concern is Martensen's assertion that Descartes's method of doubt was not "a doubt about this or that but about everything" (JC, 322-24).

Kierkegaard playfully explores the presuppositions of this third ("historical") thesis in such a way as to show its inner self-contradictions (JC, 133-35). If older philosophy had not begun with doubt, and yet still qualified as philosophy, then it would appear that doubt is not essential to philosophy, and therefore recent philosophy could also start with something other than doubt. This would be the case, for example, if one were to claim that Descartes and other modern philosophers just happened to begin their philosophizing with doubt: the thesis is thoroughly historical, but it is also trivial. On the other hand, it might be claimed that modern philosophy had instituted doubt as a new yet necessary beginning for all future philosophy. In this case, doubt would become essential rather than trivial in relation to philosophy. This would have the effect of transforming the third thesis into the ahistorical first thesis—that true philosophy begins with doubt—and, at the same time, relegating all older philosophy to the status of pre- or pseudophilosophy.

Climacus considers this a very sloppy conceptual state of affairs, but decides to persevere nonetheless and ask how, if modern philosophy begins with doubt, it came to do so. Did it occur by accident or by necessity? Here he again encounters the same problem (JC, 136-38). Either all true philosophy necessarily begins with doubt; or doubt became the starting point for philosophy at a particular historical moment. But that would mean that modern philosophy *began* to "begin with doubt" by accident, and then the whole claim is merely a trivial and misleading contradiction of the first thesis, due to the indignity that it appears to claim that "the essential happened by accident" (JC, 136). If, on the contrary, modern philosophy *began* to "begin with doubt" by necessity, then it must have begun with doubt all along, meaning that it must be "in continuity with an earlier philosophy" (JC, 137). In other words, only if the modern entry of doubt into philosophy were the consequence of a cause—that is, of an earlier philosophy—could it be considered necessary. Yet, in order for the thesis to avoid triviality, one would have to presuppose that a "leap" had occurred from the earlier causative philosophy-without-doubt to the modern consequence of a philosophy-requiring-doubt.

In short, Climacus finds himself frustrated in his effort to understand the third ("historical") thesis without either collapsing it into the first ("philosophical") thesis or rendering it "a historical triviality" (JC, 139). He finds that others take the first path, failing to distinguish between the two theses at all. With a marvelous stroke of Kierkegaardian irony, Climacus is described as pondering modern philosophy as a mystery that is "simultaneously the historical and the eternal, . . . a union similar to the union of the two natures in Christ" (JC, 139-40). He also satirizes Hegel by observing that such a union of eternal truth with the historical could occur only if "philosophy's historical progress was absolutely identical with the idea's own movement.[8] But then such a step forward would not be a historical movement" (JC, 140).

The result of all these dialectical machinations is, for Climacus, both confusion and a presentiment:

> He had the presentiment that it [the first thesis] must be something out of the ordinary; he had the presentiment that to be a

---

[8]Robert L. Perkins discusses, with frequent reference to *Philosophical Fragments* and *Concluding Unscientific Postscript*, how Kierkegaard and Hegel differ from each other and from the Greek skeptical tradition on the matter of doubt in "Beginning the System: Kierkegaard and Hegel," in *Akten des XIV Internationalen Kongresses für Philosophie* (Vienna: Herder, 1968) 478-85.

philosopher these days must be something indescribably difficult. If modern philosophy is like that, it must, of course, be the same for the individual philosopher. Thus the individual philosopher *must become conscious of himself, and in this consciousness of himself also become conscious of his significance as a moment in modern philosophy; in turn modern philosophy must become conscious of itself as an element in a prior philosophy, which in turn must become conscious of itself as an element in the historical unfolding of the eternal philosophy* (JC, 140).

Climacus finds this thought so "enormous" and Sisyphean that it is difficult to think "correctly and definitely" (JC, 140). Ever the dialectician, he also discerns that it is so deceptive in its positive appearance that it is actually an expression of skepticism, for it reduces philosophy to the realization that "the individual's knowledge was always merely knowledge about himself as a moment and about his significance as a moment" (JC, 141). This comment signals that the primary concern of the passage quoted above—indeed, of the entire chapter—is not the abstract issue of modern philosophy but the concrete question of the modern philosopher. To be sure, modern philosophy must become conscious of itself as an element within eternal philosophy. But that claim is only the corollary of the more important insight, namely, that every individual philosopher comes to philosophy as a distinct "moment" in the Hegelian sense of a cognitive-historical perspective (but without the connotation of grasping a systematic totality). It is not granted to philosophical persons to comprehend the relation of the historical to the eternal in philosophy: that is "reserved for the deity" (JC, 142). All that is available to ordinary mortals is a realistic self-awareness about their own particularity as individuals who have specific questions and presuppositions. Any insights they might have into eternal truths will come to them only in and through their concrete particularity.

The second chapter deals with the first thesis, the "philosophical" statement that "philosophy begins with doubt." Climacus is, we are told, attracted to this thesis, for one of his primary objectives is to begin to philosophize, and this thesis tells him how to do that. In contrast, the third thesis is merely an historical claim and the second simply stipulates that doubt must have happened before philosophy begins, but not how that beginning can be accomplished.

Immediately Climacus spies an inversion: just as the apparently historical third thesis does not make sense until it is collapsed into the philosophical first thesis, the philosophical first thesis conceals within itself an historical presupposition! The basis for this claim is the general observation that "doubt is precisely a polemic against what went before" (JC, 145). Climacus reflects upon how this assertion of discontinuity between any philosophy and the antecedent philosophy contrasts with the assumption of continuity between them expressed in the Greek belief that "philosophy begins with wonder" (JC, 145). The next paragraph presents his conclusion that the first thesis turns out to be so historical as to be "identical" with the third. Although he does not fully explain his reasoning, it appears to have two aspects: his observation that the demand that philosophy begin with doubt is not true of Greek (=premodern) philosophy; and his belief that both the first and the third theses embroil the would-be philosopher in the paradoxical relation of the eternal to the historical (the subject of *Philosophical Fragments*).

Once again, Climacus's central concern is not to speculate about philosophy but to begin to philosophize, and so he goes on to the question of how the single individual relates to the first thesis. Whereas reflection upon the third thesis had led to the realization that every individual must relate to philosophy as a particular moment, here reflection upon a general philosophical formulation results in the conclusion that, if philosophy really does *begin* with doubt, then no existing individual can ever make an actual beginning in philosophy at all!

Climacus first reports how happy he had at first been to learn from "one of the philosophizers" that "'[t]his thesis does not belong to any particular philosopher; it is a thesis from the eternal philosophy, which anyone who wishes to give himself to philosophy must embrace'" (JC, 147). But his happiness is short-lived, for he soon realizes that an eternal philosophy must either be abstract and beyond time, and thus have no beginning at all; or it must carry its history hidden within itself waiting to be transfigured into eternal life; but then the "eternity" of philosophy is merely an expectation for the future. In either case, the single individual in the here-and-now is given no help at all in learning how to get started in philosophy. Climacus finds some comfort in the threefold

Hegelian distinction between the "*absolute* beginning," which is the concept of absolute spirit that governs and unfolds in a total philosophy; the "*objective* beginning," in which the concept of being is still utterly indeterminate; and the "*subjective* beginning," in which an individual consciousness "elevates itself to thinking or to positing the abstraction" (JC, 149). Climacus immediately sees that only the third or subjective beginning offers him any hope in his effort to find an entry into philosophy. Moreover, he realizes that doubt should not constitute a fourth discrete beginning, and so he attempts to identify doubt with the self-elevation that defines the subjective beginning. This leads him to yet another problem he cannot resolve, for it implies that elevation above, say, sense perception, is equivalent to doubting sense perception, an implication that he firmly rejects. Doubt and elevation are not identical, Climacus insists. If they were, why would two expressions be used for them (JC, 150)?

Climacus next asks: "How does the single individual who enunciates that thesis [that philosophy begins with doubt] relate to it?" Although here he returns to the question of whether the thesis expresses an eternal truth, as do mathematical truths that, once learned, can be grasped as eternally true, the real issue for him is rather the relation between the individuality of the person who claims that philosophy begins with doubt and the thesis itself. Climacus can find no reason for viewing this thesis on the mathematical model. Rather, he likens it to religious and ethical theses that can be enunciated, he assumes, only by one who has authority (JC, 152-53).[9]

The importance of such a subjective relation ("authority") between the person who enunciates the first thesis and the thesis itself becomes clearer in the final section of chapter 2, where

---

[9]Johannes does not explain what he means by authority. Given his analysis of doubt, however, it is safe to assume that he would agree with the view advanced by Kierkegaard in *On Authority and Revelation: The Book on Adler, or a Cycle of Ethical-Religious Essays*, trans. Walter Lowrie (Princeton NJ: Princeton University Press, 1955). My reading of that text can be found in "Who Sets the Task? Kierkegaard on Authority," in *Foundations of Kierkegaard's Vision of Community: Religion, Ethics, and Politics in Kierkegaard*, ed. George B. Connell and C. Stephen Evans (Atlantic Highlands NJ: Humanities Press, 1992) 18-32.

Climacus asks: "How does the single individual who receives that thesis relate to the one who enunciates it?" Once again, the contrast is with mathematical claims, in relation to which the individuality of their proclaimer is a matter of indifference. Anticipating the discussion of Socratic knowledge in *Philosophical Fragments*, Climacus concludes that such indifference cannot prevail here, for anyone who taught another to begin with doubt would immediately have to be doubted by the pupil. This transfer of knowledge could not be an impersonal transaction, for the learner who wants to begin to philosophize (that is, to doubt) would immediately have to "slay" or "sacrifice" (by doubt) the very teacher who had so generously shared the knowledge of how to begin (JC, 155)!

Climacus sadly concludes that the thesis that philosophy begins with doubt posits "a beginning that kept one outside philosophy" (JC, 156), particularly such a one as Climacus, who would rather not philosophize than have to slay his teacher. In other words, the thesis is not one that individuals are able to appropriate. To begin with doubt would jeopardize the very relationship that made philosophy possible. Just as Climacus's reflection upon the third thesis led him to conclude that philosophy requires a certain self-awareness on the part of the philosopher, so here his discussion of the first thesis has resulted in a consideration of the subjective nature of every genuine approach to philosophy. Indeed, the thrust of *Johannes Climacus* could be stated as the claim that philosophy as such is an empty abstraction; the only concrete reality is that of persons who philosophize. Unlike mathematical truths, the theses of philosophy are always related to the identity of those who discover, propound, and live by them.

Climacus gives relatively little attention to the remaining (second) thesis, that "in order to philosophize, one must have doubted." His transition to it is a logical one, for he concludes that the thesis that philosophy begins with doubt is incoherent and that therefore doubt must precede the beginning of philosophy, which is, in fact, what the second thesis states (JC, 156). But he does not manage in the third chapter to advance beyond what he had already established in the second. After an ironic discussion of how much he appreciates the demand for a difficult period of preparation (doubt), and how it resembles other forms of asceticism required of novices in the contemplative life,[10] Climacus simply falls back upon the idea that the second thesis about doubt elevates the learner above the teacher, or at least obliges the learner to doubt the teacher because the teacher demands it. Thus he must strike out on his own with the *de omnibus dubitandum est*, without the comfort of a relationship with a teacher:

> My visionary dreams about being a follower have vanished; before I was allowed to be young, I became old; now I am sailing on the open sea. The prospects I once conjured up about the relation of this thesis to philosophy have been blocked. I do not know a thing about the relation of this thesis to anything else. I can only follow its path; "like one who rows a boat, I turn my back toward the goal." (JC, 159)

* * *

There is a very short and quite unpolished pars secunda in *Johannes Climacus*, which consists in a consideration of the possibility of doubt in more philosophical terms. Significantly, this section confirms what has already been established in the first part of the book, namely, that doubt can be comprehended only as a phenomenon that includes subjectivity. Here the point is argued in terms of the trichotomous nature of consciousness: whereas mere reflection deals in simple dualities, consciousness is a "third" that relates a subject (who is conscious) to an object (or sense impression). The relation—consciousness—is what makes doubt possible (JC, 169).[11] Reflection, with its abstract dualities, can be objective and disinterested, but every concrete consciousness always goes beyond mere reflection to include the subjective factor of personal interest (JC, 170). In simpler terms, doubt is a possible path for a person who

---

[10]Gary Hatfield argues that "Descartes's use of the meditative mode of writing was not a mere rhetorical device to win an audience accustomed to the spiritual retreat. His choice of the literary form of the spiritual exercise was consonant with, if not determined by, his theory of the mind and of the basis of human knowledge." See "The Senses and the Fleshless Eye: The *Meditations* as Cognitive Exercises," in *Essays on Descartes' Meditations*, ed. Amélie Oksenberg Rorty (Berkeley: University of California Press, 1986) 47.

[11]Josiah Thompson stresses the importance of the *dual* nature of consciousness. He asserts without explanation that this duality leads to despair. See "The Master of Irony," in *Kierkegaard: A Collection of Critical Essays*, ed. Josiah Thompson (Garden City NY: Doubleday Anchor, 1972) 154.

is attempting to choose between the two poles of a dichotomy (for example, reality and ideality). In order to doubt, there must be the two poles in conflict, which is why a doubting consciousness "presupposes reflection" (JC, 169); and there must be a conscious person who has an interest in choosing between the two poles. We could say that, just as Climacus points away from abstract philosophy to the particular philosopher, he also points away from abstract doubt to the concrete doubter.

Climacus, then, disagrees with Judge William about the nature of doubt. Whereas the Judge believes it to be a disinterested activity of objective thought, Climacus relegates all disinterested, objective thought to the realm of abstract reflection, and maintains that doubt as an activity of concrete consciousness that always involves subjective interest. If Climacus is correct, then the grandeur of doubt praised by Judge William is an illusion, a claim to objectivity that betrays profound self-deception on the part of the doubter.[12] Doubt is not, as the Judge claims, a "qualification of necessity" (EO, 2:212). Doubt is a profoundly personal choice made by a single individual in complete freedom.

This subjective freedom is the point of the only discussion of doubt to be found in the two published works attributed to Johannes Climacus. In the "Interlude" section of *Philosophical Fragments*, he insists that doubt and faith are contrary passions—acts of the will performed in freedom (PF, 81-84).[13] Also relevant is the discussion of authority in *Concluding Unscientific Postscript*, where Climacus argues that "the historical point of view" of Christianity,

---

[12]Illusion also involves wish fulfillment and an indifference to scientific verification, as Sigmund Freud argued in *The Future of an Illusion*, trans. W. D. Robson-Scott, rev. James Strachey (Garden City NY: Doubleday Anchor, 1964) 48-49. Both of these characteristics could no doubt be demonstrated for Judge William's views on doubt. Interestingly, Freud himself denied that all illusions are false by definition, and then went on to use the word "illusion" in such a way as to make clear that illusions are, after all, *de facto* false in his view (*Future*, 49, 60, 73, 79, 86). For an analysis of self-deception that is much closer than Freud's to that of Kierkegaard, see Lloyd H. Steffen, *Self-Deception and the Common Life* (New York: Peter Lang, 1986).

[13]There is a helpful analysis of this passage in C. Stephen Evans, *Kierkegaard's Fragments and Postscript: The Religious Philosophy of Johannes Climacus* (Atlantic Highlands NJ: Humanities Press, 1983) 263-65.

whether based upon the Bible, the Church, or "the proof of the centuries," is spuriously objective, for Christianity always deals with the individual alone (CUP, 1:23-49).

Yet the Judge's initial insight remains true, profoundly true in a sense that he himself does not seem to realize: "Doubt is thought's despair; despair is personality's doubt" (EO, 2:211). Insofar as the Judge means that doubt is a merely intellectual, objective way of knowing objects, and that despair alone enters into the personal, subjective path of the self, Climacus has shown him to be wrong. But as an analogy, as a statement of the parallelism between doubt and despair according to which each is a vicious circle within its own realm—the realm of thought for doubt and the realm of the self for despair—the Judge has articulated a profound truth. As for a transition from doubt to despair, that will require one of Kierkegaard's famous leaps, for the two realms are so disparate that our tendency to view despair as an intensification of doubt betrays a confusion of categories, however much language may invite it. We can only surmise that the self-deceptions and self-contradictions of a too ambitious method of doubt will lead some individuals beyond merely bipolar reflection to a deeper awareness of the role of the self in doubt, and thus into a stage of self-doubt within which that leap toward the reality of despair might occur. Although the leap from doubt to despair lies hidden in the space between the texts by Climacus and Anti-Climacus, *The Sickness unto Death* may yield some hint of how Kierkegaard envisions going beyond the illusory grandeur of doubt.

The Good News of Despair beyond Doubt

In attributing *The Sickness unto Death* to Anti-Climacus, Kierkegaard employed a pseudonym that implies a significant degree of opposition to the teachings of Climacus. On the issue of doubt, however, their relation seems rather to be one of complementarity.[14] Whereas Climacus explores the nature of doubt in *Johannes*

---

[14]Although this point seems to support the Hongs' contention that Climacus and Anti-Climacus are not really opponents (JC, ix-xn), I think that they do generally represent irreconcilable positions. On this question, see Stephen Crites, "*The Sickness unto Death*: A Social Interpretation," in *Foundations of Kierkegaard's Vision*

Climacus but never deals with despair (he mentions it only once, when discussing *Either/Or* in *Postscript* [CUP, 1:254-58]), Anti-Climacus is silent about doubt in his book on despair. From Judge William, however, we have learned that the two concepts stand in analogous and inverse relations to one another when viewed in terms of thought and personality. Moreover, as Climacus has shown, doubt as a method cannot fulfill its own promise. This implies that it may ultimately lead to despair. Anti-Climacus can be understood as picking up where Climacus leaves off, for he shows that despair develops into an awareness of the self that it stands in a fundamental misrelation to itself. It is, in Judge William's formula, "personality's doubt," the doubt of a self about itself as a self. A brief look at the text of *The Sickness unto Death* will show how this is the case, and how it brings about a closure for the person in doubt.

According to Anti-Climacus in his preface, despair is treated throughout the book as a disease and not as a cure. Yet it is also like the Christian notion of death, which is the way that Christians describe "the state of deepest spiritual wretchedness" even while they affirm that "the cure is simply to die, to die to the world" (SUD, 6). The difference is in the object: spiritual wretchedness occurs when one denies the need to die to the world. In other words, the disease manifests itself when one rejects the cure. This implies that the sickness unto death of despair is the expression of the fact that the despairing individual is refusing to despair! Only despair can lead a person through and beyond despair.

Once again, it is the object that makes the difference. In the early stages of despair, before the self has even become aware of the reality of despair, it finds itself in a state of profound self-rejection. Whether by escaping into imaginative fantasies in order to deny its own finitude, or by seeking the shelter of anonymity and constricted horizons so as to avoid the burden of its infinitude, the self is frantically fleeing a genuine dimension of its being (SUD, 29-35). In the same way, the manic self strives to live in a world of unlimited possibilities and no necessity, whereas the depressive can see only the fateful bonds of necessity without any hope of

---

of Community, ed. Connell and Evans, 144-48, esp. n. 8.

new possibilities (SUD, 35-42). In these four conditions the self remains ignorant that it is, in fact, in despair. As Anti-Climacus puts it, however, "it makes no difference whether the person in despair is ignorant that his condition is despair—he is in despair just the same" (SUD, 44).

This lack of self-awareness points to an area where doubt and despair might overlap. Doubt understands itself to be intellectual, detached, and object-oriented. It is, according to Climacus, unaware that it is really a personal, interested, and subject-driven free choice. Likewise, these still unconscious stages of despair are merely "intellectual" in the figurative sense that a person in them tries to identify the total self with a fantastic infinitude, an anonymous finitude, a manic possibility or a depressive necessity. Yet none of these efforts can ever succeed, for each is based upon a denial of the individual's total personal being. They are "detached" in an equally figurative sense, for their entire goal is to escape from one aspect of who they really are, and to remain ignorant of the extent to which this goal is actually dominated by a profoundly interested self. Finally, they focus upon their fantasies, their boundaries, their possibilities or their fate, but always as something other than the self, as an object which they as self seek to possess, without once asking if perhaps the real source of their anguish is rooted in the self as subject. The dialectic here is one of self-doubt, doubt not simply about the self's capacity to perform this or that action, but paralyzing doubt before an unacknowledged dimension of the self. As in all doubt, attention is directed toward an object. But in the self-doubt of unconscious despair that object is an aspect of the self that the self cannot tolerate, whether finitude, infinitude, necessity or possibility.

Anti-Climacus does not discuss how an individual can make the transition from unconscious despair to despair as consciousness. The transition no doubt qualifies as leap, as a hiatus in the systematic continuity that reason seeks. To move from unconscious despair to conscious despair is a leap by which the self finds itself face to face with its own self for the first time, and, also for the first time, the self abandons forever the illusory grandeur of doubt. From conscious despair, in the forms of spiritlessness, weakness, and defiance, a second leap will take the self to despair as self-consciousness in relation to the problem of

sin. Even then, the cure for despair is not complete, for consciousness of sin as a possibility or even as a personal problem does not
yet constitute confession and repentance of sin and the forgiveness
necessary to effect a genuine cure. Indeed, it often happens that
the realization of despair as a misrelation with God (sin) can lead
to an attempted rejection of God altogether. In a surprising and
disturbing manner, *The Sickness unto Death* closes with just such a
rejection. The further development of sin-consciousness as
confession and repentance of sin is described by Anti-Climacus in
his other work, *Practice in Christianity*.[15]

In the meantime, however, a definition of despair has been
stated and developed: "The misrelation of despair is not a simple
misrelation but a misrelation in a relation that relates itself to itself
and has been established by another, [namely] . . . the power that
established it" (SUD, 14). Here we see clearly that despair is
indeed personality's doubt about itself as a self, or as a relation
that relates itself to itself before God. If personality is the self, and
the self is, as Anti-Climacus declares on the page before the
passage just quoted, a relation of binary relations (eg, the physical
and the psychical) that relates to itself (by consciously choosing to
be a particular version of that relation), despair occurs whenever
that self doubts or rejects the particular relation which it finds
itself to be. Despair is indeed personality's doubt, but not doubt in
the merely intellectual, objective, and external sense that Judge
William used the term. Despair is a doubt that has turned inward
and transcended itself in the realization that the object of its doubt
is equally the subject of its doubt, and that this identity of subject
and object is the dialectic of despair. Whereas doubt is directed
toward concepts, objects, hopes, and dreams that are outside the
self, despair is directed toward the self alone.

* * *

The illusory grandeur of doubt leads Climacus to implicit
despair, and despair leads Anti-Climacus to God as the ground of

---

[15]This further development is analyzed as part of a dialectical and structural
continuity between Anti-Climacus's *The Sickness unto Death* and *Practice in
Christianity* in my *Kierkegaard's Dialectic of Inwardness: A Structural Analysis of the
Theory of Stages* (Princeton: Princeton University Press, 1985) 214-41.

human identity. Thus despair is, like death, both the sickness and the path to a cure, for it is a misrelation-with-self before God that, when confessed as sin, is healed by grace. The cure for despair is found not by running away from it but by identifying totally with it in sin-consciousness as the prerequisite to being delivered from it in redemption. Doubt may estrange the self from its world, but despair reveals that the root of all estrangement is the self's alienation from itself as a creature of God. Despair confirms what Climacus's philosophical analysis had already established: that doubt is never merely intellectual and never a "grandeur" of dispassionate thought. Doubt is an act of the will that, when directed toward God, is really a symptom of unconscious or conscious despair.

Has Kierkegaard then totally subverted doubt? No more than contemporary postmodern deconstructors can totally subvert faith or any of its logocentric affirmations. Indeed, if anything is totally subverted by the argument of *Johannes Climacus*, it is the posture of most efforts at deconstruction, whether postmodern, modern, or even premodern. To deconstruct a text usually means to root out the subterranean self-contradictions within the text as an object of analysis, and to expose the other—the author—to a mirror that will reflect unacknowledged and unintended ruptures within his or her argument and/or self-understanding. The discourse of deconstruction always remains, like the discourse of doubt, impersonal, intellectual, and object-oriented. In showing that, for all its pretensions to objectivity, doubt is inexorably personal, interested, and based upon a self's free choice, Climacus succeeds in exposing this self-contradictory premise within deconstruction as a program. Insofar as deconstruction makes a virtual cult of the method of doubt, it unwittingly subverts doubt by refusing to doubt doubt itself. What survives the unintended subversion is only a projection and a parody of doubt's self-importance, like the fantasies of a self that despairs of its own finitude, or the manic rush of one who despairs of necessity. Deconstruction, like all doubt, can transcend its own self-limitations only by realizing that all of its activity—whether directed toward objects, other persons, or itself—is a matter of intense personal interest and free choice. The primary task of doubt is the deconstruction of its own illusory grandeur.

11

Kierkegaard and Anselm

John D. Glenn, Jr.

The *Philosophical Fragments* was written primarily as a challenge to certain features of the intellectual and spiritual life of mid-nineteenth-century Danish "Christendom." Yet some essential elements of the *Fragments* can be more fully understood if they are also considered in a broader historical context. Here I want specifically to suggest that Kierkegaard (or "Climacus"[1]) is in various ways engaged in an implicit dialogue with the thought of Anselm of Canterbury, the "father of Scholasticism." The two thinkers differ markedly in their positions on rational argument for the existence of God and on the general relation between faith and philosophical understanding—although there are indications that, in composing the *Fragments*, Kierkegaard was influenced by certain literary aspects of Anselm's writings. Most crucially though—and this will ultimately be the main focus of my essay—they differ in their treatments of the central Christian mysteries of the Atonement and the Incarnation.

The Ontological Argument

The most obvious relation between the *Fragments* and Anselm's thought is that Climacus offers a pointed, although brief, critique of the ontological argument, which Anselm originated in his

---

[1]In discussing the *Fragments*, I will refer to Climacus when commenting on specific passages in the text, but to Kierkegaard where I believe his intentions can be discerned in and through the text.

Proslogium. Although it is Spinoza's rather than Anselm's version that is specifically referred to, Kierkegaard's notes show that he also had Anselm in mind.[2]

The *Proslogium* is written in the form of a petitionary prayer; Anselm asks God to help him to understand "that thou art as we believe; and that thou art that which we believe." And he continues, "we believe that thou art a being than which nothing greater can be conceived." He proceeds to argue that such a being exists at least "in the understanding" even of one who says "there is no God." Yet such a being cannot exist in the understanding *alone.* For "then it [could] be conceived to exist in reality; which [would be] greater." But this would be a contradiction; we cannot conceive of a being greater than that than which nothing greater can be conceived. Hence "there exists a being, than which nothing greater can be conceived, and it exists both in the understanding and in reality."[3] And having in this fashion argued for the divine *existence,* Anselm proceeds to derive a formula for establishing the divine *essence* or attributes—that "God is whatever it is better to be than not to be."[4]

According to Climacus, the ontological argument involves a fundamental circularity: "The whole process of demonstration . . . becomes an expanded concluding development of what I conclude from having presupposed that the object of investigation exists" (PF, 40).

This remark is actually made in reference to *all* the theistic "proofs." Applied specifically to the ontological argument, it adopts the line of criticism hinted at by Aquinas, and developed most fully by Kant. Aquinas—referring specifically to the Anselmian version of the argument—says that the existence of God

---

[2]See PF, 190.

[3]Anselm, *Proslogium,* in *Basic Writings,* 2nd ed., trans. S. N. Deane with intro. by Charles Hartshorne (La Salle IL: Open Court Pub. Co., 1962) 7-8 (*Proslogium,* 2). (Because this work has gone through various printings, with different pagination, I will state in parentheses, following page number citations, the number of the chap. in which the cited passage appears, using CDH 1 for book 1 of *Cur Deus Homo* and CDH 2 for book 2.) The argument I have summarized is the argument of chap. 2 of the *Proslogium.* Recent defenders of Anselm have tended to stress what they take to be a distinct argument in chap. 3 of that work.

[4]See Anselm, *Basic Writings,* 11 (*Proslogium* 6).

cannot be proved in such a fashion "unless it be admitted that there actually exists something than which nothing greater can be thought; and this precisely is not admitted by those who hold that God does not exist."[5] Kant, similarly, criticizing modern rationalist versions of the argument, says that "'*Being*' is . . . not a real predicate;" to assert it is not to add a predicate to a subject, but rather to "posit the subject in itself with all its predicates."[6]

The *Fragments* develops this line of criticism in somewhat more specific terms by suggesting that, in inferring God's existence from his perfection, the ontological argument involves a confusion between "ideal being" and "factual being." That is—to employ a distinction which takes on more explicit importance in the *Postscript*— the ontological argument reasons illegitimately to *existence* from what is properly a determination of *essence*.

Faith Seeking Understanding

A second, more general respect in which Anselm is significant for the *Philosophical Fragments* is that he explicitly avowed a rationalistic conception of the proper method of theological reflection. This he expressed in the phrase "faith seeking understanding"[7] —that it is proper to seek rational proof for elements of Christian faith. His use of Augustine's formula "*credo ut intelligam*" ("I believe so that I may understand")[8] is another expression of the same theme. His attempt not only to prove God's existence but also to establish a formula for determining the divine attributes can be seen as exemplifying this method.

Regarded from the standpoint developed in the *Philosophical Fragments*, where Climacus says that in faith the understanding

---

[5]Thomas Aquinas, *Summa Theologica*, I.q.2, a.1; in *Basic Writings of St. Thomas Aquinas*, vol. 1, ed. A. C. Pegis (New York: Random House, 1945) 20.

[6]Kant, *Critique of Pure Reason*, trans. Norman Kemp Smith (London: MacMillan & Co. Ltd., 1963) 504–505 (A598-99/B626-27).

[7]This was the first title that he gave to the work he later entitled *Proslogium*. See Anselm, *Basic Writings*, 2 (preface to the *Proslogium*).

[8]See Jørgen Pedersen, "Credo ut intelligam," in *Bibliotheca Kierkegaardiana* 5 (*Theological Concepts in Kierkegaard*), ed. Niels Thulstrup and Marie Mikulová Thulstrup (Copenhagen: C. A. Reitzels Boghandel, 1980) 113-16.

"steps aside" (PF, 59), the formula "faith seeking understanding" involves what is at best a crucial ambiguity regarding the status of faith, and at worst an implicit devaluation of it. While the formula does acknowledge at least a *temporal* priority for faith in its relation to theological (or philosophical) reasoning, at the same time it *could* be taken to imply that faith is merely a "temporary function,"[9] a stance which is essentially *superseded* by the attainment of philosophical understanding. This can hardly have been Anselm's intention,[10] but it was the direction taken by Hegel and his followers, who are the primary objects of Kierkegaard's polemic in the *Fragments*, as well as in such works as *Fear and Trembling* and the *Postscript*. Thinkers who would "go beyond" faith,[11] he suggests, misunderstand both human existence and the role of faith in it.

The Form and Strategy of Their Work

The connections I have so far indicated between Anselm's writings and Kierkegaard's involve points of disagreement between them. Yet there are hints of a relation that is more positive, although limited. These concern, in particular, similarities between the literary form and strategy of the *Philosophical Fragments* and Anselm's *Cur Deus Homo* ("Why God [Became a] Man"[12])—Anselm's account of the Incarnation and the Atonement. These similarities suggest that Kierkegaard, in writing the *Fragments*, modeled certain of its features on those of Anselm's work.

---

[9]This is a phrase employed by Climacus at CUP, 1:609. See also his satirical remarks about the individual who claims to have "understood himself in his believing" (CUP, 1:211).

[10]See, e.g., his distinction between "living" and "dead" faith in the *Monologium*: "living faith believes *in* that *in* which we ought to believe; while dead faith merely believes that which ought to be believed"; *Basic Writings*, 141 (*Monologium*, 77).

[11]See the frequent uses of this phrase in *Fear and Trembling* and the *Postscript*.

[12]For the use of the article here, see Hopkins and Richardson's remarks concerning "the false impression that, on Anselm's view, God assumed unindividuated human nature and thus became Man as such," in *Anselm of Canterbury*, vol. 3, trans. Jasper Hopkins and Herbert Richardson (Toronto: Edwin Mellen Press, 1976) 254.

First, there is the *hypothetical* form taken by both works in their treatments of Christian dogma.[13] Anselm says that his course of reasoning will proceed *Christo remoto*—with Christ being, as we might say, "bracketed." He will reason, that is, as if "the incarnation of God, and the things that we affirm of him as man, had never taken place." He will, however, presuppose certain other basic doctrines of the faith—"that man was made for happiness . . . and that no being can ever arrive at happiness, save by freedom from sin, and that no man passes this life without sin."[14] Through this procedure, Anselm will attempt to prove the necessity of God's having become a human being—of the Incarnation.

Johannes Climacus adopts an analogous procedure in the *Fragments*. Until the two concluding paragraphs of his work, he ironically pretends not to have heard of either Christ or Christianity! And he, too, proceeds hypothetically, considering (or, at least, purporting to consider) simply as a "thought–project" whether there is a coherent alternative to the Socratic conception of our relation to eternal happiness. He asks, specifically, whether eternal happiness *could* be dependent on historical knowledge and a decision made in time. This possibility is found to make sense only on the presupposition of *sin*. And given this presupposition, Climacus, like Anselm, says that only if God becomes a human being can human beings attain eternal happiness.

There is another, less significant, but still interesting similarity between the *Fragments* and *Cur Deus Homo*. For Anselm's work is couched as a dialogue with the monk Boso. Similarly, the *Fragments* contains brief dialogues with an imaginary interlocutor who, like Boso, voices objections which an intelligent reader might be expected to raise to the argument of the work, and also stands for

---

[13]It is this hypothetical procedure that places both *Cur Deus Homo* and *Philosophical Fragments*, in a sense, on the "borderline" between theology and philosophy. That Anselm makes the presuppositions noted here can be regarded as qualifying his theological rationalism to some degree.

[14]*Basic Writings*, 201 (CDH 1.10). Anselm adds also "the other things, the belief of which is necessary for eternal salvation."

the reader in his or her growing comprehension of its implications.[15]

Incarnation and Atonement:
Anselm and Kierkegaard on "Why God Became Man"

The most significant relation, however, between Anselm's work and the *Fragments* does not lie in their expository form or textual strategies, but in their varying treatments of the central Christian mysteries of the Incarnation and the Atonement. That "God was in Christ reconciling the world to himself" (2 Cor. 5:19) has been the Christian Church's affirmation since New Testament times. But the New Testament writers expressed the reality and work of Christ, and especially the Atonement, in various terms—"ransom," "propitiation," "redemption," "deliverance."

Later Christian thinkers have built on these bases in different ways. The differences between Anselm's and Kierkegaard's approaches to these matters will be my focus in the remainder of this essay.

In *Cur Deus Homo*, Anselm very meticulously worked out what is sometimes called the "substitutionary satisfaction" theory of the Atonement, and of the fundamental reason for and significance of the Incarnation. This became more-or-less the predominant theory in the Western Church for some centuries following.[16] For this reason, *Cur Deus Homo* has been probably as important in the history of Christian theology as has the ontological argument in the history of Western philosophy—and it would have been virtually impossible for Kierkegaard, the honors theology graduate, to treat these matters without having in mind the main lines of Anselm's account.

Anselm's basic mode of reasoning is well known. As I noted above, he explicitly accepts certain basic presuppositions—that hu-

---

[15]That Kierkegaard was familiar with Anselm's account of the Incarnation and the Atonement is attested by Thulstrup: see his commentary to the earlier edition of the *Philosophical Fragments*, trans. David Swenson, rev. Howard V. Hong (Princeton: Princeton University Press, 1967) 198–99.

[16]See Gustaf Aulén, *Christus Victor*, trans. A. G. Hebert (London: S.P.C.K., 1931) 109–11, 139-49.

man beings are meant for eternal happiness, but that sin stands in the way of this happiness. In his conception of sin, as well as that of the Atonement, Anselm makes use of notions such as "debt," "honor," and "penalty"—themes that some commentators connect to the feudal system, others to Roman law, others to the penitential system of the medieval Church.[17] And for a contemporary reader, his terms often seem to carry basically economic connotations.

The beginning point is the notion of *debt*. Considered apart from or prior to sin, every human being, as God's creature, owes God a debt: "Every wish of a rational creature should be subject to the will of God."[18] Conceived in these terms, sin is failure or refusal to pay this debt, to render the honor which is due to God. To sin is to "dishonor" God.[19]

Anselm holds that Adam and Eve, and through them their descendants, are guilty of such sin. Here he clearly accepts the Augustinian conception of original sin as involving *inherited* guilt—a concept which he does not attempt to explain in *Cur Deus Homo*. But it is treated later in his *The Virgin Conception and Original Sin*.[20] In that work, he argues that since, at the time Adam and Eve first sinned, human nature was wholly present in them, their sin became chargeable to human nature, and thus to all their natural[21] descendants. To the objection that it is unjust to punish infants for their ancestors' sins, he responds with an analogy: if a man and his wife have been awarded some high estate, yet commit a crime on account of which they are deprived of it, no one can reasonably argue that it should be inherited by their children. It is likewise, he suggests, for the descendants of Adam and Eve.[22]

---

[17]See *Anselm of Canterbury*, 3:vii.

[18]*Basic Writings*, 202 (CDH 1.11).

[19]Anselm makes it clear, though, that this in no way diminishes the honor of God; see *Basic Writings*, 208 (CDH 1.15).

[20]See *The Virgin Conception and Original Sin*, in *Anselm of Canterbury*, 3:139-79.

[21]He holds that Jesus is *supernaturally* descended from them, and hence not subject to original sin. See *The Virgin Conception and Original Sin*, 157–60.

[22]*The Virgin Conception and Original Sin*, 171-72, 177-78. For further discussion—and very cogent criticism—of Anselm's argument here, see Jasper Hopkins, *A Companion to the Study of St. Anselm* (Minneapolis: University of Minnesota Press, 1972) 208-209.

The fact of sin means, according to Anselm, that the human being has incurred an *additional* debt to God, above and beyond that
debt which he owes simply by virtue of being God's creature. Like
anyone who has unjustly taken away what belongs to another, the
sinner "ought to give something which could not have been demanded of him, had he not stolen what belonged to another."[23] If
the human being, regarded simply as a rational creature, owes
God everything he is, has, or can do, the human being as a sinner
owes *all* this, *plus* a penalty for his original fault (or default). (To
use an economic analogy, it is as if the sinner owes everything he
could ever possibly own—plus interest!) This makes his plight to
all appearances insoluble. But even this does not sufficiently state
the penalty which the sinner owes. For there is "no greater injustice" than that "the creature should take away the honor due the
Creator."[24] The sinner's debt is, in other words, *infinite.*[25]

How, then, can this debt be paid?[26] *Only* if *God* becomes *man,*
Anselm answers. Only the "God-man" (*deus-homo*) can make the
payment. He must, on the one hand, be man, for it is man who
owes the debt;[27] but he must also be God, for only then can the
payment be something of *infinite* value—namely, his very life.

There is more to Anselm's account. He explains that, insofar as
the "God–man" gives up "so great a good in itself so lovely" this
gift can "avail to pay what is due for the sins of the whole
world."[28] As sinless, the "God-man," in giving up his life, clearly
performs a supererogatory deed, and thus deserves a reward. But,

---

[23]*Basic Writings,* 202-203 (CDH 1.11).

[24]*Basic Writings,* 206 (CDH 1.13).

[25]See *Basic Writings,* 229 (CDH 1.21).

[26]And Anselm's reasoning is that if the sinner cannot make payment, the
honor of God requires that he be punished. (*Basic Writings,* 207; CDH 1.13).

[27]This means that, on Anselm's account, although God did not become Man
as such, but *a* man (see n. 12, above), the fact that Adam's (and Eve's) sinful actions implicated human nature as such is somehow mirrored in Christ's atoning
actions. If this were not so, the sacrifice could (contrary to Anselm's reasoning)
have been made by a being who was in no manner human, and his (or her)
reward transferred to human beings. (Anselm's account does—see below—envi-
sion a transfer of Christ's reward to human beings.) There are, I think, some unresolved tensions in Anselmian theology at this point.

[28]*Basic Writings,* 263 (CDH 2.14).

being himself divine, he needs nothing. Therefore, his reward—the reward due the Son from the Father[29]—can rightly be bestowed upon others, namely "those for whose salvation, as right reason teaches, he became man."[30] In paying what he does not owe, substituting himself for them, he makes satisfaction for their debts, and the way to eternal happiness is again open to them. And so the ethically very problematic notion of *inherited guilt* stands at the beginning of Anselm's account—and the equally problematic notion of *transferred merit* at its end.[31]

It does not seem right to move from Anselm's thought to Kierkegaard's work as if nothing of importance which is significant for understanding their differences occurred in the centuries between them. The problem, of course, is that so much occurred! But the intervention of Hegel's thought is crucial—*especially* insofar as it incorporated major tendencies in the whole development of Western cultural and spiritual life. In particular, increasing secularization, a process which was furthered by the Renaissance, the Reformation (despite the Reformers' intentions), and the Enlightenment, together with a tendency to emphasize society or humanity in an abstract sense to the neglect of the worth and responsibility of concrete human individuals, reached a kind of apex in the thought of Hegel and his followers.

I have already mentioned the way in which Anselm's "faith seeking understanding" is transformed, in Hegel, into a viewpoint in which philosophical understanding is regarded as essentially supplanting faith. In Hegel's thought, too, the Christian doctrine of the God-man becomes a doctrine of the unity of divinity and humanity at large—and, earlier in the decade in which *Philosophical Fragments* appeared, it was further "demythologized" by the "left-Hegelian" Feuerbach into a humanistic reduction of divinity to humanity.

---

[29]I cannot here discuss Anselm's account of the Trinity.

[30]*Basic Writings*, 284-85 (CDH 2.19).

[31]That it is not merely reward, but also *merit* that is somehow transferred from Christ to human beings is implicit at various points in Anselm's reasoning: see esp. *Basic Writings*, 224-25 (CDH 1.19), where he compares sinful man to a pearl that has been cast in the mire, and must be cleansed before it can appropriately be restored to its owner's treasury.

Feuerbach, in fact, presented a proto-Freudian account[32] of God as a "projection" of human nature outside itself—and suggested that (to state the matter in Freudian terms) in the doctrine of the Incarnation the "latent content" of the idea of God was becoming manifest. "In the Incarnation," Feuerbach wrote, "religion only confesses what in reflection on itself, as theology, it will not admit; namely that God is an altogether human being."[33] And in the thought of both Hegel and Feuerbach the reality of sin is treated in a way which would clearly be objectionable to Anselm, as it was to Kierkegaard. For Hegel, sin seems to be a necessary element in the dialectical progression of the divine-human Spirit. Feuerbach also tends to discount the seriousness of sin, suggesting that being overly concerned over one's own sins—like desiring one's own immortality—reflects an overemphasis on the human *individual* at the expense of the human *race*. The individual may be a sinner, he says, but the race as a whole is perfect; the individual may be mortal, but the race is immortal.[34]

In the *Philosophical Fragments*, though, Kierkegaard is not writing so much against these thinkers *per se* as he is struggling with a general tendency which they in part represented, in part furthered[35] through their ideas—namely, the increasing secular complacency of European (and, most proximally, Danish) "Christendom," which for the most part continued to think of itself as Christian while forgetting the real core of the Christian message, and implicitly devaluing individual existence and Christian faith and life. Such attitudes are, I believe, the primary object of the *Fragment*'s polemic; and reminding its readers of who they are

---

[32]It would be fairer, strictly speaking, to say that Freud developed a neo-Feuerbachian account. But however the matter is stated, I would not want to slight the differences between the two. Where for Freud the "original" of what is "projected" as God is the human *father*, for Feuerbach it is our human *essence*. A brief account of Freud's early interest in Feuerbach is given in Peter Gay, *Freud: A Life for Our Time* (New York: W. W. Norton & Company, Inc., 1988) 28-29.

[33]Feuerbach, *The Essence of Christianity*, trans. George Eliot (New York: Harper & Row, 1957) 56.

[34]Ibid., 152–59.

[35]Here I refer more to Hegel and Hegelianism, which had attained considerable influence in Denmark. The ideas of the "left-Hegelian" Feuerbach had not.

(sinners) and of who they professed to be (Christians) is the purpose of what could be called its *maieutic*[36] dimension.

This maieutic-polemic intention, as well as its self–conscious opposition to the Hegelian "system," accounts for much of the fragmentary character of the *Fragments*. And I believe this should be kept in mind in comparing its content to that of Anselm's work. For Anselm, although in many ways a modest man, in his various writings was working out what would today be called a systematic theology. Kierkegaard had no such aspiration. Among other things, this means that we must be careful to refrain from concluding that what is not explicitly stated in his work is, even implicitly, denied.

Another feature of the *Fragments* which colors, and in a sense limits, its approach to its topics is the fact that Climacus delineates the Christian position (not named as such until his concluding paragraphs) specifically in distinction from "the Socratic" standpoint. The two positions are contrasted in terms of their answers to the question whether "eternal happiness" is, or is not, attainable through "historical knowledge" and temporal decision (PF, xxiii). This question is itself approached through consideration of whether "truth" can be acquired in time. So the rhetoric of the *Fragments* is framed in terms which are basically *cognitive* or epistemological—as distinct from, for example, *Fear and Trembling*, which is in many respects parallel to the *Fragments*, but in which the basic contrasts are drawn in terms which are primarily *volitional* and ethical.[37]

Yet Climacus's statement of the Socratic standpoint functions, I believe, as a paradigm of any conception[38] which holds that human beings have, within themselves, the capacity to achieve

---

[36]I am using this term in a very loosely Socratic sense, for "bringing out" of human beings what they already know or are. Here see Climacus's statement that, "even if a divine point of departure is . . . given, [the Socratic maieutic relation] remains the true relation between one human being and another" (PF, 10). Kierkegaard clearly conceived his own task among his contemporaries as analogous to Socrates' task among his.

[37]I.e., in *Fear and Trembling* faith is delineated primarily in its relation to desire for earthly happiness, resignation, and "the ethical."

[38]Or, at least any *coherent* conception. There are ample indications that Climacus regards Hegelianism as fundamentally *in*coherent: see PF, 10, 111, and the whole critique of Hegelian logic in the "Interlude," PF, 72–88.

fulfillment—or "salvation." Climacus remarks that the question whether the truth can be learned "was a Socratic question or became that by way of the Socratic question whether virtue can be taught—for virtue in turn was defined as insight" [PF, 9]. This indicates that what is fundamentally at issue here is human fulfillment as a whole, including its moral-religious dimension, rather than simply cognition *per se*. Climacus is not so much concerned with knowing the truth as with *existing in* the truth—a point which is made more explicit in his discussion of "subjectivity" in the *Postscript*.

I referred above to the hypothetical procedure which is followed in both *Cur Deus Homo* and the *Fragments*, and to the fact that both accounts presuppose the reality of sin. But this is true in a somewhat different sense in the *Fragments*. Here the reality of sin is assumed only in the (unnamed) position which Climacus contrasts with the Socratic standpoint. Sin is regarded as the fundamental presupposition without which we can make no sense of the possibility that historical events, and a decision made in time, could be decisive for one's eternal happiness—since sin itself is conceived as a breach made, in time, between the existing human being and eternal truth. And, consistent with the cognitive terms in which the argument of the *Fragments* is framed, sin is regarded as being in "untruth"—yet as being in untruth "through one's own fault" (PF, 15).

The *Fragments* does not, at this point, refer explicitly to the notion of *original* sin. And the spirit of the passage just quoted militates against this notion—*if* it is taken to refer basically to guilt inherited from Adam. Like Anselm, Kierkegaard does take up the question of original sin in a separate work—*The Concept of Anxiety*, which appeared under another pseudonym, "Vigilius Haufniensis," only four days after publication of the *Fragments*.[39] Vigilius's account of sin is significantly different from the conception of original sin taken over by Anselm from Augustine. For he claims that *every* human being is an "original" sinner; each originates sin in his or her *own* life. We are not sinners *because* Adam was a

---

sinner, but *as* Adam was a sinner.[40] Yet, at the same time, we stand in relation to the race and its past. We "inherit" sin in the sense that one's "leap"[41] into sin can be occasioned (though Vigilius insists it is not *caused*) by situations which have been shaped by the sins of others, and in particular through one's anxious awareness of the possibilities which these sins exemplify.[42]

How, then, are the Incarnation and the Atonement—the reality and work of Christ, although of course Climacus does not refer to him by name—treated in the *Philosophical Fragments*? Climacus's account is developed, fundamentally, in three stages. First, Christ is considered, in Climacus's "Thought-Project," as a "teacher"—yet a teacher essentially different from the Socratic. Then, in "The God as Teacher and Savior," which Climacus calls a "poetical venture," he is envisioned as "the god in time"—as God Incarnate. Finally, in a "metaphysical caprice," he is regarded through the "category" of "the absolute paradox." The elements of, and the relations between, these different determinations are crucial for understanding how the *Philosophical Fragments* bears on the central Christian mysteries.

Reasoning under the hypothesis that—contrary to what Socrates assumed—the human "learner" is, due to sin, bereft of "the truth," Climacus says that the learner needs a teacher essentially different from Socrates. This teacher can be no mere "midwife," who helps to bring out a truth which one already in some sense possesses. He must not only bring the learner the truth, but must also "provide him with the condition for understanding it" (PF, 14). And, insofar as this is a fundamental

---

[40]"Through the first sin, sin came into the world. Precisely in the same way it is true of every subsequent man's first sin, that through it sin comes into the world." (CA, 31)

[41]See CA, 37: "innocence is always lost only by the qualitative leap of the individual."

[42]It is such facts that allow Vigilius to make some sense of the Augustinian conception of inherited sin. Nevertheless, as I understand *The Concept of Anxiety*, Vigilius does not regard original sin as, strictly speaking, inherited. For an excellent discussion of issues involved here, see Lee Barrett, "Kierkegaard's 'Anxiety' and the Augustinian Doctrine of Original Sin," in *International Kierkegaard Commentary: The Concept of Anxiety*, ed. Robert L. Perkins (Macon GA: Mercer University Press, 1985) 35-61.

transformation of the learner—a kind of re-creation—the teacher can only be "the god himself" (PF, 14–15).

The "Thought-Project," however, explains neither *why* nor *how* this teacher would bring the truth. These questions are taken up by Climacus in "The God as Teacher and Savior." Unlike the Socratic teacher, who stands in a relation of fundamental equality with the learner, the *divine* teacher, Climacus says, "needs no pupil in order to understand himself." *If* he does, then, "make his appearance," he must be moved to do so not by necessity, but by *love*. (PF, 24-25). Moreover, "just as his love is the *basis*, so also must love be the *goal*. . . . The love, then, must be for the learner, and the goal must be to win him, for only in love is the different made equal, and only in *equality* or in unity is there *understanding*" (PF, 25; my emphases).

Yet here "equality"—that is, a state of affairs in which the learner is not coerced, but in some sense freely participates in and contributes to the relation[43]—and "understanding," in which he has confidence that he is, despite his sin, the object of "the god's" love, are difficult to achieve. Using the well-known analogy of a king who "loved a maiden of lowly station," Climacus suggests that the desired relation cannot be achieved by the god's appearance "in glory" to the learner; this would make the relation coerced and one-sided; no "equality" in any sense could result. Nor can the desired relation be achieved through immediate glorification of the learner instead; this would only lead to *mis*understanding; the learner would forget the fact that he is a sinner, and would not understand that he is nevertheless loved. How, then, is the desired relationship possible? Climacus responds:

> If, then, the unity could not be brought about by an ascent, then it must be attempted by a descent. Let the learner be X, and this X must also include the lowliest. . . . In order for unity to be effected, the god must become like this one. He will appear,

---

[43]This is, I think, the sense of "equality" that is suggested by Climacus's consideration of the difficulties involved. Since he later speaks of sin as the "absolute difference" (PF, 47) between "the god" and the human learner, it is clear that the equality *ultimately* aimed at is one in which the learner is free from sin. (See CUP, 1:490-92, for further thoughts on how "love's equality" expresses itself in the human relation to God.)

therefore, as the equal of the lowliest of persons. . . . the god will appear in the form of a *servant*. But this form of a servant is not something put on like the king's plebian coat, which just by flapping open would betray the king . . . —but it is his true form. For this is the boundlessness of love, that in earnestness and truth and not in jest it wills to be the equal of the beloved. (PF, 31-32)

The basic "rationale" of the Incarnation is, on this conception, *love*. One may object that what Climacus offers here is poetry, not theology—as if there were not, of necessity, a good deal of poetry in theology. And it must remembered that he continually allows the exposure of his pretense to be the unwitting discoverer of these matters. The "poetry" of the "poetical venture" is not his, Climacus says, but "the god's," and is thus no mere poetry, but *truth*. "The poem was so different from every human poem that it was no poem at all but *the wonder*" (PF, 36).

Yet "the wonder" is, from another perspective, a *paradox*. And it is this determination which Climacus considers in the "metaphysical caprice" offered under the title of "The Absolute Paradox"—which is one of the most difficult sections of Climacus's work to interpret. Remarkably, it does not even offer an explicit statement of what the "absolute paradox" *is*. The reference to a "metaphysical caprice" might seem to indicate that the paradox should be conceived of as involving fundamental metaphysical categories—as, for example, the paradox of the *infinite* God becoming a *finite* human being. But these are not terms which Climacus employs. Other terms for conceiving this paradox are more closely suggested by the text. Is it that the *eternal* truth, or the eternal god, comes into existence *in time*? Or that "the unknown"—that which transcends the reach of human understanding—reveals itself, makes itself *known*? Or perhaps it is that "the absolutely different," that from which human beings are absolutely different because of "the absolute difference of sin," becomes *like* them, "wanting to annul this absolute difference in the absolute equality" (PF, 47).

This is, I believe, closer to the core of Climacus's fundamental meaning.[44] The "absolute paradox" seems, in short, to be basically what was suggested in Climacus's "poem"—that, despite our sin,[45] God loves human beings so much that he becomes human to express that love, to free them from sin, and to make eternal happiness possible.

There are other considerations which suggest that this is the proper reading of Climacus's text. He poses the question of whether "the truth" can be learned, and posits "the god in time" as "teacher." Yet he says little concerning just what "the truth" is—*what* it is that the teacher *teaches*. Only in a section of the *Fragments* entitled "The Situation of the Contemporary Follower" does Climacus really address this question. And here he says that "the god's presence is not incidental to his teaching but is essential. The presence of the god in human form—indeed, in the lowly form of a servant—*is precisely the teaching* . . . " (PF, 55; my emphasis).

The god's "teaching" is, it seems, rather like what contemporary philosophers call a "performative utterance." What the god *says*—that he loves the sinner and wants to establish a relationship with him—he at the same *does*; he *enacts* this love by himself taking on the human condition. Love is not merely, as Climacus has said, the *basis* and the *goal* of the teacher's teaching; it is also its essential *content*.

---

[44]Climacus seems relatively uninterested in the strictly metaphysical dimensions of the "absolute paradox." As to whether God *could* become a human being, he says simply that "it is the omnipotence of resolving love to be capable of that of which neither the king nor Socrates was capable"—namely, being "the equal of the beloved" (PF, 32).

[45]As I read this section of the *Fragments*, it involves a distinction between an *initial* paradox, which has to do with the encounter between the human being and the God as absolutely *different from* him, and the *absolute* paradox, which has to do with the God becoming *like* him, so that he may become like the God. Given Climacus's characterization of the "absolute difference" as *sin*, the initial paradox is thus, fundamentally, that of human alienation from God due to sin, and the absolute paradox concerns the God's becoming man in order to express love even for the sinner, and to make reconciliation possible.

I have referred to the fact that the *Fragments* is just that—fragmentary, no philosophical system *or* work of systematic theology.[46] Its account of its basic themes is, moreover, shaped by its polemic and maieutic purposes, and by the fact that the Christian "position" is here treated in juxtaposition with Socratic conceptions. This means that there is much which relates to its themes which is *not* said—although not, thereby, denied. Some attention to what is not said may, then, be in order.

One notable omission in the *Fragments* is any reference to the distinction between the First and Second Persons of the Trinity—which is crucial in Anselm's account of Christ's sacrifice, which he must make *as* Incarnate Son *to* the Father. Trinitarian Christianity is not denied in the *Fragments*, but it is not essential to Climacus's approach to the Incarnation and the Atonement.

Moreover, the *Fragments* does not explicitly refer to the *Crucifixion*—the sacrifice which, for Anselm, was the whole point of the Incarnation and the essential means by which the Atonement was accomplished. (Nor does the *Fragments* mention the Resurrection.) Climacus *does* say that "the god must suffer all things, endure all things, be tried in all things, hunger in the desert, thirst in his agonies, be forsaken in death, absolutely the equal of the lowliest of human beings—look, behold the man!" (PF, 32-33)

This passage of course alludes implicitly to the Crucifixion. But that a literal Crucifixion was a necessary part of the story of "the god in time" is not asserted—perhaps because of Kierkegaard's belief in human freedom. For the *Fragments*, the basic sacrifice made by "the god" does not consist in the Crucifixion, but in the Incarnation itself—in that, out of love, "the god" freely submits himself to the conditions of human existence, and to the possibility that the human "learner" may (to his own loss) reject the relation which is offered. Climacus continues:

---

[46]In the *Postscript*, responding to a reviewer, Climacus speaks of the *Fragments* as involving a "parody of speculative thought"—from which yet emerges "old-fashioned orthodoxy in its rightful severity." He adds that "the presence of irony" in a discourse "does not necessarily mean that . . . earnestness is excluded" (CUP, 1:275-77).

The suffering of death is not his suffering, but his whole life is a story of suffering, and it is love that suffers, love that gives all and is itself destitute. What wonderful self–denial to ask in concern, even though the learner is the lowliest of persons: Do you really love me? (PF, 33)

I have said that the *Fragments* involves a treatment of both the Incarnation and the Atonement, but have said little specifically about how it treats the latter. In fact, the term "Atonement" does not occur in the newer translation of the *Fragments*. It was used once in the older translation, where Climacus, reflecting on the "properties" of the "teacher," says that he can be called "Saviour" and "Redeemer," and that "when the Teacher gives [the learner] the condition and the Truth he constitutes himself an Atonement, taking away the wrath impending upon that of which the learner has made himself guilty."[47] The new translation (probably more appropriately, and closer to the original biblical term[48]) speaks instead of a *"reconciler"* (PF, 17). Climacus's stress is not on a substitutionary sacrifice, but a communication of love and an offer of reconciliation.

One characteristic of the works published under the pseudonym Johannes Climacus is that—despite their stress (particularly in the *Postscript*) on the subjective "appropriation" of Christian truth—they say little about the concrete character of the Christian life, about what it is to *live* as one who has, in some fundamental (if yet imperfectly realized) sense, been freed from sin.[49] Yet an account of this life is implicit, I think, in his identification of love as not only basis and goal, but *content* of "the god's" activity—as

---

[47]This passage is on p. 21 of the older translation, cited above. What Climacus takes this "wrath" to be—whether it is actively administered divine punishment, or loss of "eternal happiness" per se—is not really clarified. It is also worth noting that, in the *Postscript*, Climacus explicitly *refuses* to attempt a description of the latter: see CUP, 1:392-93. The only thing to be said of eternal happiness, he suggests, is that "it is the good that is attained by absolutely venturing everything" (CUP, 1:427).

[48]See D. M. Baillie, *God Was in Christ* (London: Faber and Faber Ltd., 1948) 187.

[49]For Anselm, of course, we are freed from sin in the sense of having the debt of original sin discharged through Christ's sacrifice. We are to respond through imitation of Christ's obedience: see *Basic Writings*, 280 (CDH 2.18b).

"the truth." The life which is thereby made possible—in which one's self-incurred alienation from the truth is healed—is essentially, it seems, the life of one who accepts himself or herself as loved by God, and who returns this love. But what this involves is delineated more concretely only in later works—especially, as I read Kierkegaard, in *The Sickness unto Death* and *Works of Love*, where love of God, (the right kind of) love of oneself, and love of one's neighbor are proclaimed as inseparable.[50]

Niels Thulstrup has suggested that one difference between Anselm and Kierkegaard is that Anselm affirmed, and Kierkegaard denied, the *necessity* of the Incarnation.[51] This is, I believe, essentially correct—although, strictly speaking, not quite accurate. Anselm does speak of "necessity" here, but he means a *conditional* necessity[52]—that, having created human beings with the intention that at least some of them should have eternal happiness, God must, in order to fulfill his plan, become a man to redeem them from sin.

In his denial of the necessity of the Incarnation, Climacus's main point is that it is God's free act, to which "the learner" should respond in gratitude and love. And here we come to a fundamental difference between Anselm and Kierkegaard, a difference which is closely bound up with all the other differences which I have discussed. For Anselm gives very little attention to what might be called the subjective dialectic of faith, to the factors which qualify the believer's—or the non–believer's—*response to* the divine action. Yet these are crucial stresses of the *Fragments*.

Anselm's theory is sometimes referred to as the "objective" theory of the Atonement. And he does describe it in very "objective" terms—as if it were a kind of legal transaction or cosmic ritual played out before an onlooking crowd. Here, in fact, his treatment seems to have an affinity with the medieval

---

[50]I take "willing to be itself" in the sense that Anti-Climacus uses the phrase (SUD, passim) to refer to what can rightly be conceived as a form of love for oneself. For Kierkegaard's account of the relation between love of oneself, love of God, and love of one's neighbor, see WL, 39, 113, 351-52.

[51]See Thulstrup, in the earlier translation of the *Fragments* cited above, 198–99.

[52]See *Basic Writings*, 244 (CDH 2.5).

celebration of the Mass,[53] when the celebrant was often the only partaker. One's only decision is whether he will, in Anselm's term, "subscribe to the condition...laid down"[54] by God in order to receive pardon. (For Climacus, of course, the appropriate response is *love*.) And Anselm gives no attention to resistance or doubt—to "offense"—as a possibility on the part of the potential believer.

To Anselm's "objective" theory of the Atonement, various "subjective" theories have been contrasted—such as the "moral influence" theory attributed to Abelard,[55] and similar accounts developed later by Enlightenment and post-Enlightenment theologians.[56] These typically speak of Christ as affecting human beings by his example of self-sacrificing love—and thus they do put more stress on the believer's response than did Anselm.

Yet although the treatment of the Incarnation and the Atonement in the *Fragments* is not "objective" in the manner of Anselm's, it is also—contrary to what a superficial understanding of Kierkegaard might lead one to expect—not "subjective" in the sense just described. As it is treated in the *Fragments*, the Atonement is not a cosmic ritual enacted before a gazing populace. But neither is Christ's life and death simply the presentation of an inspiring example; Kierkegaard, like Anselm, takes sin too seriously[57] to think that it can be cured simply by example.

---

[53]I believe I have seen this affinity noted elsewhere.

[54]*Basic Writings*, 267 (CDH 2.16).

[55]In his *The Logic of Divine Love: A Critical Analysis of the Soteriology of Peter Abelard* (Oxford: Oxford University Press, 1970) Richard E. Weingart argues persuasively that accounts of Abelard's position have consistently oversimplified it.

[56]See Aulén, *Christus Victor*, 112, 149-59. Aulén distinguishes from both the Anselmian (or, more generally, what he terms the "Latin") doctrine and the "subjective" view what he calls "the classic idea" of the Atonement. His exposition of the classic idea—which he argues is the predominant view in the New Testament, the early Church Fathers, and Luther—is complex, and although in some respects the account developed in the *Fragments* is close to that idea, it differs in others. (E.g., as Aulén expounds the classic idea it depicts the Atonement as a victory over cosmic evil forces, and conceives it as involving "a change . . . in God's own attitude" [22]; neither of these themes is present in the *Fragments*.)

[57]A journal entry written several years after the *Fragments*, at a time when Kierkegaard had become somewhat more rigorously orthodox, is worth consulting in this connection; in particular, it shows an appreciation of certain elements that he finds in Anselm's position: see JP, 1:532.

I have suggested that the Incarnation—the "absolute paradox"—is essentially, for Climacus, a *communication* of God's love *to* the human being. Its dialectics are, then, the dialectics of communication and of interpersonal relations—with (on one side, at least) the possibilities of misunderstanding and offense which these seem inevitably to involve. The human "learner" is (at least, *per hypothesis*) in "untruth," and alienated from "the god," through his own fault. "The god" nevertheless loves him, desires to establish a right relation with him, and becomes like him in order to communicate this love. But offense is always possible. The human being may haughtily refuse to admit his fault. Or he may allow himself to be so overcome by it that he cannot believe that he is truly loved as he is. These—and not reaction to any purely "metaphysical" paradox—are, as I read the *Fragments*, the basic forms of "the offense."[58]

As Christian thinkers, of course, Anselm and Kierkegaard have much in common. And their common ground is by no means exhausted in saying that neither would accept the secular optimism represented by thinkers such as Hegel and Feuerbach. Yet their differences are marked. The categories in terms of which Anselm approaches his topics are primarily those of abstract reflection; his search is for universal rational truths; his understanding of the work of Christ is based on impersonal law. While not entirely dismissing the value of these things, Kierkegaard's categories are personal, dramatic, and historical. He tells (with a unique mixture of poetry, playfulness, and pathos) a story—which he suggests is somehow *our* story—of self-incurred blindness to truth and alienation from God, and of divine grace and love beyond all expectation. For him the story of the Incarnation and the Atonement is, it seems, *all* a story of love. The question he poses is whether one can, and will, *believe* it, and answer love with love.

---

[58]Climacus says that "the offense *comes into existence* with the paradox" (PF, 51). If the paradox is essentially that "the god" loves the sinful human being enough to take upon himself the human condition in order to communicate this, then the offense is essentially a reaction to that communication. Here see the treatment of offense in *The Sickness unto Death*, esp. SUD, 83–86.

12

Johannes Climacus and Aurelius Augustinus on Recollecting the Truth

George Pattison

In setting out to solve the questions posed on the title page of *Philosophical Fragments* ("Can a historical point of departure be given for an eternal consciousness; how can such a point of departure be of more than historical interest; can an eternal happiness be built on historical knowledge?") Johannes Climacus draws out two contrasting views of truth and of our human apprehension of truth. The one, which he identifies with Socrates, he calls "recollection," the other, which is linked to Christianity, he calls "faith." The doctrine of recollection answers the question "Can the truth be learned?" by assuming that the learner is already implicitly in possession of the truth in such a way that the function of the teacher is simply to be the midwife who helps this truth to the birth of conscious recognition. In this way both the teacher and the moment in which knowledge of the truth becomes conscious (the "historical point of departure") are of no more than passing significance, mere occasions by means of which the learner makes the transition from an unconscious to a conscious self-relation to truth, a transition involving no change in the essential nature of either learner or truth. Although in the context of *Philosophical Fragments*, where Socrates is put forward as the exemplary teacher of the doctrine of recollection, this doctrine is associated with belief in the preexistence of the soul, it is clear that Johannes Climacus understands that there may be forms of the doctrine which do not require any such archaic buttressing. For he would have been able to see among contemporary idealists (and even among their critics) a view of truth which equated the discovery of truth with the progressive self-discovery of the human race in such a way that the "Absolute Idea" of history or the "Species Being" of the race came to perform a logical function comparable to that of preexistence in the Socratic scheme of things. The doctrine of faith, by way of contrast, teaches that outside that relation to truth which only the teacher can initiate the learner is in untruth to such an extent that he cannot even know that he is in untruth. Faith consequently holds that both the teacher and the moment are of decisive and unsurpassable significance. Indeed, the teacher must be none other than the God himself as Saviour, the moment the "fulness of time" of the Incarnation, the previous state of the learner not merely untruth but "sin," and that relation in which the learner embraces the truth faith itself (with its accompanying shadow: "offense").

All this, of course, is no more than what any didactic summary of the argument of *Philosophical Fragments* might say. The question to be asked here, however, is this: is Climacus correct in equating the distinction between these two views of truth—a distinction which, it should be said, is for him always strictly hypothetical, being made under the rubric "thought experiment" (not "dogma")—with Socrates and Christianity; or, to ask the question another way: is he correct in claiming that Christianity must repudiate the doctrine of recollection?

There would seem to be at the very least strong historical reasons for refusing to allow this claim without further examination. For the Augustinian tradition of Catholic Christianity (often said to be the most significant intellectual and spiritual strand within the complex event known as Western Christianity) seems to offer something remarkably akin to the doctrine of recollection as described by Climacus. In order, then, to examine what a Christian doctrine of recollection might mean, let us turn to Augustine himself, focussing on two works, *The Teacher* and the *Confessions*[1]

---

[1]The text of *The Teacher* can be found in Augustine, *Earlier Writings*, trans. and ed. John H. S. Burleigh, The Library of Christian Classics (London: SCM, 1953). References will be given in the text following the symbol "T." Recent literature that deals with it includes M. Burnyeat, "Wittgenstein and Augustine's *De Magistro*," in *Proceedings of the Aristotelian Society*, suppl. vol. (1987); C. Kirwan, *Augustine* (London and New York: Routledge, 1989, 1991) chap. 3, "The Nature

The Teacher is a short work written approximately two years after Augustine's acceptance of baptism at the hands of Ambrose, Bishop of Milan, at Easter AD 387, and after his return to North Africa. Poignantly it takes the form of a dialogue with his fifteen year old son Adeodatus, who died shortly afterwards and to whom *The Teacher* was to be Augustine's best memorial (see also *Confessions* IX, 6). The detail of the dating of the text is significant insofar as it signals that what we are dealing with is "early" Augustine, that is to say that it is the work of an Augustine still strongly influenced by the ideals of Platonism yet determinedly "Christian." The dialogue begins (as, we may say, *Philosophical Fragments* begins) with a purely philosophical question:

"*Augustine.* —What do you suppose is our purpose when we use words?" To which Adeodatus replies, "the answer that occurs to me at the moment is, we want to let people know something, or we want to learn something" (T, 69). It soon emerges, however, that words not only function as a means of communicating hitherto unknown information but also as a means of *reminding* either the speaker or the listener of things which he or she already knows. For words are but signs of realities which exist outside the realm of language. This is equally true in the case of material realities with which we are acquainted through the senses and in the case of spiritual realities which can be known only by the "inner man," the mind itself. Thus Augustine explains to Adeodatus that words "bid us look for things, but they do not show them to us that we may know them. He alone teaches me anything who sets before my eyes, or one of my other bodily senses, or my mind the things which I desire to know" (T, 94). In relation to material things this means that if we are to engage in meaningful conversation about things which are not immediately present and cannot therefore be immediately *shown*, then language must rely on memory:

---

of Speech," 35ff.; G. O'Daly, *Augustine's Philosophy of Mind* (London: Duckworth, 1987)—both the discussion of memory in chap. 5 and the section "Signs, Communication, and Knowledge" (pp.171ff.) are relevant to the *De Magistro*; G. C. Stead, "Augustine's *De Magistro*: a Philosopher's View" in *Signum Pietatis*, ed. A. Zumkeller (Wurzburg: Augustinus Verlag, 1989).

> So in the halls of memory we bear the images of things once
> perceived as memorials which we can contemplate mentally and
> can speak of with a good conscience and without lying. But these
> memorials belong to us privately. If anyone hears me speak of
> them, provided he has seen them himself, he does not learn from
> my words, but recognizes the truth of what I say by the images
> which he has in his own memory. (T,96)

Language, then, as a means of communicating truth, depends
entirely on the possibility of shared realms of experience. If this is
lacking then the most that words can do is to inspire belief,
according to the picture we are able to form of what the words say
on the basis of our previous experience and according to our
assessment of the authority of the speaker. In relation to spiritual
things (and it is, of course, these which most concern Augustine)
the situation is not dissimilar. For "if my hearer sees these things
[which we look upon directly in the inner light of truth] himself
with his inward eye, he comes to know what I say, not as a result
of my words but as a result of his own contemplation" (T, 96). As
was the case in Johannes Climacus's presentation of the Socratic
doctrine of recollection, the teacher thus becomes a mere occasion
of the act of learning. "Even when I speak what is true and he sees
what is true, it is not I who teach him. He is taught not by my
words but by the things themselves which inwardly God has made
manifest to him" (T, 96f). Here too, those who are unable to share
this experience in themselves will arrive no further than belief.[2]
But who is the teacher in this situation? It is none other than Truth
itself, which in its absolute and unchanging self-identity stands
entirely unmoved by all relativities—and this Truth is Christ:

> We listen to Truth which presides over our minds within us,
> though of course we may be bidden to listen by someone using
> words. Our real Teacher is he who is so listened to, who is said
> to dwell in the inner man, namely Christ, that is the unchange-

---

[2]Augustine concedes (quoting Isaiah, "Unless ye believe, ye shall not know")
that there are many things we cannot, strictly, *know*, such as the biblical story of
the three youths in the fiery furnace, but which may nonetheless be extremely
useful for us to believe. Two years after *The Teacher*, Augustine found himself
defending *The Usefulness of Belief* (*De Utilitate Credendi*) in the treatise of the same
name.

able power and eternal wisdom of God. To this wisdom every rational soul gives heed, but to each is given only so much as he is able to receive, according to his own good or evil will. (T, 95)

The closing words of this passage point towards what later develops into major "Augustinian" themes. But, whilst acknowledging a grading in the ability of different individuals to attend to what Adeodatus later calls the "Secret Oracle" there is a clear implication here (as throughout *The Teacher*) that the human mind *is essentially capable of learning the truth* and that *remembering* ("bringing to mind") *is the means by which that learning occurs*— whether we are talking about remembering as reenvisioning the stored mental images of past experiences or as "remembering" the illumination which eternal Truth shines forth in the mind. A corollary of this argument is that any act of learning truth is in some way "taught" us by Christ, the Secret Oracle, Truth itself. This had indeed already been argued by Augustine in an earlier work, *The Soliloquies*, in which he defended the value of the classical curriculum of the liberal arts on the grounds that since such education had to do with truth it could function as a kind of preparation for the gospel, stimulating an aptitude and a taste for truth which, since truth is one and indivisible, may lead ultimately to a full beholding of truth as Christ.[3] Our capacity for learning truth is in this way an anticipation, a *prolepsis*, of our capacity for learning Christ and, in Christ, (to borrow the phraseology of Johannes Climacus) "the God."

There is an obvious objection to all this that Augustine was at this stage of his career more Platonic than Christian—or, conversely, that the admission of a variation in the capacity for truth among different individuals, a variation determined by the orientation of the will, is a Trojan Horse whose content must end with the destruction of the Platonic ("recollection") model of learning truth. This is because the greater the division between God and humanity brought about by the operation of the evil will the less human beings will be capable of learning truth, with the consequence that if the archetypally "Augustinian" view of original sin as having brought about for each individual an innate bias towards the evil

---

[3]See, Augustine, *The Teacher*, 17-63.

will is accepted (and that is, after all, putting it in a fairly moderate form—more extreme statements are readily available) then the capacity for learning truth *cannot* be assumed to exist in each individual. Sin is, perhaps, not the only factor serving to differentiate the Christian from the Platonic models of learning the truth. One might think also of the *personal* quality of the Who who is Truth in the Augustinian view of things—a quality which is determinative for the whole literary and rhetorical character of the *Confessions*. Nonetheless, the issue of sin is decisive (and is, of course, of peculiar relevance in this comparison with Johannes Climacus).

With the question concerning Augustine's Platonism in mind let us move on to what is his most renowned discussion of "memory," in *Confessions* book 10, a discussion that opens with the question, "What do I love, when I love God?" (10.6.7)[4]. Memory is quickly identified as the faculty whereby we might best pursue the answer to such a question, for in memory is to be found all knowledge of whatsoever things the subject knows:

> men go out and gaze in astonishment at high mountains, the huge waves of the sea, the broad reaches of rivers, the ocean that encircles the world, or the stars in their courses. But they pay no attention to themselves. They do not marvel at the thought that . . . I could not even speak of [these things] . . . unless I could see them in my mind's eye, in my memory. . . . (C, 216)

But memory (as *The Teacher* had already shown) does not merely have to do with the retained traces of sense experience recalled in language; it also has to do with what later philosophy would call *a priori* truths of reason, or with our own subjective feelings. "The power of memory is great, O Lord. It is awe inspiring in its profound and incalculable complexity. Yet it is my mind: it is my self" (C, 224).

And God? God must, Augustine reflects, *be more than* the self, so that whoever wishes to find God must ascend above memory. But, he asks, "where will the search lead me? Where am I to find you? If I find you beyond my memory, it means that I have no memory of you. How then am I to find you if I have no memory

---

[4]Augustine, *Confessions*, trans. and ed. R. S. Pine-Coffin (Harmondsworth: Penguin, 1961). Further references are given as "C" in the text.

of you?" (C, 224). At this point he breaks off from impassioned introversion and pauses to reflect on the parable of the woman who searches for a lost coin (Luke 15), a reflection which leads him to what is, in effect, the starting point of *Philosophical Fragments*. For how, he asks, could the woman have ever found the coin unless she had remembered it? "Otherwise, when it was found, how would she have known whether it was the one she was looking for? ... We do not say we have found what was lost unless we recognize it, and we cannot recognize it unless we remember it" (C, 224-25). This conundrum is then applied to the soul's search for God, a search which is again channelled through the mind's relation to truth.

> See how I have explored the vast field of my memory in search of you, O Lord! *And I have not found you outside it.* [My emphases: GP] For I have discovered nothing about you except what I have remembered since the time when I first learned about you. Ever since then I have not forgotten you. For I found my God, who is Truth itself, where I found truth, and ever since I learned the truth I have not forgotten it. (C, 230)

Now, in the preceding pages of the *Confessions* Augustine has argued that even those whose minds are in most respects turned away from God in some sense continue to love truth. For, he claims, all desire happiness and though many seek for happiness (as they think) in things other than God they do nonetheless wish for their happiness to be based on truth: the concept of truth transcends the varying contexts in which it is applied because it is presupposed even in those cases in which we make false judgements—intellectual or existential—concerning what is true. If I can talk about "what I *really* want from life" (and Augustine assumes that we can all engage in such talk) then I am presupposing some kind of standard by which to measure the "truth" of whatever proposals I myself or my interlocutors come up with. The sensualist or the idolator *in some sense* holds that what he does is "true" or is based on a true conception of the way things are. "There is still a faint glow of light in man," Augustine concedes, "Let him walk on, for fear that darkness may engulf him" (C, 229).

All this suggests that when Augustine refers to "the time when I first learned about [Truth]" he is not talking about a particular moment or point in time. The moment, in this sense, does *not* have decisive significance but is subsumed into the recollective process of the memory (/mind) which is always and from the very beginning in some kind of relation to truth, without which (as Augustine understands the situation) mental life would not be possible.

Yet the conundrum of the woman and the lost coin is not resolved so easily, for (as we have noted) Augustine is convinced that God is not exactly "in" the memory in the same manner in which all other things can be "in" it. God as Truth is invested with a dimension of transcendence which the capacity of the knowing human subject alone cannot encompass: "you are not the mind itself, for you are the Lord God of the mind" (C, 231). Where then, he asks again, could he have found God? "Where else, then, did I find you, to learn of you, unless it was in yourself, above me? . . . you are Truth, and you are everywhere present where all seek counsel of you" (C, 231).

This "answer" to the riddle may seem to suggest that Augustine is wanting to have it both ways: both that the mind "remembers" God in such a way that it is able to recognize him when it "finds" him (so that, to say it again, the moment lacks decisive significance) and that God transcends the mind in such a way that only he can provide the condition whereby the subject can come to know him. In terms of Climacus's distinction between recollection and faith, The Socratic and Christianity, it may at this point look as if Augustine is simply failing to grasp the Christian nettle. The drama of Platonic recollection and the drama of Christian redemption are simply laid out alongside each other without any clear decision being made between them and equally without any clear principle of integration being offered.

Nonetheless, there are grounds for arguing that Augustine's exposition of the relationship between God, memory and truth is a coherent exposition in an intellectually rigorous form of the Christian understanding of certain key dynamics of the human situation. This is, of course, to move the ground of the discussion from epistemology to anthropology, from philosophy to theology—though Climacus might well not have any problem with that. Indeed, it would not be hard to argue that Augustine's account of the human situation "before God" has provided a paradigm for the most significant of all later accounts in the Western Christian and post-Christian tradition (at least until well into the nineteenth century);

that the kind of "conversion story" told by the *Confessions*, a story involving complex interactions between the "natural" ascent towards truth and the "encounter" with divine Truth, or between the "before" and "after" of the convert, is (after Paul's "Damascus Road") *the* exemplary "conversion story"—nor, as later sections of Book X show, is it a story which fails to register the decisive role of Jesus Christ as Mediator. Indeed, Book X closes with an extraordinary blending of the Platonic discourse concerning knowledge with the Christian discourse concerning redemption:

> Lord . . . you know how weak I am and how inadequate is my knowledge: teach me and heal my frailty. Your only Son, *in whom the whole treasury of wisdom and knowledge is stored up*, has redeemed me with his blood. *Save me from the scorn of my enemies*, for the price of my redemption is always in my thoughts. I eat it and drink it and minister it to others; and as one of the poor I long to be filled with it, to be one of those who *eat and have their fill*. (C, 251-52)

None of this may help to solve Augustine's (and Climacus's) problem at a purely philosophical level (and the *Postscript* is there to remind us that Climacus himself did not regard this as the decisive level) but it might strengthen the claim that he is not merely regurgitating an undigested blend of Pagan and Christian concepts (Climacus's "bad marriage") but is speaking a distinctively new and a distinctively Christian language. Nor is the case for Augustine merely historical, i.e., based on the historical fact that his thought became normative in Western Christianity. Rather, if Augustine became authoritative for the Church it was because his account of the human situation was, in its own terms, persuasive. Part of this persuasiveness may well lie precisely in the way in which he treats the dilemma which has been at the centre of this discussion, the dilemma which is also Climacus's starting point, namely: whether the truth can be learned, whether (that is) the human subject, as such, has a capacity for truth and, therewith, a capacity for God. Over against Climacus's distinction between two systematically opposed responses to this question ("recollection" and "faith") it could be one of the strengths of Augustine's argument that far from resolving the dilemma one way or the other he is driven to restate it at another level in such a way that a logical and philosophical brain teaser comes to disclose a fundamental existential and religious question. In this way of looking at it the very ambiguity of Augustine's response, an ambiguity which allows the question to remain a question whilst moving it forward to a theological level, is part of both its human and its Christian persuasiveness. Climacus's work, on the other hand, is haunted by the criticism that it tends in the direction of *in*humanity, that the "point of contact" between divine and human is severed so completely that we are left wondering "for whom could such a faith be actual? who could live such a version of Christianity?" By "inhuman" I here mean something akin to what Hegel would have called "abstract," that *is*, lacking in the concreteness proper to a psychosomatic social entity such as a human being. Whilst not all commentators are scrupulous in observing the distinctions between the pseudonyms (nor even between the pseudonyms and their "author" Søren Kierkegaard), so that Climacus may suffer to some extent from "guilt by association," there is little doubt that he contributes to that tendency in Kierkegaard's writing which has provoked the kind of criticism I am alluding to. Examples of this may be found among Kierkegaard's own contemporaries (for example, H. L. Martensen, *Christian Ethics: General Part* [Edinburgh: T.&T. Clark, 1871] 217-36), in the heyday of existentialism (Karl Barth, *Church Dogmatics* III/2 [Edinburgh: T.&T. Clark, 1960] 113, and, from a very different view point, Colin Wilson, *Religion and the Rebel* [London: Gollancz, 1957] 231-40), and down to the present (Patrick Gardiner, *Kierkegaard* [Oxford: Oxford University Press, 1988]). Augustine, on the other hand, tells us most forcefully who his subject is, making the anthropological, existential dimension integral to his whole manner of proceeding—and (to repeat) in this respect his refusal to "solve" the ambiguity of the conundrum about learning the truth is very much part of his strength.

Does this "inhuman" lack of appropriate ambiguity mean that Climacus is in danger of losing (or has already lost) a vital element of authentic Christian theology? Let us not (as Climacus himself might have put it) be too hasty at this point. If Climacus "solves" the question about truth in a manner as clear-cut as (according to his account) the doctrine of recollection "solved" it, this does not immediately brand his book as unambiguous. Nor do we need to restrict the possibilities of fruitful ambiguity to the question of the paradox (a paradox is not, in itself, necessarily ambiguous). For when we have to do with an editor as careful as Climacus's editor Søren Kierkegaard, the reader must be alert to the possibility that the *content* of the communication is only one part of its significance—and a part which should never be taken on its own. Here I would offer two observations, the first of which relates to the philosophical context of *Philosophical Fragments*, the second of which has to do with its character as *indirect* communication.

First, then, it is clear that Augustine was not a foundational thinker for Kierkegaard in the sense of determining the intellectual context of his work.[5] Of far more immediate significance was the tradition of German idealism and, above all, Hegelianism.[6] This was in a distinctive manner, however, a philosophy of recollection. The journey of Spirit traced in Hegel's work, a journey leading from immediacy to Absolute Knowledge, is described in a variety of ways by Hegel. It is, for instance a journey powered by negation, the continually repeated negation of all elements of immediacy, as intuition is surpassed in the direction of rationally structured and articulated knowing; or, it is a process of enrichment in which the purely abstract, one-dimensional character of immediate intuition is enriched and made ever more concrete by its successive mediations; or, it is also a process of *recollection*. In this respect Hegel makes great play on the double meaning of the German term *Erinnerung*, which embraces the ideas of both "remembrance" and "internalization." The process of *Erinnerung* is a process which leads from the exteriority of sense experience to the interiority of pure thought precisely—and this is the burden of Hegel's phenomenological method—by making an exhaustive recollection/remembrance of the totality of the experiences of consciousness. The stages of Spirit can thus be contemplated as ever more refined ex-

---

[5] See JP, 1: 179-81. Apart from the fact that he does not seem to have had a serious historical interest in Augustine (compared, say, to his interest in Socrates) it is clear that both at the philosophical and cultural levels he is likely to have regarded Augustine as making precisely the kind of confusions with which he reproached both Idealist philosophy and "Christendom."

[6] Though not exclusively. Ponder, e.g., the following quotation from Kant: "For the concepts and principles required for eternal life cannot really be learned from anyone else: the teacher's exposition is only the occasion for him to develop them out of his own reason." Kant, *The Conflict of the Faculties*, trans. and ed. M. Gregor (New York: Abaris, 1979) 63.

pressions of the essential ideal truth. In this way, for instance, the "true" content of visual art is recapitulated in a more refined way in the "inner" spiritual medium of language (i.e., in poetry); the "true" content of Greek religion, a content commensurable with the depiction of the God in sensuous human form (as in the cult statue), is recapitulated in a more refined form in Christianity, whose proper medium is that of the thoughts of the heart; the "true" content of religious thought—which, according to Hegel is by definition representational and pictorial ("picture thinking")—is recapitulated in a finally adequate form in philosophy and, above all, in philosophical logic which sets out the thoughts of God prior to the creation of the world.[7] It is this concept of philosophy as recollection that lies at the heart of that most poetic of all Hegel's aphorisms: that the work of philosophy

> appears only when actuality is already there cut and dried after its process of formation has been completed . . . it is only when actuality is mature that the ideal apprehends [the] same real world in its substance and builds it up for itself into the shape of an intellectual realm. When philosophy paints its grey in grey, then has a shape of life grown old. By philosophy's grey in grey it cannot be rejuvenated but only understood. The owl of Minerva spreads its wings only with the falling of the dusk.[8]

Here, as elsewhere, Hegel casts recollection in an eschatological mould: for his is the recollective view on history from the standpoint of the end of history. Without here venturing to decide the issue it is at least clear that there might well be readings of Hegel—and these could include readings with which Kierkegaard was familiar and, arguably, his own reading—in which the process of recollection is described in such a way as to minimize or even lose sight of the existential context of recollection. In Augustine's *Confessions*, on the other hand, the recollecting subject does not presume to stand at the end of history but is still very much searching for an explanation of life from within the midst of life. For Augustine's restless heart recollection is a task to be under-

---

[7]See, George Pattison, *Kierkegaard; The Aesthetic and the Religious* (London: Macmillan, 1992) 11ff.

[8]G. W. F. Hegel, *Philosophy of Right*, trans. and ed. T. M. Knox (Oxford: Clarendon Press, 1978) 12-13.

taken, renewed and pursued again and, again, a never-ending story—and even when, in *The City of God* we are given a glimpse of "the end" it is an end "which has no end," i.e., God himself, who surpasses all the limits of human understanding.[9] The closure of Hegelian recollection, in other words, also (though in an opposite way from that of Climacus) loses the vital ambiguity of the Augustinian version. Augustine's God is not the endpoint from which the the knowing human subject is able to survey the sweep of time in one great act of remembrance of things past but rather the endpoint, the limit, the boundary, the confinium, to which, again and again the knowing subject comes in his quest for truth: God as Truth is rather the presupposition which the thinker is unable to make for himself—whereas for Hegel it is the starting point which is always already made.

But what has all this to do with *Philosophical Fragments*? Simply this: that—as the *Postscript* was to make even clearer—the "target" of *Philosophical Fragments* is not (of course) Socrates but idealist philosophy as such and, historically, this means German idealism as the contemporary form of that philosophy. The continuous eulogy of—not Socrates alone, but—"the Greek" way of doing philosophy throughout *Philosophical Fragments* should at least warn us of this however: that the contemporary idealism which is confronted here was a philosophy of closure, of complete immanentism, of total recall, to a quite unprecedented degree and that it was precisely this extreme loss of ambiguity, this insistence on "cut and dried" definition which demanded the kind of conceptual clarification which Climacus put on offer. His work, in short, is "corrective." If we were to take the text on its own, in isolation, it might well support a one-dimensional reading in the direction of an inhuman and incomprehensible view of faith, itself an extremely "closed" view. If, on the other hand, the text is read as critical and polemical throughout then the very clarity of its argument—the refusal of recollection—far from denying ambiguity enables ambiguity to reappear on a philosophical scene desiccated by the precision logic of the system. The similarity of such a conclusion to "what every student knows about Kierkegaard" should not disturb us—

---

[9]Augustine, *City of God* (Harmondsworth: Penguin, 1972) 1091.

and, in any case, it is not all there is to be said. The converse of this, it should be added, is not that Hegel is therefore "outside" Christianity but rather that Hegel and Climacus together—precisely in their mutual contradiction—mark out the opposite boundaries of "classical" (Augustinian) Christian thought, with particular regard to the issues of faith, knowledge and truth.

My second reflection is this: that the form of indirect communication seriously qualifies the content of *Philosophical Fragments*. As Climacus himself noted with regard to the review of *Philosophical Fragments* which appeared in a Berlin theological journal, "the impression that the pamphlet is . . . didactic . . . is the most mistaken impression one can have of it" (PF, xx). For, he says, the whole trick of the book has to do with

> the contrast of form, the teasing resistance of the imaginary construction to the content, the inventive audacity (which even invents Christianity), the only attempt to go further (that is, further than the so-called speculative constructing), the indefatigable activity of irony, the parody of speculation in the entire plan, the satire of making efforts as if something *ganz Auszerordentliches und zwar Neues* (altogether extraordinary and even new) were to come of them, whereas what always emerges is old-fashioned orthodoxy in its rightful severity. (PF, xx-xxi)

What is important here is not simply the last phrase ("what always emerges") but the fact that this phrase, the statement of "old-fashioned orthodoxy," is qualified by everything that has gone before: the contrast of form, the inventive audacity, irony, parody and satire. In this way "old-fashioned orthodoxy" is not asserted, stated or taught (didactically) but raised *as a question*, or, as Kierkegaard might have put it, raised *in the subjunctive mode*.[10] In this connection the indirect communication of *Philosophical Fragments* is interestingly qualified by the appearance of "Søren Kierkegaard" on the title page as the book's editor (in contrast, for example, to the kind of pseudonymity of *Either/Or*, *Fear and Trembling*, and *Repetition*. This could be taken as a sign of the beginning of the end of the aesthetic authorship, the speaker beginning to emerge in his proper person from behind the pseudony-

---

mous mask. Equally, however, it could be read as giving a fresh spin to the pseudonymous uncertainty, since it poses yet another question to the reader. For in the light of this declared editorship we not only find ourselves asking, "How seriously does Johannes Climacus want us to take his book?" but also, "Does Søren Kierkegaard want us to take Johannes Climacus seriously?" Thus the very presence of Søren Kierkegaard, editor, further undermines any didactic reading.

Finally (and in terms of the focus of this essay), it is important that "old-fashioned orthodoxy" is raised as a question by means of the Socratic question concerning truth, by which we are alerted to the possibility that the truth of orthodoxy—of Christianity—may well only become a question *for us* insofar as we are ready to be concerned with the prior question of truth as such. With that we are back once more—or at least close once more—to Augustine, the philosopher in search of faith, the man of faith seeking understanding. This will not surprise those readers who have noticed that even the notorious chapter on the paradox (notorious, that is, among commonsense philosophers) states that it is the understanding itself which seeks its own downfall; in Augustinian terms: the mind which is in search of truth seeks that limit which both transcends it and establishes it in its quest. But whether the text of *Philosophical Fragments* "contains" such a direct communication regarding the innate *nisus* of the mind in the direction of truth or not, the form of indirect communication enables us to raise the question of such a doctrine without doing violence to the clear contrary indications to be found within the text itself. It must be emphasized that "to raise the question" is not, of course, the same as saying "this is what the text teaches"; that would be to return to the didactic reading of the Berlin reviewer. What we may say, however, is this: that as a question, as an essay in subjunctivity, *Philosophical Fragments* (always in polemical contrast to Hegel and all his works) returns us to the central theme of Augustine's Christian philosophy, namely, truth, and our relation to it. In doing so it reminds us (again with rather than against Augustine) that great as the debt of affection and of gratitude which we owe to those who are our human teachers and guides, the quest for truth is one in which I can make no other human being answerable for my insights or resolutions and from which no other human person can absolve me. Addressing (as always) his God, Augustine writes, "you made us for yourself [———— and "the dash ought to be as long as the radii of the earth's orbit" (JP, 5: 5141)] and our hearts find no peace until they rest in you" (C, 21). "To seek after God," as the title of one of the *Upbuilding Discourses* reminds us, "constitutes man's highest perfection." Neither Augustine nor Kierkegaard, however, offer guarantees as to whether or not you or I will find our peace or find our God: *that* is between ourselves and God. What they further agree in is that *if* we do, then *what* we find will be truth. In that dis/agreement let us leave them.

13

The Paradox of Faith
in Philosophical Fragments:
Gift or Task?

Lee Barrett

Søren Kierkegaard, or at least his pseudonym Johannes Clima-cus, has provided ammunition for two opposed theological inter-pretations of the relation of human and divine agency in the matter of human salvation. Paradoxically, modern champions of both Augustinianism and Pelagianism have discerned a kindred spirit in Climacus. Some interpreters of Climacus have discovered in his writings an Augustinian description of "faith" as an uncon-ditional gift from God, while others have detected a Pelagian view of faith as a human task and accomplishment. Much of the evi-dence for both views is contained in *Philosophical Fragments*. This essay will investigate the question of how this one text can support such divergent construals.

I shall argue that Climacus is neither a doctrinaire Augustinian nor a pure Pelagian. Furthermore, he is not an advocate of any of the alleged mediating positions which presupposed speculative theories of the interaction of divine grace and human freedom. Climacus undercuts the basic foundations upon which all these doctrinal options were based. Rather than answering the question of the relationship of divine and human agency, he redescribes the issues in such a way that the question evaporates. Climacus's view of the way religious concepts come to have meaning rules out any systematic, theoretic resolution to the seeming paradox of grace and freedom and even renders such a resolution unnecessary.

It will be necessary to consider the views of those interpreters who do regard Climacus as advocating a particular theological theory of grace and freedom. Some commentators applaud Climacus's profound emphasis of divine grace and his exposure of human incapacity apart from grace, two themes which have been central to the followers of Augustine. For example, M. Holmes Hartshorne argues that Kierkegaard ironically used Climacus's spiritually strenuous themes of "the leap" and "subjectivity is truth" to show the reader through indirect communication that salvation by such heroic action is beyond human ability. The discouraged reader should recognize that people cannot "leap" into faith in that superhuman manner and learn to await the "miracle of grace."[1] For Hartshorne, Kierkegaard's project was intensely Augustinian, seeking to drive the reader to despair over his own efforts to respond to the incarnation and to fall back upon the sustaining power of God's grace moving the will. "Grace" for Hartshorne suggests an empowerment of human capacities, or even the bestowal of a new capacity, for which the individual can take no credit. Similarly, other expositors have found Climacus's talk of God "supplying the condition" of faith as directly implying an Augustinian reliance upon prevenient grace, a position which was congruent with Kierkegaard's own espoused views.[2] The optimistic Pelagian assessment of human capacities is seen to have more in common with Kierkegaard's Hegelian opponents.

Other commentators, however, have discovered in Climacus, and in Kierkegaard himself, an emphasis upon faith as an act of human autonomy which has affinities with Augustine's adversary Pelagius. Mark C. Taylor, for example, remarks, "It is of central importance for Kierkegaard's argument that man himself be responsible for faith."[3] According to Taylor, God only provides the possibility of faith by presenting a possible object for faith, the incarnation, while human beings must freely decide to actualize

---

[1]M. Holmes Hartshorne, *Kierkegaard, Godly Deceiver* (New York: Columbia University Press, 1990) 28-44.

[2]See Gregor Malantschuk, *Kierkegaard's Thought*, trans. Howard and Edna Hong (Princeton: Princeton University Press, 1979) 143-44, 246-58.

[3]Mark C. Taylor, *Kierkegaard's Pseudonymous Authorship* (Princeton: Princeton University Press, 1975) 314.

this new possibility. Similarly, existentialist expositors of Climacus discern in *Philosophical Fragments* the foreshadowing of their own radically volitional view of existential commitments. Individuals come to have life-orienting beliefs by willing to have them. More moderate interpreters detect a "semi-Pelagian" or "synergistic" position in Climacus, arguing that God's grace is partly responsible for the genesis of faith in the individual while the human will is partly responsible. In this mediating view grace and will must cooperate in order for faith to appear. Perhaps Climacus was proposing that the individual must freely develop sin-consciousness in order to receive the gift of faith, or at least that the individual must freely embrace and utilize the gift once it is offered.

Climacus himself is responsible for this dizzying plethora of interpretations. Not one of the preceding interpretations is implausible. With ostensible inconsistency Climacus mingles the language of human passivity with the language of human agency. Sometimes having faith sounds like something one does, and sometimes it sounds like something which happens to one. Sometimes it sounds like making a deliberate decision to get married and at other times it sounds like unexpectedly falling in love. He insists that "faith is not an act of will" (PF, 2) and then proceeds to proclaim that belief is "an act of freedom" (PF, 83). (The same Danish word "Tro" can be translated as either "belief" or "faith.") Sometimes Climacus's emphasis of the fact that only the god can give the "condition" of faith seems to point in the direction of Augustine's view of predestination. At other times Climacus's attention to the "leap" character of faith appears to have more in common with Pelagius's defense of free will and human responsibility. As a result, some commentators have emphasized either the "condition" language or the "leap" language at the expense of the other, while others have posited a division of labor between the two. It is not surprising that Louis Pojman concludes, "the reader may be forgiven if he wonders whether Kierkegaard could not have done more to reconcile his categories."[4]

---

[4]Louis Pojman, *The Logic of Subjectivity: Kierkegaard's Philosophy of Religion* (University AL: University of Alabama Press, 1984) 92.

It is no accident that both the language of faith as a gift and the language of faith as a task are present in Climacus's text. The theological debates concerning the relation of divine and human agency were certainly not unknown to Kierkegaard himself or to the religious culture of early nineteenth-century Copenhagen. Rationalists influenced by Kant stressed the inviolability of human freedom as a necessary condition of all morally relevant acts, including commitment to Christianity. H. N. Clausen, the leading figure in the faculty of theology at the University of Copenhagen, propounded a Kantian defense of autonomy and called for the free commitment to duty. Bishop Mynster, who profoundly influenced Kierkegaard's father, somewhat reduced the strenuousness of this orientation by proposing that the individual must freely resolve to strive for spiritual perfection before God's grace can become efficacious.[5] The sincerity of the effort would compensate for the deficiency of the results. Some pietists, on the other hand, adhered to the more traditional teaching that God must move the will, but considered the unaided attainment of penitent sin-consciousness to be a necessary precondition for God's activity. This view was particularly prevalent among those influenced by the style of spirituality which had emerged from the University of Halle. Other pietists took a more moderate view and overtly embraced synergism, regarding God's grace as assisting the human will's naturally inadequate but sincere efforts. The more populist form of pietism influenced by the Herrnhut movement went so far as to describe conversion as the individual's own act. To further complicate the theological situation, the stalwart defenders of moderate confessional orthodoxy continued to proclaim the priority of God's grace and the bondage of the sinful human will. The young Kierkegaard encountered this view during his childhood study of Bishop N. E. Balle's widely used *Catechism in the Evangelical Christian Religion*.[6]

---

[5]See Bruce H. Kirmmse, *Kierkegaard in Golden Age Denmark* (Bloomington: Indiana University Press, 1990) 100-35.

[6]N. E. Balle, *Laerebog i den evangelisk-christelige Religion* (Copenhagen: n.p., 1791). See W. von Kloeden, "The Home and the School," in *Kierkegaard's View of Christianity*, ed. Niels Thulstrup and Maria Thulstrup (Copenhagen: C. A. Reitzels Boghandel, 1978) 11-16.

The problem of grace and freedom received the most attention in Hans Martensen's celebrated critique of Schleiermacher's treatment of predestination. Kierkegaard heard Martensen lecture on Schleiermacher while Martensen served as Kierkegaard's tutor. Martensen subsequently elaborated his position in his *Christian Dogmatics*, a mediating work which tried to avoid the extremes of divine determinism and unqualified human autonomy.[7] Martensen differentiated himself from the Pelagian claim that human volition can choose to enact the will of God, a position which he associated with the spirit of contemporary rationalism in Denmark. Kierkegaard would have encountered such an emphasis of human autonomy during his attendance of H. N. Clausen's lectures on dogmatics and would have recognized Clausen as one of the targets of Martensen's critique. Martensen also criticized the Augustinian position which he associated with Schleiermacher, claiming that it led to the pernicious view that grace works upon the individual through natural necessity and rules out any role in the salvific process for the "freely choosing self-determining ego."[8] He lamented the unfortunate turn taken by Lutheran orthodoxy toward the "Calvinist" view that God predestines individuals to salvation and damnation without regard to their future faith or unbelief. Martensen also eschewed the allegedly semi-Pelagian "synergism" of Melanchthon, a position prevalent in the Danish church. Over against these views, Martensen proposed that the human will is only free to resist grace; it can take no credit for assisting the operation of grace. God's gracious activity is exclusively responsible for the genesis of faith, but human agency is exclusively responsible if the gift of this faith is rejected. Martensen concludes, "the native natural will possesses the power to withstand or resist grace, but not the power of surrendering itself to grace."[9] By proposing this view, Martensen approximated the position of the seventeenth-century theologian Jacob Arminius, who restricted natural freedom to the ability to resist grace. The care with which Martensen sorted through the theological options indicates the

---

[7]H. Martensen, *Christian Dogmatics*, trans. William Urwick (Edinburgh: T.&T. Clark, 1866).

[8]Ibid, 365.

[9]Ibid, 359.

extent to which the issues of grace and human freedom were embedded in the contemporary disputes between rationalists, pietists, idealists, and confessionalists. These theological controversies formed a significant part of the context for the composition of *Philosophical Fragments*.

I shall argue that Climacus's remarks about divine grace and the human response cannot be identified with any of the above doctrinal positions which were available in his intellectual environment. In one way or another, all of them regarded the tension between the language of "gift" and the language of "responsibility" as an issue which was amenable to a theoretic solution. All of the options treated the relationship between divine and human agency as a matter which could be clarified by specifying exactly how much causality could be ascribed to God and how much to human individuals. In order to accomplish this, each position had to elaborate a metaphysical framework in order to describe and compare the interaction between the two sorts of causality.

Climacus, however, does not propose to synthesize God's initiative and the human response in a theological theory. He does not approach the problem of understanding grace and faith as a systematic theologian at all. Climacus's persistent and vehement objections to philosophic systems apply with equal force to theological systems. The pervasive antisystematic thrust of Climacus's work cannot be exaggerated. It is significant that the polemic against systems is not only enshrined in the book's title but also frames the main text, occurring prominently both in the preface and in the concluding pages. Climacus introduces the work by protesting that what is offered here is "only a pamphlet" (PF, 5) and describes himself as a "loafer" who "dances lightly in the service of thought" as opposed to the pundits who ponderously tinker with the intricacies of the weighty system (PF, 7). Similarly, in the conclusion of the final chapter Climacus contrasts the frivolity of his own fragmentary pamphlet with the gravity of the system (PF, 109). This antisystematic nature of his approach informs his treatment of the issue of grace and freedom; he "dances lightly" through the opposed theories of rival doctrinal systems without pausing to embrace a permanent partner.

For Climacus, the relation of divine and human agency as discussed by the theologians had become a putatively speculative problem. Theologians invented theories to integrate freedom and grace in the way that natural scientists might develop theories to account for seemingly discrepant data or logicians might develop new systems of logic to accommodate apparent conundrums and paradoxes. For Climacus, the matter of God's interaction with humanity is not amenable to a theoretic solution at all. Entertaining a theory would be like having an "opinion" about a conceptual puzzle. The mood of holding an opinion is not conducive to religious pathos (PF, 7). A new doctrinal formulation is not the answer, and Climacus does not proffer any new doctrines. To attempt to clarify this issue through the development of a new doctrinal system would produce a fundamental distortion of the concepts involved.

For Climacus, the meaning of a religious concept is not a function of its location in a theoretic system. In *Concluding Unscientific Postscript* Climacus reflects:

> What does that mean—objective faith? It means a sum of tenets. But suppose Christianity is nothing of the kind; suppose that, on the contrary, it is inwardness, and therefore the paradox, in order to thrust away objectively, so that it can be for the existing person in the inwardness of existence by placing him decisively, more decisively than any judge can place the accused, between time and eternity in time. (CUP, 1:215)

In the same work Climacus insists that "Christianity is not a doctrine" but rather is an "existence-communication" (CUP, 1:379-80). In so far as it is appropriate to talk of Christian "doctrines," the purpose of such language is to help the individual "exist in" the doctrine. Accordingly, the concepts of "grace," "freedom," and "responsibility" can only be grasped in their proper passional contexts, as they are used to shape human lives. Their meaning is rooted in the specific activities of exhorting, praising, trusting, and repenting which constitute their natural environment. With this in mind, Climacus sets out to illumine the passions, concerns, activities and moods which are constitutive of the meaning of these Christian concepts. By clarifying the contexts in which these concepts are used and the purposes for which they are used the possible theoretic inconsistencies do not even arise. Under the ironic guise of a "thought-experiment," Climacus "indirectly" describes the employment of these concepts in the Christian life. Climacus's understanding of grace and human responsibility can only be grasped when the rhetorical strategies and passional purposes of his remarks are taken into account.

In *Philosophical Fragments* Climacus elucidates the use of two themes deeply embedded in the Christian tradition: dependence upon God's grace and active growth in faith. By sorting out the passional purposes of each theme Climacus shows that they need not conflict with each other or generate logical contradictions. Clarity about the appropriate contexts for the use of each of these Christian themes obviates the need for a theoretic integration of divine and human agency. Familiarity with the appropriate passions, moods, interests, and emotions which give the concepts meaning replaces the quest for a resolution by means of a theological system.

The grateful celebration of God's grace working within the individual may be the more dominant of the two themes in *Philosophical Fragments*. The entire work could be construed as an investigation of the logic of gratitude, trust, and dependence. The first chapter establishes this theme as the foundation and each subsequent chapter adds a more detailed specification. Of course, the clarification of the logic of gratitude proceeds through the ironic indirection of Climacus's thought experiment, in which he pretends to deduce a set of doctrinal concepts suspiciously reminiscent of Christianity from a single proposition. Climacus's hypothetical project is cast in the form of an extended transcendental deduction. The author asks what must be the case if the "moment" is to have "decisive significance" in the religious life of the individual. This is equivalent to an inquiry concerning the necessary conditions for the possibility of "rebirth" or "becoming a new person." Part of the force of "decisive significance" here is the injunction to be grateful, to never forget that the new birth is a gift. Climacus writes, "If the situation is to be different (from Socratic recollection), then the moment in time must have such decisive significance that for no moment will I be able to forget it, neither in time nor in eternity" (PF, 13). The playful exploration of "decisive significance" alerts the reader to the possibility of trusting and relying upon a power which does not originate in the individual's own volitional activity.

In order to probe the ramifications of "rebirth," Climacus pits the decisiveness of the moment against the recollection of inward truth. If the moment of coming to know the truth is to have significance, the learner must have been devoid of truth. The actualization of a potential for truth residing in the individual would only give the moment the importance of an accidental catalyst. If the learner lacks the potential for truth, the learner cannot even be regarded as searching for truth. Climacus observes, "Now if the moment is to acquire decisive significance, then the seeker up until that moment must not have possessed the truth, not even in the form of ignorance, for in that case the moment becomes merely the moment of occasion; indeed, he must not even be a seeker" (PF, 13). The learner cannot even possess the "condition" for understanding the truth once it is revealed. Climacus elaborates, "Along with it (the truth), he (the teacher) must provide him (the learner) with the condition for understanding it . . . because the condition for understanding the truth is like being able to ask about it—the condition and the question contain the conditioned and the answer" (PF, 14). Possessing the condition would be equivalent to having the ability to ask the appropriate question. For Climacus, any question implies an awareness of a range of possible answers. The capacity to question rightly would indicate that the inquirer is oriented to the truth. However, the learner must be viewed as polemically poised against the truth. Far from being a pilgrim questing for truth, the individual naturally delights in illusions and error. Climacus thus rules out any doctrinal stance which would allow the individual to take credit for the preparation for grace, even if that preparation were nothing more than the search for religious answers. For example, the *facere quod in se est* position of many late medieval nominalists insisted that God gives grace to those persons who strive their hardest with their natural abilities to make progress in the struggle for righteousness and truth. Such an attitude had reappeared in certain forms of Danish pietism and in the sermons of Bishop J. P. Mynster and was discussed extensively in contemporary text books on the history of doctrine.[10] For

---

[10]See K. G. Bretschneider, *Handbuch der Dogmatik* (Leipzig, 1823); and Karl Hase, *Hutterus redivivus*, (Leipzig, 1839).

Climacus any preparation for grace could jeopardize the decisiveness of the moment. The individual would be grateful to God for the gift of grace, but grateful to oneself for becoming eligible to receive the gift. But if the moment is to have decisive significance, the recipient can take no credit for being in a position to receive grace. The logic of absolute gratitude, trust, and dependence requires the denigration of the previous life situation. Gratitude is maximized if salvation is not only a gift, but also a gift which was neither expected nor sought. Trust and dependence are maximized only if the individual's inherent capacities are in no way credited with the attainment of the "eternal happiness."

The subsequent chapters of *Philosophical Fragments* elaborate other dimensions of the decisiveness of the moment and the maximization of gratitude. The second chapter focuses upon the content of the salvific moment in order to engender gratitude not only for the fact that it occurs but also for what specifically does occur. This involves the claim that not only is the gratuitous bestowal of the gift of truth unexpected but also that the nature of the gift is unheralded and unwanted. In fact, the content of the gift reveals why the learner was polemically poised against it and oriented toward error. Again, the argument takes the form of an ironic transcendental deduction which actually serves to clarify the meaning of the concept "incarnation." The peculiarities and possible flaws in the argument do not militate against its value as an exercise in conceptual analysis.[11] The chapter asks what must be the case with the god if there is to be a possibility of new birth for the individual in the decisive moment. In effect Climacus is exploring the divine conditions for the possibility of religious conversion. Because only the god could effect such a birth, and because the god could not be motivated by any need to effect such a birth, it follows that the god can be moved only by love. Furthermore, because love seeks equality and understanding, and because this equality can only be achieved through a descent of the god, it follows that rebirth involves a relationship with the god not as the exalted one but as the humbled one. The god does not want to be

---

[11]See Robert C. Roberts, *Faith, Reason, and History: Rethinking Kierkegaard's Philosophical Fragments* (Macon GA: Mercer University Press, 1986) 15-29.

loved and adored only "as the omnipotent one who preforms miracles" but as "him who humbled himself in equality with you" (PF, 33). Climacus concludes that loving the god in the form of a servant is a project which could not have occurred to any human being; it is not commensurate with ordinary human hopes and desires. The prospect of the god seeking a relationship of mutuality and empathetic understanding with humanity is alien to natural conceptions of divinity. The incarnation was not what the human race was expecting, nor was it what humanity, left to its own abilities, could naturally accept and embrace. The self-humbling of the god is an offense and an inscrutable mystery to humans disposed toward self-exaltation. The passional point of Climacus's dialectical maneuvers is that the appropriate mood for grasping the meaning of "incarnation" is shock, amazement at the extraordinary nature of God's love. According to Climacus, the incarnation is supremely terrifying, "for it is indeed less terrifying to fall upon one's face while the mountains tremble at the god's voice than to sit with him as his equal, and yet the god's concern is precisely to sit this way" (PF, 34-35). On the other hand, it is also "the most won-drously beautiful thought" which comes as a "felicitously fore-shadowing word" (PF, 36). Once again, gratitude requires the recognition of the gracious initiative of God, this time for pre-senting humanity with an opportunity beyond the race's most extravagant aspirations. The incredible and inestimable nature of the gift suggests that it be regarded as unwanted and unexpected prior to its reception.

The third chapter intensifies the grateful response by present-ing the very consciousness of sin, the awareness of the human problem, as a gift rather than as an achievement. Again Climacus employs an ironic dialectical strategy to make his conceptual point. The need for a revelation of sin is deduced from the paradoxical desire of thought to collide with the "unknown." Human reflective, imaginative, and valuational powers have a mysterious yearning for something which transcends and limits the provisional world of meanings they have constructed. If the unknown is "the differ-ent," then that which is different must reveal the nature of the dif-ference. Climacus writes, "Just to come to know that the god is dif-ferent, man needs the god and then comes to know that the god is absolutely different from him" (PF, 6). The incongruity between the ways of the god and the values of ordinary human "under-standing" cannot be discovered through a spiritual or intellectual quest. If this difference between the individual and the god can be described as sin, then only the god can bring consciousness of sin. The importance of the moment and the maximization of gratitude require that the very awareness of humanity's situation of guilt and debility be regarded as a gift. The understanding of the hu-man problem itself is due to the operation of grace. Contrary to the claims of some late medieval theologians with whom Kierkegaard would have been familiar through his use of Bretschneider that "attrition," self-generated fear of punishment and despair over one's sinfulness, must precede the reception of grace, the individu-al can take no credit for the efficacy of his remorse.[12] Climacus here parts company with many of the pietists, especially those in-fluenced by the Halle movement, who did see a humanly achieved despair over sin as a necessary preliminary to the encounter with forgiveness. The reader is implicitly warned to take no pride in his dissatisfaction with his moral and religious failures. A contrite heart should be an occasion for thanksgiving, not self-congratula-tion.

The fourth and fifth chapters concerning the situations of the contemporary and secondhand followers explore the nature of faith, the passionate encounter with god-the-teacher. In so doing, Climacus portrays the felicitous response to this incarnate god as being itself a gift from the god. The previous chapters had focused upon the absence of prior conditions preparing the individual for the advent of faith; this portion of the text stresses the gratuity of the birth of faith in the individual. The argument is based upon the epistemic ambiguity of the god's incognito. If the object of faith is the god in the form of a servant, it follows that the identity of the god is not directly discernable. Faith is not indubitable objective knowledge. It is neither the immediate awareness of sensory exper-ience nor is it an inevitable inference from historical data. Of course, the god furnishes some clues about his divine identity, but

---

[12]Bretschneider, *Handbuch der Dogmatik*, 475-76.

these intimations do not compel a believing response.[13] All such hints of an extraordinary identity do not constitute a sufficient condition for the genesis of faith. Neither the testimony of contemporaries nor the longevity and resilience of the subsequent ecclesial tradition make the divinity of the teacher any more probable. The subjectivity of the individual must be transformed in order for the individual to apprehend the god hidden in the form of the servant. The claim that divinity seeks out fellowship with the lowly would not seem plausible to natural common sense. It is incongruent with ordinary human hopes and desires which assume "exaltation" to be the basic dynamic of life. Consequently, no one can discern the divinity in the external form of the historical person unless one is given the "condition" by the god. "Condition" here suggests a new set of concerns, passions, attitudes, and aspirations discontinuous with the individual's old patterns of emotion, valuation, and action. Climacus insists, "The person who through the condition becomes a follower receives the condition from the god himself" (PF, 100).

In this context Climacus eschews volitional language. The transformation of subjectivity which makes the recognition of the god possible must not be construed as an act of will. The individual does not simply decide to develop faith. Climacus observes, "It is easy to see, then (if, incidentally, the consequences of discharging the understanding need to be pointed out), that faith is not an act of will, for it is always the case that all human willing is efficacious only within the condition" (PF, 62). Acting occurs within a passional matrix of particular desires, yearnings, and aspirations. For Climacus, human willing is motivated by the passional orientation of the individual's life. Faith cannot be willed precisely because the requisite motivational patterns are lacking. The individual's currently operating subjectivity does not dispose the individual to embrace the god-as-servant. If faith were construed as the fruit of volitional activity, this would presuppose a preexisting passional orientation toward faith. The existence of such a con-

---

[13]See C. Stephen Evans, *Kierkegaard's Fragments and Postscript: The Religious Philosophy of Johannes Climacus* (Atlantic Highlands NJ: Humanities Press, 1983) 257-58.

dition in the learner has already been ruled out because it, like any innate capacity, would militate against the decisiveness of the moment and constitute a return to the Socratic position.

The basic thrust of all these observations in the last two chapters of *Philosophical Fragments* is that faith, the happy passion, the capacity to respond to the lowly god, should be welcomed with gratitude and trust in the god. The individual should rely upon the god and nothing else. Church traditions and historical testimonies must not be accorded causal power in the awakening of faith, for the believer "is not indebted to someone else for something but is indebted to the god for everything" (PF, 102). All saving efficacy must be ascribed to the god. It is the god who gives the condition and "opens the eyes of faith" (PF, 65). The god as teacher not only gives himself to the learner but also gives the learner the ability to respond to that momentous encounter. The learner can take no credit for the awakening of faith in the learner's heart.

All of the themes which have been examined so far combine to reinforce a sense of divine activity and human passivity. Climacus develops all of them in order to maximize gratitude for the gift of eternal happiness. The general rule for the maximization of gratitude is to take no credit for anything. The individual should humbly view the individual's self as owing everything to the god. The possibility of rebirth is a gift, the presence of the god in the form of a servant is a gift, consciousness of one's own sin is a gift, and the advent of faith itself is a gift. Climacus's ironic dialectical exercises have a profound homiletical purpose: to wean the reader away from reliance upon the reader's own powers and to foster grateful trust in the power of the god. Anything which might compromise reliance and gratitude, whether it be trust in the profundity of one's inherent spiritual potential, in the purgative benefits of one's own contrition, in the reliability of historical testimonies, or in the venerability of church traditions, must be rejected.

On the other hand, a countervailing dynamic permeates Climacus's work: the call to take the incarnation of the god with maximum seriousness. The increase of passionate concern about one's response to the mystery of the humble god is a second, equally important purpose of the text. The rhetorical thrust of much of the latter sections of *Philosophical Fragments* is designed to augment the reader's vigilance about the quality of the reader's own existence.

This involves an implicit warning to assume responsibility for the basic shape and orientation of the reader's own life.

The two themes of maximum gratitude and maximum seriousness interweave in Climacus's text in complex ways. Sometimes one theme will dominate a lengthy section, while at other times both themes will be suggested by a single passage. Often the two can even be juxtaposed in creative tension. In order to better understand Climacus's purpose, it will be necessary to factor out and separately examine the theme of the maximization of seriousness.

The call to seriousness and responsibility makes almost no appearance in the first chapter, which focuses entirely on the need for rebirth and luxuriates in the language of passivity. However, the second chapter's exposition of the god's adoption of the form of a servant suggests both the need for and the unguaranteed nature of a human response. This occurs in the context of an elaboration of the extent and depth of the god's love. Climacus writes, "Oh, to sustain heaven and earth by an omnipotent 'Let there be,' and then, if this were to be absent for one fraction of a second, to have everything collapse—how easy this would be compared with bearing the possibility of the offense of the human race when out of love one became its savior" (PF, 32). The possibility of the individual's being offended is a function of the hiddenness of the god's divinity. The god's assumption of the form of a servant entails that the learner may not discern the divine identity. In these passages the focus is not on the dire consequences of being offended, but on the willingness of the god to risk being misunderstood. The god's willingness to suffer the pain of possible misunderstanding is a testimony to the extent of the god's love. The god loves enough to become vulnerable, investing himself in a relationship which might not blossom in mutuality. The force of these passages is to encourage the reader to take the god's love seriously, to appreciate its costliness. The god has risked defeat; a happy relationship is not guaranteed. The reader must never take the god's incarnated love lightly, as if it were merely one more painless manifestation of the god's invincible power.

The third chapter and its appendix further explore the motif of the possibility of the learner's offense. Sometimes the language of "the leap" functions to stimulate a sense of responsibility for one's relationship with the god. Ironically, the same considerations which often are used to foster gratitude for the "condition" are also used to engender an active desire to avoid offense and cultivate the "happy passion." They serve as a warning concerning the reader's perilous situation, threatened by the natural liability to offense. A "leap" is necessary and offense is possible because knowledge of the god is neither immediately given nor available through inferential procedures. It is impossible to reason with certainty from any alleged works of the god to the existence of the god. Immediate awareness is limited to the existence of a thing; sensory perception cannot discern that a thing has the quality of being an effect of something else. The connection between causes and effects is never directly perceived. By making these general epistemological claims, Climacus is setting the stage for the *a fortiori* argument that no evidence can render the recognition of the god in the form of the servant inevitable. None of the acts attributed to the god indubitably prove themselves to be the products of divinity. The life of the servant, no matter how many miracles may accompany it, does not manifest itself as the effect of divine causality. If recognition is not necessary, then nonrecognition is always possible. The possibility of offense is logically tied to the mode of the god's incarnation. In these contexts Climacus's remarks indirectly alert the reader to the dangers and the likelihood of offense. The alarmed reader should strive to avoid actualizing this unhappy possibility. At times Climacus goes so far as to use overt agential language to encourage critical self-scrutiny in the reader. Although offense is a "suffering" dependent upon the prior action of the god, it "is always active to the extent that it cannot allow itself to be annihilated (for offense is always an act, not an event)" (PF, 50). Without directly exhorting the reader, such observations entice and provoke the reader to assume responsibility for succumbing to the offense. One should not dismiss offense as a tragedy which inevitably befalls a victimized human nature. The wary reader should be on guard against submitting to the offense's temptations.

The use of the language of personal agency recurs in the final two chapters' exposition of "faith," the happy encounter between the paradox and the understanding. Here Climacus uses active verbs to describe the response to the paradox. The understanding "surrenders itself" as the paradox gives itself (PF, 54). Similarly, faith occurs in the moment "when the understanding steps aside and the paradox gives itself" (PF, 59). The "Interlude" reinforces the theme of faith as a responsible action. Climacus writes, "it is now readily apparent that belief is not a knowledge, but an act of freedom, an expression of will" (PF, 83). "Belief" (which could also be translated as "faith") and doubt are not two modes of cognition, but are opposed attitudes toward the possibility of having a conviction (PF, 84). The doubter decides to refrain from drawing conclusions because of a passionate desire to avoid error and deception. The suspended commitments of the skeptic are willed; they are not a necessary reasonable response to the available data. The believer, on the other land, decides to risk the possibility of being mistaken in order to make an epistemic commitment. Both doubt and belief are seen as intentional dispositions of the subject. Doubting and believing are long-term policies adopted by the subject for which the subject can be held accountable. The reader is invited to compare the reader's self to the skeptic, to probe his doubtings in order to discover the interior sources of his or her refusal to commit himself. The reader cannot be exculpated by attributing a lack of faith to the paucity of evidence. The problem resides in the passional life of the subject, and the subject should be disturbed enough to attend to the absence of the requisite passions.

The final chapter implicitly functions to admonish the reader to be vigilant about the maintenance of faith. Climacus reiterates the contention that neither the accumulation of more eyewitness reports of the god's works nor the multiplication of testimonies to the god by subsequent generations compel faith. The passage of time, including the entire history of the church, does not make faith more certain. Consequently, faith can never be regarded as an assured, permanent possession. Climacus warns, "If the contemporary generation of believers did not find time to celebrate triumphantly, then no generation finds it, for the task is identical, and faith is always in conflict, but as long as there is conflict, there is the possibility of defeat" (PF, 108). The believer can never be smug in the guaranteed further continuation of faith. The alerted reader should develop the necessary self-concern to cultivate the passions which make the perdurance of faith possible.

It has been shown that the two themes of gratitude/trust and self-concern/responsibility are both prominent throughout Climacus's text. If they are taken to be context-neutral truth claims about the world, particularly about the relation of divine and human agency, they could ostensibly conflict. As context-neutral propositions they could be combined with other context-neutral propositions to generate two series of logical entailments. The two series generated by the original two themes might not be compatible. For example, the theme of total reliance upon God's grace and the correlative use of passive language could imply that God's grace irresistibly moves the human will, if it were assumed that total reliance is only possible in the case of irresistible efficacy. In conjunction with the observation that some people seem to have faith and others do not, this could imply that God must have predestined some people to salvation and other people to damnation, or at least that God has arbitrarily decided to grant grace only to a select few. If the ascription of responsibility presupposes some causal efficacy, this could also imply that human beings are not ultimately responsible for their own eternal destinies. Human volitional capacities are merely the passive instruments of divine causality. These reflections could even be pushed in the direction of theological or metaphysical determinism. On the other hand, talk of human responsibility and the need for passionate self-concern would seem to suggest that individuals should take some action which would have an impact on their eternal happiness. In conjunction with the proposition that "ought" implies "can," this would imply that the human will is free to choose such action. If freedom to choose requires the absence of determination by prior causes, then the will must be at least somewhat undetermined. Furthermore, if this sort of causal responsibility is morally evaluable, individuals would deserve some credit for contributing to their own salvation. Either they are to be congratulated for cultivating sin-consciousness, or for cooperating with grace, or for refusing to resist grace, or at least for utilizing grace once it had been bestowed. The two series of inferences generate conflicting conclusions. In short, the theme of gratitude would imply that the human will enjoys no independent causal efficacy in matters of salvation, while the theme of self-concern could imply that the human will does indeed possess at least some causal power. Such a glaring contradiction would require mediation in a second-order theory of the interaction of the divine and human wills. Some sort of metaphysical system would be required, governed by publicly adjudicable criteria of consistency and comprehensiveness, to reconcile the discrepant first-order propositions.

However, this conceptual conundrum does not arise if the language of gratitude and responsibility is not treated as a set of passion-neutral propositions which could imply other passion-neutral propositions. Accordingly, Climacus refuses to speculate about the relative degrees to which the god and individuals are active in salvation or the modes in which they are active. If Climacus's propositions only acquire meaning and truth-value when they are used in the appropriate activities of shaping an individual's subjectivity, they cannot be regarded as ciphers in an abstract calculus. The mood which accompanies the generation of logical entailments is inappropriate to the concepts in question. In a metaphysical exploration the concepts of "grace" "sin," etc. would lose their self-involving force and hence lose their very meaning. Outside the context of specific forms of pathos, the use of these concepts would be hopelessly obscured. Their role in the formation of human lives is constitutive of their meaning and therefore delimits the range of intelligible implications they can have. The existential purposes of these statements are ingredient to their meaning. For example, the activities of trusting, hoping, thanking, etc. are part of the very meaning of the concept "God." The meaning of "God" cannot be stipulated neutrally, as if God were one being among many who might contingently happen to exist, or referred to in the way one might refer to a chair or a horse. It is part of the meaning of the concept "God" that God is to be adored, trusted, obeyed, etc. The referential use of the concept cannot be artificially separated from the worshipful activities. Accordingly, Climacus introduces the concept "the god" in the context of concern about one's own eternal happiness. His method of indirect communication is calculated to entice and provoke the reader into supplying the requisite pathos which constitutes the context for talk about "grace." It is significant that Climacus concludes the introduction by musing that "the thought of death is a good dancing partner" (PF, 8). Without such a pathos-laden dancing partner Christian concepts cannot dance.

The problem of reconciling the language of passive gratitude and trust with the language of active self-concern and responsibility does not arise if the passional contexts of the relevant concepts are taken into account. The contradiction does not appear if the two sets of contexts are not contradictory. This is indeed the case. The exhibition of gratitude and trust in the appropriate ways in the appropriate circumstances need not conflict with the self-ascription of responsibility in the appropriate ways in the appropriate circumstances. Seeing the Christian life as a gift need not conflict with seeing it as a task. Both "gift" and "task" serve as pictures or models to make sense of the individual's deepest passions and actions. The learner simply needs to develop skill in recognizing when to use each picture and how to use each picture. The learner must cultivate the art of using each picture to inform the other, so that gratitude becomes responsible and responsibility becomes grateful.

The use of dual or even multiple schemes to interpret phenomena is not unknown in other domains. For example, Ian Barbour has explored possible analogies between scientific models and theological systems.[14] At times it is heuristically useful to regard the behavior of electrons as being similar to that of waves, while at others it is more helpful to view it as similar to that of particles. No unified model can be developed to account for all of the statistical patterns which electrons exhibit. In some laboratory situations the wave model is clearly called for, while in others the particle model can make sense of the observed data. Neither model can be translated into terms appropriate to the other. They function in irreducibly different but complementary fashions. Skill is required in order to discern when to rely on which one.

In a similar way, the themes of life as a gift and life as a task could be regarded as complementary ways of construing the phenomena which constitute personal existence. Skill would be required to evaluate the passional context in order to determine whether to employ the "gift" model or the "task" model. For example, when the individual is tempted to compare favorably his

---

[14]Ian Barbour, *Myths, Models, and Paradigms* (New York: Harper & Row, 1974) 71-92.

own virtue to that of others, the gift model would be appropriate to eliminate the possibility of pride. This is the force of Climacus's denial that the individual can take credit for anything in the encounter with the teacher. The gift model would also be suited for situations in which one might brood about the inadequacies of one's own spiritual life, in order to forestall the introspective search for reassuring signs of salvation. Climacus's remarks foster trust in the power of the teacher/giver, not in the receptivity of the learner/receiver. On the other hand, the task model could be employed in contexts which encourage complacency in order to prevent the learner from taking the possession of an eternal happiness for granted. The task model could also be employed to prevent self-congratulatory comparisons between those who seem to be "elected" and those who do not.

Of course, in these instances the utility of the models would have nothing to do with their predictive or explanatory power, as is the case with scientific models. The models would not be used to suggest fruitful possibilities for empirical research. Rather, the purpose of the models would be to nourish a set of attitudes and dispositions. They would enable individuals to see life in new ways, to discern new connections between actions and events, and to evaluate themselves differently.

Unlike the sharp disjunction of the wave and particle models of subatomic phenomena, the themes of gratitude and responsibility could reciprocally influence each other. Gratitude would condition the way the individual regards the task of cultivating the life of faith. Responsibilities could be situated in a context of gratitude without either relaxing their strenuousness or without misusing them to promote self-righteousness. The project of self-salvation could be abandoned without renouncing the struggle to live out the faith. This integration of the two models does not take place through the auspices of a theoretic framework, but through the sagacity of passionate existers.

M. Jamie Ferreira has discerned a similar reciprocal interaction between the language of "leap" and the language of "passion" in Climacus's writings and in Kierkegaard's corpus in general. According to Ferreira, the concepts "leap" and "passion" can be seen "as parallel and as mutually and substantively correcting or qualifying each other."[15] Through their dynamic interaction unmediated by any theory, the two concepts make it clear that the transition to faith has both passive and active aspects. The individual's imagination holds these poles together in tension without reducing one to the other or synthesizing them through theoretical reflection. According to Ferreira, we "can live together what we cannot theoretically unite."[16] Imagination is this ability to hold opposites together without mediating them, so that the tension generates a new vision for the existing individual's life. Ferreira regards this as an instance of metaphorical activity, which is the placing of a phenomenon in two perspectives simultaneously so that one network of associations interacts with the other network of associations. In a similar way, I have argued that the language of grace and the language of responsibility can be seen as two interacting metaphorical domains of discourse. "Gift" and "task" reciprocally qualify and mutually correct each other through the imaginative activity of the faithful individual.

All this is not to say that Climacus is a noncognitivist or that his propositions are not intended to have any truth-value. He is not proposing that the themes of gratitude and responsibility only have a regulative use and make no claims about the way the world is. Although such injunctions as "Trust the incarnation" or "Cultivate gratitude for the gift of faith" do have a regulative function, they are not reducible to simple imperatives. Climacus does not treat them as stipulations unrelated to the issue of the truth about the world. In fact, the whole orientation of *Philosophical Fragments* toward the question of truth suggests quite the opposite. The factual historicity of the presence of the god in human history is of passionate concern to Climacus. Rather than recommending arbitrary behavioral policies, these regulations assume that life is hospitable to this form of interpretation and evaluation. By using

---

[15]M. Jamie Ferreira, *Transforming Vision: Imagination and Will in Kierkegaardian Faith* (Clarendon Press: Oxford, 1991) 9. Ironically, Ferreira's very helpful and sensitive account of the irreducibly metaphorical nature of Climacus's project has a tendency to mediate away the tension between the "gift" and "task" aspects of the transition to faith by specifying the ways in which certain aspects of the transition are passive and the ways in which other aspects of it are active.

[16]Ibid, 6.

them the believer gambles that the world is such that it is appropriate to construe it in terms of gratitude and responsibility. One stakes one's existence on the hope that a life of gratitude and responsibility is in accord with God's nature and purposes. Climacus is only committed to the claim that Christian concepts and propositions cannot be used referringly without the appropriate context of religious pathos. Their use in shaping religious pathos is a necessary condition for their cognitive force.

Climacus's treatment of the themes of grace, faith, and responsibility is a drastic revision of the conventional way of conceiving the theological task. Most of Kierkegaard's contemporaries viewed theology as the integration of discrete doctrinal propositions into a systematic framework. The propositions would be organized according to principles of formal logical relations. Some propositions would be seen as entailing others, some would be combined to generate more complex propositions, and some would be discovered to conflict with one another, a phenomenon which would require a higher synthesis. The framework in which the propositions were to be integrated would usually be borrowed from a metaphysical system, be it that of Aristotle, the Neoplatonists, Leibnitz, or Hegel. Climacus rejects this entire approach to theology. For Climacus, theology is the clarification of the role of religious concepts in forming human lives. Doctrines are not connected by logical relations, but by concrete activities and emotions. The synthesis of the various concepts and propositions occurs in the lives of individuals, not on paper.

This is not to say that reflection has no role to play in the effort to appropriate Christian concepts. First, reflection can dispel the power of misguided theoretic hindrances to faith. As we have seen, *Philosophical Fragments* attempts to disabuse the reader of any theological picture which discourages either thankfulness for faith or commitment to the task of nurturing faith. Secondly, reflection can clarify the basic purposes of Christian concepts. After reading Climacus's text, the reader should recognize that the language of prevenient grace should function to promote thankfulness and that the language of decision should be used to encourage self-vigilance. Thirdly, reflection can be used indirectly to stimulate and deepen passionate self-concern. Climacus's description of the alternative to the Socratic position destabilizes the complacent denizens of Christendom and awakens the troubling suspicion that their lives may be founded upon an illusion. Climacus's conceptual clarifications are laden with devices which trigger the imagination and present the powerful enticements of a qualitatively different kind of existence. The fact that eternal happiness can be experienced as both a gift and as a task is no small part of the attractiveness of the Christian life.

Contributors

International Kierkegaard Commentary 7
Philosophical Fragments and Johannes Climacus

LEE BARRETT is Professor of Theology at Lancaster Theological Seminary.

ANDREW J. BURGESS is Associate Professor of Philosophy at the University of New Mexico.

GEORGE B. CONNELL is Associate Professor of Philosophy at Concordia College.

STEPHEN N. DUNNING is Professor of Religious Studies at the University of Pennsylvania.

RONALD M. GREEN is John Phillips Professor of Religion at Dartmouth College.

JOHN D. GLENN, JR. is Professor of Philosophy at Tulane University.

C. STEPHEN EVANS is Professor of Philosophy at St. Olaf College.

GEORGE PATTISON is Dean of King's College Chapel at Cambridge University.

ROBERT L. PERKINS is Professor of Philosophy and Religion at Stetson University.

M. PIETY is a graduate student at the University of Copenhagen and Magill University.

HUGH S. PYPER is Lecturer in Biblical Studies at the University of Leeds.

HEATHER SERVATY is a graduate student in psychology at North Texas State University.

J. HEYWOOD THOMAS is Professor of Theology, emeritus, at Nottingham University.

SYLVIA WALSH is Adjunct Professor of Philosophy at Stetson University.

MEROLD WESTPHAL is Professor of Philosophy at Fordham University.

Advisory Board

Index

death of God, 138
deconstruction, 203, 222
dependence, 268, 272-81
Descartes, Rene, 8, 198, 204, 208, 210, 216n.
design, argument from. *See* physicoteleological argument.
despair, 142, 204, 206-207, 216n., 218-22
Diotima, 4-5, 10
doctrine, 137, 139, 144
doubt, 203-22
Dunning, Stephen N., 197

edification, 12
Either/Or, 13-16, 19, 92, 119, 203-208, 219, 258
Enlightenment, 2, 110, 122, 174, 231, 242
epistemology, 155-68
error, 59-60
essence, 47-49, 51, 57
eternal happiness, 227-28, 231, 233-34, 238, 240-41
ethical, the, 12, 122
Evans, C. Stephen, 42, 47n., 103, 117, 128n., 217n., 273
evidence, 72
existence, 130, 140, 193-96
experience, 59-60

faculty, 110, 116, 123
faith, 39-41, 43-45, 64, 68, 73, 75-77, 80-81, 83, 204, 208, 223, 225-26, 231-33, 241, 261-83. *See also* trust.
faith (and knowledge), 188-90
Faust, 203
Fear and Trembling, 13-14, 18-21, 24-28, 31, 34, 39, 92, 203, 205, 208, 226, 233, 258
Ferreira, M. Jamie, 185n.28, 281-82
Feuerbach, Ludwig, 231-32, 243
Fichte, J. G., 152, 153, 154, 161, 163
Findlay, J. N., 155
Flavius, Justinius, 1
forgiveness, 97
Fornuft, 112-21, 126
For Self-Examination, 124, 143, 208n.
Forstand, 109, 112-18, 120-21, 123, 125-27

foundationalism, 73-74, 78, 82
freedom, 46, 60
Freud, Sigmund, 217n., 231-32
functionalism, 90-93

Gardiner, Patrick, 254
Gilson, Etienne, 3
God, 58-59, 212, 221-22
God-man, 1, 6, 9, 41-42, 96, 132-33, 141, 143, 145
God, nonperceptability of, 190
God-relation, 104
grace, 222, 268-74
grammar, 158, 163, 168
gratitude, 268, 270-81
Greek philosophy, 213
Gregor, Mary J., 170
guilt, 122

Hartshorne, Charles, 224
Hartshorne, M. Holmes, 262
Hatfield, Gary, 216n.
Hegel, Georg Wilhelm Friedrich, 10, 11, 14-15, 17-19, 24-32, 48n., 92, 98, 132-33, 135-50, 153-54, 159, 163, 166, 181, 198, 202, 208, 210-11, 214, 226, 231-33, 243, 254-59
Herder, Johann Gottfried, 10
hierarchical thinking, 1, 2, 9-10, 12
Himmelstrup, Jens, 47n.
historical, the, 64, 72, 76-77.
historical knowledge, 233
history, 9-12, 54-55, 154, 166, 172, 176-78, 187-88
Hobbes, Thomas, 8
Hong, Howard, 34
Hong, Howard V., and Edna H. Hong, 53n., 57n., 58n., 109-10, 116-17, 119-20, 128, 171, 201, 209-10, 218n.
Hopkins, Jasper, 226, 229
humor/humorist, 72

illusion, 34-36, 45, 198
impossible possibility, 130, 145
improbable, the, 37, 45
incarnation, 67-68, 70-71, 76, 137, 223, 226-28, 232, 235, 237-39, 241-43, 264
incongruity, 72
indirect communication, 258-60

DATE DUE